SNIPER
IN ACTION

SNIPER
IN ACTION
HISTORY • EQUIPMENT • TECHNIQUES

CHARLES STRONGE

amber
BOOKS

First published in 2011 by
Amber Books Ltd
Bradley's Close
74–77 White Lion Street
London N1 9PF
United Kingdom
www.amberbooks.co.uk

Copyright © 2011 Amber Books Ltd.

All rights reserved. With the exception of quoting brief passages for the purpose of review no part of this publication may be reproduced without prior written permission from the publisher. The information in this book is true and complete to the best of our knowledge. All recommendations are made without any guarantee on the part of the author or publisher, who also disclaim any liability incurred in connection with the use of this data or specific details.

ISBN: 978-1-907446-29-0

Project Editor: Michael Spilling
Picture Research: Terry Forshaw
Designer: Hawes Design
Additional text: Martin J. Dougherty

Printed in China

PICTURE CREDITS:
Jonathan Alpeyric: 138 (CC Attribution Share Alike 3.0 Licence)
Amber Books: 13
Art-Tech/Aerospace: 11, 27, 65, 53, 59, 62, 67, 78, 81, 103, 112, 117, 124, 131, 139, 147
Art-Tech/MARS: 14, 24
Australian Department of Defence: 153, 158
Australian War Memorial: 36
Board of Trustees of the Armouries: 136
Bridgeman Art Library: 10 (Peter Newark's American Pictures), 26 (Stapleton Collection), 33 (Ken Welsh), 35 (Stapleton Collection)
Cody Images: 8, 12, 15, 17, 23, 28, 30, 41, 44, 49, 56, 60, 64, 70, 73, 75, 77, 80, 82, 87, 89, 94, 96–98 (all), 109, 111, 113, 116, 118, 125–128 all, 134, 152, 179
Corbis: 20 (Hulton), 22 (Hulton), 95 (Bettmann), 107 (Rob Howard), 143 (EPA/Anja Niedringhaus), 148 (Kate Brooks), 163 (In Pictures/Richard Baker), 164 (Reuters/Paul Saxby), 167 (Reuters/Chris Helgren), 172 (Reuters/Atef Hassan)
Mary Evans Picture Library: 31 (Robert Hunt Library)
Getty Images: 19 (Science and Society), 50 (Hulton), 63, 119 (Hulton), 123, 157 (Ghaith Abdul-Ahad), 161 (Giles Penfound), 184 (AFP/John D. McHugh)
LEI: 182
McMillan Group International, LLC: 149
Press Association Images: 137 (Musa Sadulayev), 142 (Zoran Sinko), 144 (Rikard Larma)
Public Domain: 43, 66, 101, 102, 108
Topfoto: 52 (Novosti)
Ukrainian State Archive: 7, 38, 42, 47, 55, 58
U.S. Department of Defense: 6, 68, 79, 84, 88, 90, 92, 105, 106, 115, 120, 121, 132, 140, 141, 150, 151, 154, 159, 165, 166, 168–171 all, 174–176 all, 181, 183, 186–187 both

Contents

Introduction   6

1. FROM SKIRMISHERS TO SHARPSHOOTERS   8

2. SNIPERS IN THE TRENCHES   24

3. THE MARKSMAN AND MANEUVER WARFARE   38

4. COLD WAR CONFLICTS   92

5. THE MODERN SPECIALIST   132

Appendices   186
Bibliography   188
Index   188

INTRODUCTION

The sniper, as this particular breed of solitary marksman is now called, is the master of many skills. He is first and foremost a marksman and supreme practitioner with a long-range rifle; he is a master of movement – able to maneuver himself into position unseen and remain undetected, often for hours, sometimes for days; he is an expert at camouflage, taking this art way beyond the skills of a regular soldier; and he has a general's ability to assess ground, fields of fire and the optimum positions to take advantage of all these.

The common snipe bird, which gives its name to the sniper, is known to be remarkably difficult to find on the ground, because of the way it conceals itself in long grass and its well-camouflaged nest and because of its erratic flight. These skills enable both the snipe and the sniper to survive. Concealment from the enemy mixed with deadly accuracy of aim make the sniper an extremely effective weapon and creates a hugely disproportionate effect on the enemy. A sniper is capable of literally reaching the enemy's heart with

INTRODUCTION

his unseen hand, striking terror into all those around. Not only can the unseen bullets of the sniper keep large numbers of troops pinned down and too afraid to move, they can also eliminate key personnel and thus create an instant impact on the chain of command and morale of the enemy.

This mortal efficiency has caused the sniper to be respected, feared and loathed. The sniper seems akin to an assassin, although in military terms his aims are no different to any other of the fighting arms. A machine-gunner blazing away may hit targets almost at random. An artilleryman is unlikely to see the effects of his shells. A submarine captain is inured from the terror and devastation wreaked by a torpedo and an airman is similarly detached from the damage and victims below. The cold hand of the sniper, however, has a personal and clinical quality that sets it apart.

This book will chart the development of the sniper through history, from the early roots of the sniper as a master of fieldcraft and hunting. Those with the skills to stalk animals and shoot them at long ranges, such as the American frontiersmen, possessed the natural skills to hit human targets from concealed positions. The book examines the personal characteristics and motivations of the sniper through the years and highlights some of the leading snipers in history. The book charts the development of sniping in different wars, how it was used by smaller forces to have a disproportionate effect on larger ones and how it was also used by world powers struggling to contain insurgents in Iraq and Afghanistan. In between are some of the great battles of World War I and World War II, including the stalemate at Stalingrad when the sniper was king.

The book also analyzes the tools of the sniper's trade, from the British Baker and Whitworth rifles of the nineteenth century, through the Lee-Enfield, M-1 Garand, Gewehr 41 and Mosin-Nagant rifles of World War I and World War II to the M82A1 Barrett of the twenty-first century.

Opposite: U.S. Marine Corps scout/snipers at Marine Corps Development and Education Command. Both snipers wear ghillie suits, developed from the camouflage originally used by Scottish ghillies, which enables them to blend effectively with their surroundings and also breaks up their profile. The Marines are equipped with the M40A3 sniper rifle.

Right: A Soviet sniper of 21st Army on the Stalingrad front in the winter of 1943, wearing a snow camouflage tunic over layers of cold-weather clothing. He carries a Model 1891/30 Mosin-Nagant bolt-action rifle with a x4 magnification PE sight as well as binoculars for observation.

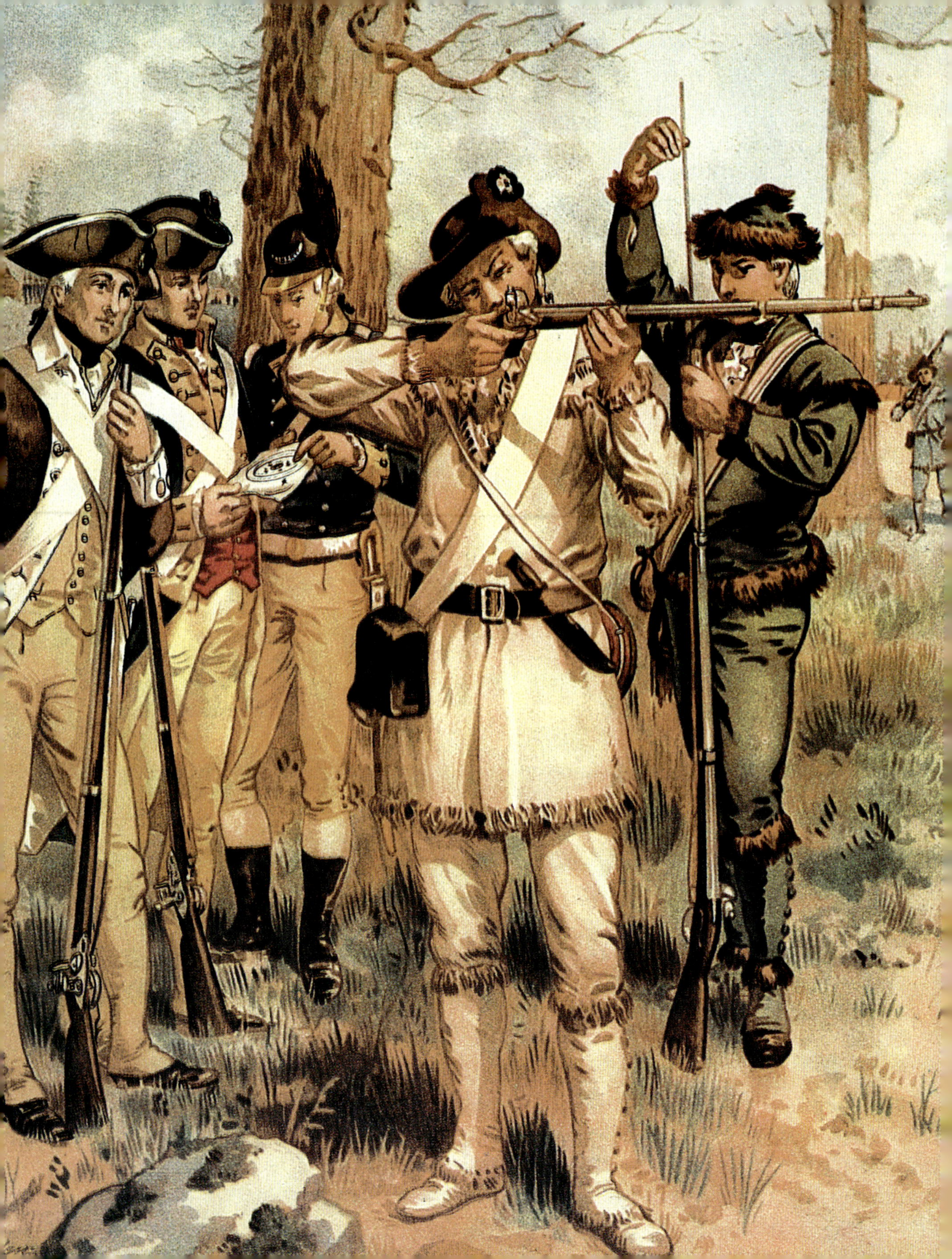

CHAPTER ONE

FROM SKIRMISHERS TO SHARPSHOOTERS

The name Timothy Murphy may not have the same resonance in American folklore as, say, Daniel Boone but the two had much in common. Both were sons of immigrants from the British Isles – Murphy from Irish and Boone from English and Welsh parents. Both were backwoodsmen and frontiersmen, used to hunting for a living, familiar with the ways of Indian tribes and used to surviving for many days on their own. Both men were emblematic of a young country and of the topsy-turvy approach to authority with which that country liked to associate itself. It was an attitude that would continue in later years to create the legend of the Wild West.

Opposite: *A member of Morgan's Sharpshooters, founded by General Daniel Morgan, fires a Pennsylvania rifle during shooting practice. The brown-fringed buckskin coat and trousers provided an element of camouflage while also being practical and easy to move in.*

FROM SKIRMISHERS TO SHARPSHOOTERS

In the American War of Independence (1776–83), during the defense of the Middle Fort in Schoharic Creek in September 1780 against the forces of the British under Sir John Johnston, Timothy Murphy, although of relatively junior rank, imposed his will on both his own commander and the British who were attempting to parlay. Against the orders of his commander, Murphy fired two shots over the heads of the British truce party, forcing them to withdraw and then threatened to shoot anyone in the fort who attempted to run up a flag of surrender. Although Murphy undermined his commander, who resigned his command, the fort was held. Murphy had demonstrated some of the characteristics of the sniper. Although on this occasion he did not shoot to kill, effectively he held his own forces and the British under the power of his rifle. He showed the independence, resilience and self-confidence of the sniper who can literally call the shots. On another famous occasion Timothy Murphy's shots would be dead on target and effectively decide the course of a battle.

MORGAN'S SHARPSHOOTERS
Daniel Morgan (1736–1802) was a pioneer of Welsh immigrant roots who gave his name to one of the most significant and effective units to fight in the American War of Independence – Morgan's Sharpshooters.

Below: *This painting shows Morgan's Sharpshooters at the Battle of Saratoga, one of whom is up a tree (top right), sighting the enemy and preparing to shoot. (By American artist H Charles McBarron.)*

KENTUCKY RIFLE

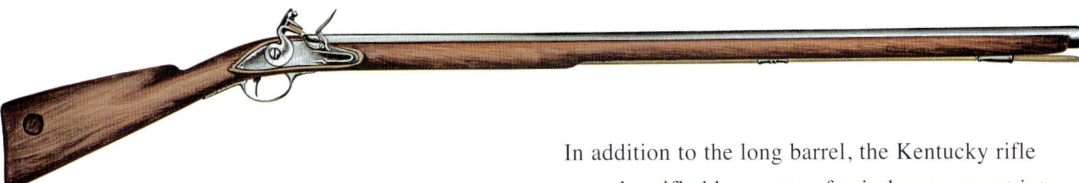

Country of Origin	North American colonies
Caliber	15mm (0.60in) approx.
Overall length	1651mm (65in)
Barrel length	889mm (35in)
Weight	variable

In addition to the long barrel, the Kentucky rifle was also rifled by means of spiral grooves cut into the inside of the barrel. This caused the bullet to spin which maintained a more accurate flight on its way to the target.

Morgan first assembled his team of snipers in 1775 before the siege of Boston. Although Morgan was captured later at the siege of Quebec in Canada in 1775, he returned to active service in 1777 as part of the 11th Virginia Regiment. Later, Morgan took part in the battles of Saratoga, which included the incident involving one of his most famous sharpshooters, Timothy Murphy.

In the second Battle of Saratoga in October 1777 the British General Burgoyne was supported by General Fraser. Fraser's men were confronted by Morgan's Sharpshooters, among whom was Timothy Murphy. It is said that General Benedict Arnold, recognizing the danger from Fraser and his men, went up to General Morgan and ordered him to dispose of Fraser. According to the story, Morgan assigned Timothy Murphy to perform one of the first recorded sniper actions. Murphy is said to have climbed a tree and taken careful aim with his rifle at a range of 275m (300 yards). He squeezed off a shot and the British general fell from his horse, mortally wounded. Murphy is then said to have shot the British officer Sir Frances Clarke. The effect on British morale was immediate and as fatal as the shots that had been so carefully delivered. Resistance began to crumble and the British retreated. Saratoga is considered to be a turning point in the American War of Independence. At the Battle of Cowpens in 1781, Morgan showed his true mettle as a general and made maximum use of the skill of his sharpshooters. The British walked into a devastating fire at long range from Morgan's Sharpshooters who then reloaded and delivered another volley at short range. The result was a clear American victory.

The Kentucky Rifle

Perhaps the weapon that is most emblematic of the American frontiersman is the Kentucky rifle. Sometimes known as the Long Rifle or Pennsylvania Rifle, this weapon probably originated with German immigrant gunsmiths and was characterized by a long barrel that could be between 89–127cm (35–50in). The reason for the long barrel was to provide better accuracy over long ranges. In the huge expanses in which the frontiersmen operated, accuracy at long range was at a premium.

Rifling, the long barrel and a relatively narrow bore gave the Kentucky rifleman a range of about 275m (300 yards), which gave him a huge advantage in approaching game unawares. It goes without saying what advantage an unseen rifleman could have over an approaching human enemy. As the American settlers could not always match the advancing British columns of troops head on, they compensated by using highly accurate fire while the British were in their range but when they were out of range of British fire. Accurate fire from a Kentucky rifle could knock out a man at 228m (250 yards) whereas the British standard-issue Long Land Pattern "Brown Bess" musket only had an effective range of 46–91m (50–100 yards).

FERGUSON'S RIFLE CORPS

Good shooting skills were not confined to the American frontiersmen, however. Major Patrick Ferguson (1744–80) was a Scottish officer who served in the 70th Foot and was an early exponent of light infantry tactics. He also gave his name to a novel breech-loading rifle that made the task of firing and reloading from concealed positions much easier. Although the rifle was only produced in limited numbers and had several defects, it proved to be a groundbreaking design and was later perfected by other manufacturers.

Like his adversary, Morgan, Ferguson organized a group of men drawn from various light infantry units called Ferguson's Rifle Corps. The rifle corps was eventually disbanded because of the number of casualties it suffered. The reason for this was simple: they were always in the thick of the action.

It is said that Ferguson once had none other than General George Washington in his rifle sights but that he chose not to pull the trigger because at the time the General had his back to him, which troubled his sense of fair play. If Ferguson had pulled the trigger, one solitary sniper could have not only changed the course of the American War of Independence but of world history as well.

THE FRENCH REVOLUTIONARY AND NAPOLEONIC WARS 1792–1815

Having been given the runaround by the American Revolutionaries and ultimately defeated, the British were not long in learning their lesson. The British Army was relatively small and in the war against revolutionary France they would need to develop the best possible tactics to counter the sheer weight of French columns.

A new rifle was commissioned, designed by Ezekiel Baker, which, although it did not have the accuracy and range of the Kentucky rifle, at least provided British forces with a more accurate rifle and with greater range than the standard Long Land Pattern "Brown Bess" musket.

The 95th Rifles

With the new rifle, and following the initiatives of people like Patrick Ferguson and Colonel Coote Manningham, a new corps of riflemen was introduced, to be known initially as the 95th Rifles. This regiment was distinguished from regular line

Left: *A British soldier of the Peninsular War manning a redoubt carries the "Brown Bess" British Land Pattern flintlock musket. As this only had an effective range of up to 91m (100 yards), riflemen were issued with the more accurate Baker rifle.*

FROM SKIRMISHERS TO SHARPSHOOTERS

infantry by wearing a dark green uniform, which made it easier to camouflage themselves. The men were all proficient with rifles and some of them were crack shots. Taking a leaf out of the book of the American sharpshooters, the British riflemen would demoralize and create confusion among advancing French forces by picking off officers and NCOs before they came into contact with the regular troops.

The 95th quickly became an elite that attracted a strong following from more adventurous and independent-minded young men. After all, the skirmishers were not confined by the formalities of columns and could use more initiative than was possible in serried ranks. "Hurrah for the first in the field and the last out of it, the fighting 95th!" was a cry that attracted men like the Scots farmer's son John Kincaid whose exploits would later inspire the successful Sharpe series of stories by Bernard Cornwell. To give a sense of the importance of this new regiment, it not only fired the first shots in the first battle of the Peninsular War, which took place in Portugal and Spain from 1808, but it took part in every battle all the way up to and including Waterloo.

> *"Hurrah for the first in the field and the last out of it, the fighting 95th!"*

The Light Division, of which the 95th was part, also included the Portuguese *caçadores* – a name that literally means "hunters." Under Robert "Black Bob" Craufurd, they set up a chain of outposts and communications which enabled them to closely monitor the movements of the enemy and to intervene when necessary. This close knowledge of the ground and ability to observe the enemy unseen is very much the role of the sniper.

One soldier of the 95th was particularly prominent for his marksmanship. Thomas Plunkett had served with the regiment in a disappointing campaign in

Above: *Contrasting with the scarlet uniform of the regular British infantry, a soldier of the 95th Rifles is dressed in dark green uniform with black accoutrements. He has a shoulder belt and carries a Baker rifle which could be fitted with a long brass-hilted sword bayonet.*

THE FERGUSON RIFLE

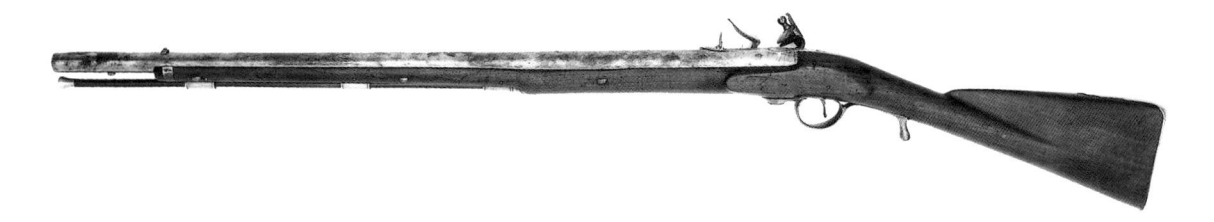

Country of Origin	Great Britain
Caliber	17.27mm (0.68in)
Overall length	1200mm (47.25in)
Barrel length	800mm (31.5in)
Weight	5kg (11lbs) excluding bayonet

Patrick Ferguson adapted a French design of rifle of 1720 called the de la Chaumette. The redesign involved a breech plug that was lowered by turning the trigger guard. The ball was then inserted, followed by the powder. Any excess of powder was cleared by the screw when it was rotated back into place. This mechanism enabled a much higher rate of fire than with ordinary muzzle-loaders and trained soldiers could fire up to 10 rounds per minute. The Ferguson rifle had some weaknesses, one of which was that the stock was not strong enough and often cracked in the area of the lock.

South America which included an unsuccessful attack on Buenos Aires. Plunkett is said to have shot a Spanish officer and also a soldier carrying a white flag in an incident reminiscent of his fellow Irishman Timothy Murphy.

Later Plunkett was with the 95th under Sir John Moore on the famous retreat to Corunna in northern Spain. On January 3, 1809, in its usual position of being the last off the battlefield, the 95th was covering the retreat of the British Army, which had become somewhat disorderly. The French pursuers were very close and, as they reached a bridge at Cacabellos in the mountains of Galicia, the French cavalry under their commander Auguste-Marie-François Colbert, attacked. Various accounts suggest that at this point Thomas Plunkett ran out towards the bridge and took up a position where he could aim at the French officer. Plunkett killed Colbert with his first shot and then killed another French officer who came to Colbert's aid. The effect on the French cavalry was immediate. The shock of losing their commander sent them reeling back and the solitary sniper Thomas Plunkett could return to his grateful comrades who had been saved from a nasty scrap with the enemy.

Sniping at Nelson

The Battle of Trafalgar in 1805 marks two significant events: Britain's greatest naval victory and the death of her greatest naval hero, Admiral Horatio Nelson.

After attacking the combined French and Spanish fleet led by Admiral Villeneuve, Nelson's flagship HMS *Victory* became closely engaged with the *Redoutable*, commanded by Captain Lucas. The French captain was an able individual and his men were well trained. Many sharpshooters were sent up to the tops of the French ship to pick off targets below. One of these shot Nelson, who died shortly afterwards, having been taken below. According to Robert Southey, who wrote a biography of Nelson, the shot was taken from a range of about 14m (15 yards). The crew of HMS *Victory* began to avenge the death of their admiral and fired back at the Frenchmen. Lieutenant John Pollard and Midshipman Francis Edward Collingwood are credited with shooting the man who shot Nelson along with many of the sniper's comrades.

THE AMERICAN CIVIL WAR 1861–65

By the time the American Civil War was underway, the rifle was no longer the preserve of elite sharpshooters but was standard issue. However, some rifles were better than others and sharpshooting and sniper tactics would evolve so that targets could be picked off at ever greater distances.

Berdan's Sharpshooters

In a similar way to Daniel Morgan and his sharpshooters of the American War of Independence, Hiram Berdan (1824–93) organized sharpshooter regiments for the Federal Army that were dressed in a similar way to the British 95th Rifles, wearing a green uniform with black facings. Hiram Berdan described it as consisting of:

a green cloth coat, with black metal buttons – pants of same color and material. Goatskin

Below: *Admiral Horatio Nelson is shot by a French sharpshooter on the quarterdeck of HMS* Victory *at 1:15, October 21, 1805. It is thought that the fatal shot was fired from the mizzen topmast of the* Redoutable, *commanded by Captain Lucas.*

leggings [sic], and hair outside. 2 pair strong low shoes – with leather gaiters. Grey felt hat. Grey overcoat with cape moveable and india rubber lined. The fatigue dress will be green flannel "round about" [jacket] and pants – 2 pairs grey Russia linen pants and proper under clothes.

He explained,
My reasons for selecting this uniform are that the men composing this regiment will not content to wear the common U.S. uniform; and as they will be skirmishers, they not be conspicuously dressed – the green will harmonize with the leaves of summer while the grey overcoat will accord with surrounding objects in fall and winter. The goatskin leggings are to protect the legs against snakes and briars.

Berdan also developed a rifle, though his corps were initially issued with Colt revolving rifles and later with 1000 Sharps breech-loading rifles. These were effective weapons, which in trained hands could fire up to ten rounds per minute. In addition or as an alternative to the Sharps, Union sharpshooters sometimes used a variety of sporting or hunting rifles, including the muzzle-loading Dimick sporting and target rifle and the Spencer magazine rifle. Berdan's Sharpshooters were required to pass a rigorous selection test, which included the requirement to group ten shots in succession on a target of 25.4cm (10in) diameter from 183m (200 yards). The sharpshooters were to play an important role in many battles of the Civil War. In the Battle of Gettysburg in July 1863, they were prominent in engaging Confederates on a rocky outcrop known as the Devil's Den.

Confederate marksmen

Although Berdan's Sharpshooters were well trained and well equipped, the Confederates had some natural sharpshooters in their own ranks and these made a considerable impact. Whereas the Federal sharpshooters tended to come from educated backgrounds, the Confederates fielded a large number of men who were used to hunting in the wild, and possessed tracking, concealment and rifle skills. Some of the best sniper rifles for the Confederates were produced in England. Due to a Federal naval blockade, these rifles were difficult to come by and, partly due to the difficulties in supply and partly due to the quality of craftsmanship, they were very expensive to buy. The most popular of the English rifles were the 1853 Enfield Rifle and the prized Whitworth long-range target rifle.

The Whitworth rifle was designed with a hexagonal bore and incorporated a fast-twist polygonal rifling system. It had its own ammunition, which was carefully designed to be exact and consistent in weight and size. The result was unparalleled accuracy at considerable ranges. Since the Whitworths were only allocated to the best marksmen, the combination was formidable.

Like their British counterparts, the Confederate sharpshooters were often first in the field and the last out. Unfortunately, many did not leave the field of battle at all for they were often in the most exposed positions and casualty rates were correspondingly high. Even where the sharpshooters were well concealed, their lethal effectiveness was sometimes met with a devastating response from the enemy. At the Devil's Den at Gettysburg, for example, a Confederate sharpshooter was killed by an artillery round. If the Confederate sharpshooters were less organized than their Union counterparts, they certainly had a way of dealing with criticism. General John Sedgwick was unwise enough to comment on the shooting ability of Confederate skirmish lines at the beginning of the Battle of Spotsylvania Court

Opposite: *Major-General John Sedgwick was shot in the head by a sharpshooter with a Whitworth rifle at a range of roughly 900m (500 yards). Ironically, he had just been telling his men to ignore the Confederate sharpshooters. This underlined the power of the sniper to change the course of a battle by shooting senior commanders.*

FROM SKIRMISHERS TO SHARPSHOOTERS

House on May 9, 1864, when his corps was probing forward against skirmishers. At about 910m (1000 yards) his men were already diving cover as rounds came over. In an attempt to rally his men, Sedgwick shouted, "They couldn't hit an elephant at this distance!" With these words, he fell off his horse with a bullet hole under his left eye. At that range, the bullet was likely to have come from a Whitworth rifle.

> "They couldn't hit an elephant at this distance!"
>
> Last words of General John Sedgwick, May 9, 1864

Although American Civil War battles featured incidents attributed to individual sharpshooters, such as the death of General Sedgwick, on the whole the sharpshooter regiments acted as skirmishers, their movements largely based on *Rifle and Light Infantry Tactics* by William Hardee. The skirmishing formation involved spreading out in groups of four with about five paces between each man, thus forming what has been described as a "cloud" of men. Due to the distances between the men, the skirmishers were taught to respond to bugle calls instead of voiced orders. Unlike regular soldiers of the time, when called to a halt, the skirmishers would automatically seek the nearest cover, whether behind a tree, rock or other obstacle or by falling flat on the ground. In this way, they were almost identical to the modern soldier.

THE ANGLO-AFGHAN WARS

In the novel *Kim* by Rudyard Kipling set in British Imperial India Kim says: "Now I shall go far and far into the North, playing the Great Game." Though Kim was a boy and would not have fully understood the "game," it was in fact political and military maneuvering between Britain and Russia, which resulted from Russian probing south into Central Asia and British concern about the threat to the jewel of their Empire India. The "Great Game," which lasted for about a hundred years, was partly played in the rugged and inhospitable mountains of Afghanistan and here the British and Russians met a formidable foe, the Afghan mountain tribesmen.

The British came to the conclusion that, in order to provide a buffer between India and the Russians, they should occupy Afghanistan. So, in December 1838 a large British force moved north into Afghanistan where they took over Kabul and installed a friendly ruler. The Afghans soon came to resent the British occupation. There were many reasons for this, including insensitivity towards their culture and immoral treatment of Afghan women by British soldiers. By 1841, riots had broken out in Kabul and a senior British officer, Sir Alexander Burnes, was murdered by a mob. When another British officer was killed and his body dragged through the streets, the British decided to withdraw. This was not so much the end of the nightmare for the British as the beginning. As the British occupation began to implode, the Afghans attacked British outposts. On one occasion a British brigadier formed up his men in squares, anticipating an Afghan cavalry attack, only to find his men dropping down dead all around him. The Afghans were not risking their lives in a cavalry charge but instead picking off the British soldiers from long range with their Jezails, or long-barrelled muskets. These had a longer range than the standard-issue British Brown Bess and were more accurate. The only hope the British had in this situation was their nine-pounder cannon. The Afghans knew this and carefully targeted the gun crew with their Jezails. Soon the British could do nothing but flee for their lives.

The retreat from Kabul

On January 6, 1842 the British forces began their retreat from Kabul through the treacherous passes. As soon as they left, the Afghans began to snipe at them at long range with their Jezails. This was

THE JEZAIL

The Jezail was a mostly homemade weapon adapted by Afghan tribesmen in such a way as to take advantage of existing technology (the lock and trigger mechanism was often taken from discarded or captured Brown Bess muskets) while adding certain refinements to improve range and accuracy.

The barrel was long and designed to take close-fitting ammunition. It was often rifled. The stock had a characteristic curve, which suggests it may have been designed to fit under the arm. The Jezail was often fired while supported on a forked rest to support the long barrel.

The stocks and other parts of the Jezail were often finely decorated. A Jezail could be used effectively at 457m (500 yards), whereas the Brown Bess had a maximum effective range of 137m (150 yards).

Below: Afghan soldiers watch one of their companions as he aims a Jezail, the long-barrelled musket. The Jezail had an effective range of about 457m (500 yards) and was very effective when fired from secluded sniping positions.

followed by attacks on horseback. To add to the misery of the fleeing British-Indian army, which included women, children and retainers, the Afghan winter was bitterly cold and many became victims of frostbite. After a night in the open, during which many died of exposure, they set off again but the Afghans continued to snipe at them from long range. As they approached the Khoord-Cabol Pass, the Afghans had taken up sniping positions in the rocky crags. About three thousand died in the pass.

A British soldier, Dr. William Brydon, who was the only Englishman to survive the massacre, at one point rode straight at an Afghan with a Jezail. The Jezail bullets broke his sword and wounded his pony but he managed to get away. At Gandamak, the 44th Regiment of Foot mounted a last stand and were all killed. In the words of Peter Hopkirk, author of *The Great Game: On Secret Service in High Asia*, echoing the thoughts of the British Governor-General in India, "A mob of mere heathen savages, armed with home-made weapons, had succeeded in routing the greatest power on earth."

The British response

The British had been humiliated but they managed to put a tough general in charge of a relief force that would restore some of their dignity. General George Pollock recognized the tactical advantage the Afghans held with their Jezail marksmen and he made sure his troops were not going to be served up as easy targets again. As his expedition set off through the Khyber Pass, he sent flanking columns up onto the high

Below: *The opening of the Siri Bolam Pass in 1839 on the way to Kabul by James Atkinson shows how difficult it was for the forces moving in the passes to deal effectively with their assailants in the rocks above. Tribesmen armed with the Jezail could pick off their victims at will.*

"BOB THE NAILER"

During the Indian rebellion of 1857, sometimes known as the Indian Mutiny, the city of Lucknow, capital of Oudh, was besieged by a Sepoy army. The British were defending the Residency within the city, which also contained civilians. The rebellion had been triggered by the introduction of the Enfield rifle, which required a greased cartridge. It was believed that the cartridge grease was made from beef and pork fat, which would defile the Hindu and Muslim soldiers.

About eight thousand Indian Sepoys and several hundred other native rebels besieged the Residency between July and September 1857. Apart from indiscriminate shelling, the Sepoy rebels employed a number of highly effective sharpshooters, the most famous of which became known as "Bob the Nailer," due to the fact that he used nails as ammunition.

Bob the Nailer demonstrated many of the characteristics of a classic sniper. He would lie in wait for hours, having selected an invulnerable firing position, until he saw a glimpse of a red uniform or any sign of movement. He would then literally nail his victim. There was no time of day or night when the defenders felt safe from the attentions of Bob the Nailer. Shooting back at him proved useless and eventually the defenders had to dig a tunnel under the house where the Nailer was lodged and plant a mine to blow him up.

ground. As the Afghans took aim at the troops below them, they were astonished to find themselves being fired upon from above. The British had learned their lesson, at least temporarily: to deal with snipers, use other snipers.

As the tension with Russia continued, the British were back in Afghanistan for the Second Afghan War of 1879–80. In most of the battles fought on open ground the British prevailed, but at the Battle of Maiwand in 1880 they were heavily defeated by the Afghans. There is a coda to this battle: Sir Arthur Conan Doyle's fictional character Dr. Watson, companion of Sherlock Holmes, was said to have been wounded at Maiwand by an Afghan Jezail.

THE BOER WARS

The Boer Wars (1881–82 and 1899–1902), fought between the British and the Boer farmers of Dutch descent in southern Africa, offered a familiar recipe. Here again was a substantial army trained for traditional tactics up against lightly equipped men of farming stock who used movement and concealment along with accurate shooting to make up for their inferior numbers.

The Battle of Majuba Hill in 1881 underlined the difference in approach. The British trained their soldiers to move as part of a larger unit and not to think for themselves. The Boers, on the other hand, like the American frontiersmen, were individualists, trekkers, good horsemen and good hunters.

At Majuba Hill, instead of attacking the British *en masse*, as the British might have expected them to do, the Boers made maximum use of the available cover and fired at the British from long ranges. As their comrades and officers began to fall around them, British discipline began to crumble. There was little the British could do about it. They could order their men to fire back but there seemed to be nothing visible to fire at. Blending into their surroundings, the Boers could barely be seen. The last straw for the British came when their commander, Sir George Colley, was shot by a Boer marksman when trying to organize an orderly retreat. This was classic sniper work: causing maximum confusion by taking out selected important targets. The British tried to make their escape but were sniped at from ridges as they went. The Boers had demonstrated their mastery of sniping tactics as well as fire and movement.

In the Second Boer War, at Magersfontein in 1899 and at Spion Kop in 1900, the British were also subjected to accurate fire from Boer marksmen who were either hidden in craggy knolls or concealed in well-dug trenches, invisible to the eye. Devastatingly accurate rifle fire soon sowed confusion. To add to their difficulties, developments in gunpowder technology meant that there was barely any smoke once a Boer Mauser rifle had been fired to identify the marksman's position. At the Siege of Mafeking, however, the tables were turned. Here the Boers were the dominant force and the British, commanded by the founder of the Scouts, Lord Baden-Powell, were the underdogs who survived due to ingenuity.

Although the Boers were eventually defeated, there were many lessons to be learned in the Boer War for large armies fighting against smaller ones or even against bands of guerrillas. Surprisingly, by the time of the next major war in Europe in 1914, fire and movement was all but forgotten and huge armies settled down for a static slogging match.

Opposite: *Three elements in this photograph demonstrate the effectiveness of the Boer sharpshooter: the powerful Mauser rifles, the plentiful ammunition clips and the clear sharp eyes of the natural hunter. They were also masters of camouflage and fieldcraft.*

Below: *Boer sharpshooters at the Siege of Mafeking between October 1899 and May 1900. Well concealed, and with accurate, powerful Mauser rifles, the Boers were a formidable foe.*

FROM SKIRMISHERS TO SHARPSHOOTERS

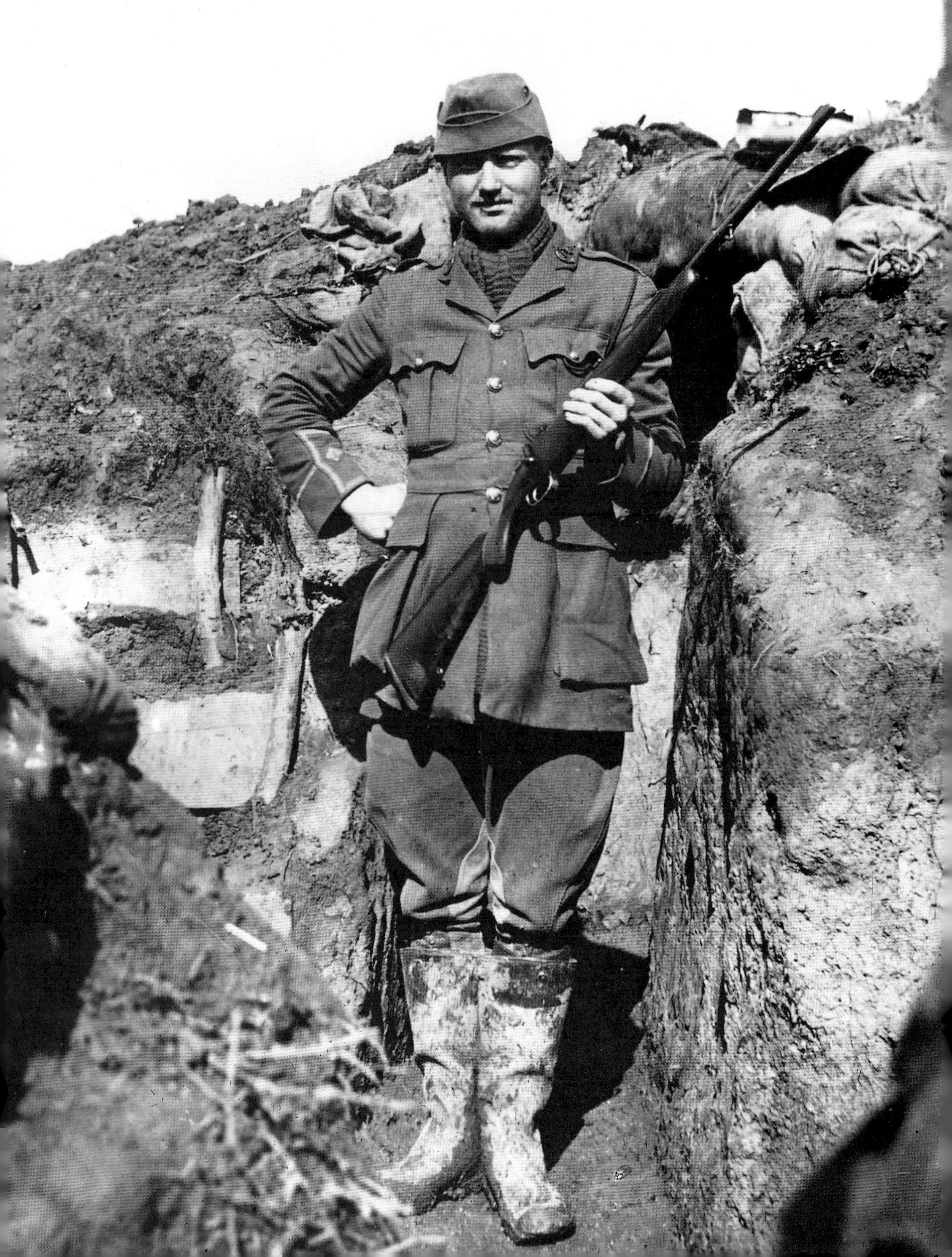

CHAPTER TWO

SNIPERS IN THE TRENCHES

In the foreword to *Sniping in France* by Major H. Hesketh-Prichard, General Lord Horne writes that "we were slow to adopt, indeed our souls abhorred, anything unsportsmanlike." The "unsportsmanlike" methods Horne was referring to included the use of gas and of sniping. The Germans were ahead of the game with regard to sniping at the beginning of World War I. In the stalemate of the opposing trench systems and with No Man's Land blasted and cratered by artillery, infantrymen had several major fears: these included going over the top and being shot down by machine-gun fire or inadvertently raising their heads above the trench line or crossing a gap and being found by a sniper.

Opposite: *This .280 caliber Ross hunting rifle was presented as a gift from Lord Londonderry to a junior officer in the 2nd Durham Light Infantry at Houplines, France, in 1915. Officers would often use their own personalized weapons, and hunting rifles made excellent sniping tools.*

Above: *A sniperscope is used by a British marksman in the trenches during World War I. The idea was to fire the rifle while remaining below the trench line but the eccentric device did not prove very effective.*

German snipers at the beginning of the war were well trained and well equipped. They were often recruited from gamekeepers, hunters and others who were well versed in long-range shooting and tracking their quarry. Apart from natural talent and training, the sniper needs excellent equipment. The German sniper had both a good rifle, the Gewehr 98, and good telescopic sights. The Germans had a wide range of manufacturers of high-grade optical sights to draw on, including Zeiss, Goerz, Hensoldt and Voigtlander. Today, Hensoldt continues to produce military sights as the military arm of Zeiss. Fitted with such sights, the Gewehr 98 had an effective range of 800m (875 yards) which, in view of the fact that opposing trenches were sometimes only 182m (200 yards) apart, provided plenty of scope. As the standard Gewehr 98 was not designed to take optics, a special production variant with an altered bolt was produced for sniping. Over eighteen thousand of these adapted rifles were issued to snipers during World War I, demonstrating the German commitment to sniping from the outset.

Ernst Junger (1895–1998) served in the 73rd Hanoverian Fusilier Regiment during World War I and his memories of the war were vividly recorded in his books *Storm of Steel* and *Copse 125*. He was soon recognized as an exceptionally brave soldier and was awarded the Iron Cross First Class and the Pour le mérite, or "Blue Max." On one occasion, as he relates in *Copse 125*, Junger went out into No Man's Land accompanied by a spotter known as "H" to try to neutralize British marksmen. After waiting patiently, an unsuspecting victim eventually came into view.

Suddenly a sound rang out – a sound foreign to this noontide scene, an ominous clinking as of a helmet or bayonet striking the side of a trench. At the same moment I felt a hand grip my leg and heard a low-breathed whistle behind me. It was H., for he had passed those hours in the same alert attention as I.

I pushed back with my foot to warn him and at the same moment a greenish-yellow shadow flitted across the exposed part of the trench. It was a tall figure in a clay-coloured uniform, with a flat helmet set well down over his forehead and both hands grasping his rifle, which was slung from his neck by a strap. It must have been the relief as he came from the rear; and now it could only be a matter of seconds till the man he relieved passed across the same spot. I sighted my rifle on it sharply.

A murmuring of voices arose from behind the screen of glass, broken now and again by suppressed laughter or a soft clanking. Then a tiny puff of smoke ascended – the moment had come when the returning post lit a pipe or cigarette for the way back. And in fact he appeared a moment later, first his helmet only, next his whole figure. His luck was against him, for just as he came in line of aim, he turned round and took his cigarette from his mouth – probably to add a word that occurred to him during the few steps he had come. It was his last, for at that moment the iron chain between shoulder, hand and butt was drawn tight and the patch pocket on the left side of his tunic

GEWEHR 98 RIFLE

This rifle was first manufactured in 1898 and remained the standard German infantry rifle throughout World War I. It was a manually operated bolt-action rifle fed by a five-round magazine. It had a relatively long barrel at 740mm (29.1in) (compared with the 640mm [25.2in] of the British Lee-Enfield), which, while less practical for close-quarters combat and rapid fire, was well suited to the sniping role.

The bolt-action system designed by Mauser proved to be extremely effective and reliable, even if it did not allow quite such a rapid rate of fire as the system on the British Lee-Enfield. In 1915, 15,000 selected Gewehr 98 rifles were adopted specifically for sniper fire. In order to mount telescopic sights, the rifle was fitted with an adapted bolt design which kept the bolt out of the way of the sight. Despite these modifications, the telescopic sight still had to be mounted relatively high in order to keep clear of the bolt action and the safety catch. The success of the Gewehr 98 sniper-modified rifle was such that in due course over 18,000 were issued.

Country of Origin	Germany
Caliber	7.92mm (0.31in)
Overall length	1250mm (49.2in)
Barrel length	740mm (29.1in)
Weight	4.09kg (9lbs)

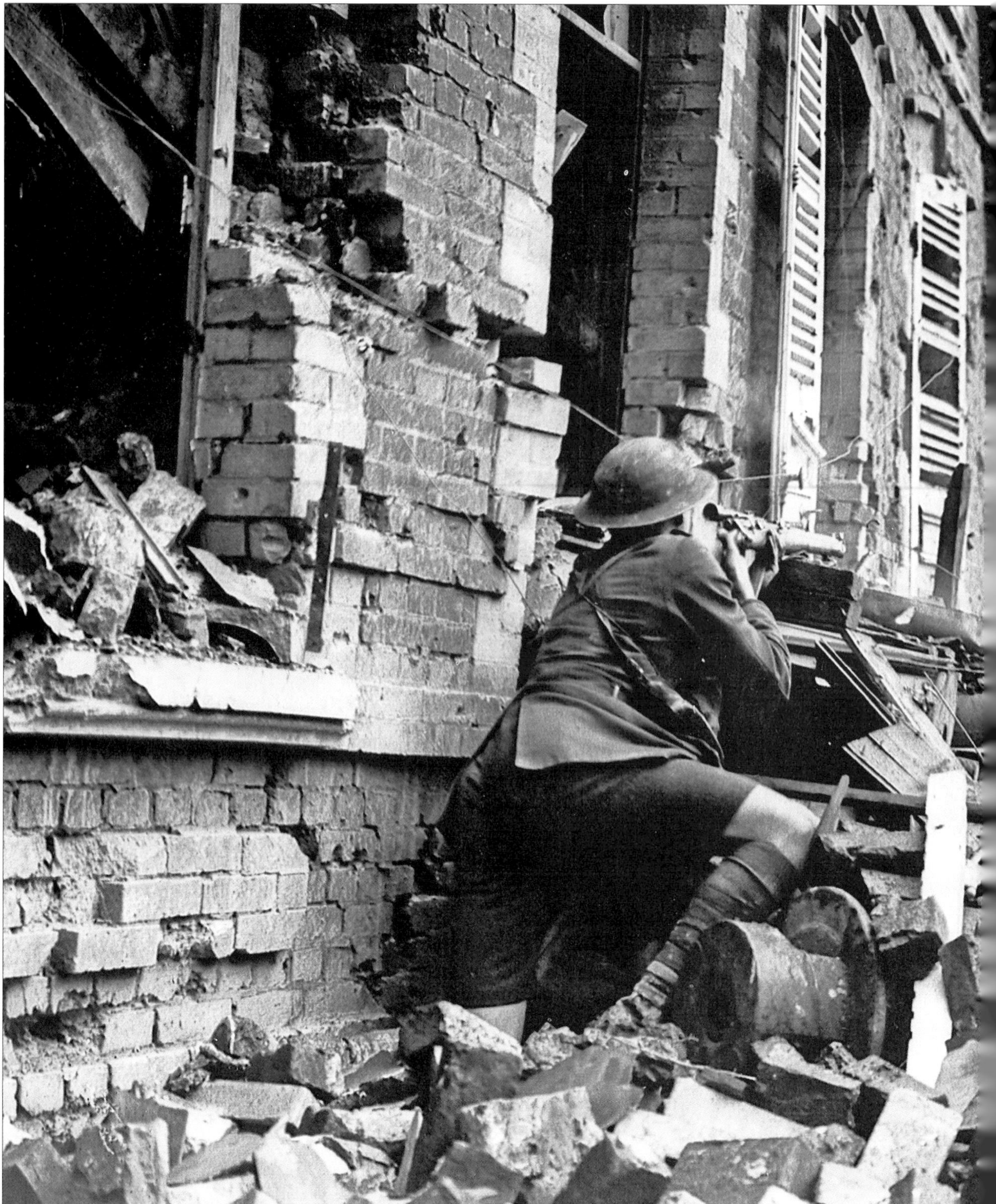

was taken as clearly on the foresight as though it were on the very muzzle of the rifle. Thus the shot took the words from his mouth. I saw him fall, and having seen many fall before this, I knew he would never get up again. He fell first against the side of the trench and then collapsed into a heap that obeyed the force of life no longer but only the force of gravity.

THE BRITISH SNIPER SCHOOL

So naive and unprepared were the British at the beginning of the war that they actually thought that their losses of men to individual rifle rounds were coincidental, in other words an enemy soldier just happened to be watching that gap when someone passed it. Little did they know that German snipers had every gap marked and that target opportunities that would be impossible for the naked eye over a standard iron sight were virtual sitting ducks for a trained sniper with advanced optics. Having come to the conclusion that, although on the face of it sniping was not cricket, it was even less sportsmanlike to allow their men to be cut down by sniper bullets, the British began to find ways to resolve the problem.

It had been discovered during attacks into German trenches that the German snipers sometimes operated from behind protective steel plates. Hesketh-Prichard obtained some of these steel plates and took them back to England. He did not want them for target practice; he wanted to discover which rifles had the power to penetrate them.

The Germans had designed the plates to be proof against standard rounds from the British issue .303 (7.7mm) Lee-Enfield but Hesketh-Prichard had access to other weapons, including rifles designed to stop an elephant. Now that the British authorities had woken up, Hesketh-Prichard was allowed to buy the weapons he needed.

Left: A British soldier armed with a Lee-Enfield rifle watches for potential targets amidst urban wreckage, Northern France, 1918.

Obtaining telescopic sights proved difficult because British industry was not as advanced as the Germans in producing this kind of equipment. The British took a pragmatic view of this problem and decided to try to obtain them from Germany. A deal was negotiated via Switzerland and the British obtained some Zeiss, Goerz and Voigtlander sights. By the end of the war, the optimum set up for a British sniper was said to be the 1914 Pattern .303, Mk 1 W(T) sniper rifle fitted with the Model 1918 telescopic sight.

Another problem was training the men to understand how to calibrate the telescopic sights and zero the weapons. Having an incorrectly adjusted telescopic sight was about as useless as not having one at all. In muddy and wet conditions, soldiers would sometimes unscrew the eye glasses in order to clear them and often refitted them incorrectly. The capstan heads of the sights were also sometimes wrongly adjusted.

On the German side, a specialist NCO was assigned to ensure that sights were properly calibrated and to fix any problems and the soldiers were also provided with written instructions.

As the momentum increased, Hesketh-Prichard managed to persuade the British high command to set up a sniping school, the First Army Sniping, Observation and Scouting School, at Linghem near Calais in 1916. At this school, selected officers were taught a range of skills, which they could then pass on to different corps and battalions in the army.

Below: *British troops at Gallipoli. The corporal in the foreground has a Lee-Enfield SMLE sniper rifle with a telescopic sight. During static trench warfare, the sniper was an important influence.*

TELESCOPIC SIGHTS IN WORLD WAR I

The first telescopic sight with a refractor lens was developed in 1880 by August Fiedler. A few telescopic sights were used for military purposes at the end of the nineteenth century but they came into their own in World War I, largely due to the development of sniping in the German army. Even so, at the beginning of the war the German army only had a small supply of these sights and many were procured second-hand from sporting and hunting rifles.

Telescopic sights presented the sniper with many advantages due to the clarity and magnification of the target. The disadvantages were that the sight itself was mounted high on the rifle and the lens could create a reflection that would attract the enemy. In muddy and wet conditions, the sights could be blurred and might also be difficult to adjust.

Pre-war, British sights were normally aperture target sights with a micro-adjustable rear sight. These were typically produced by BSA, Parker Hale, Westley Richards or Alex Martin. An official British Government tender was put out for a telescopic sight to fit the Mk. III Lee-Enfield. The Periscopic Prism Company of London and Aldis Brothers were two companies that offered to meet the requirements. Other British telescopic sights were produced by Watts, Rigby, Evans and Winchester.

Below: *The Germans began World War I with a sniper system fully organized. Here a German sniper awaits his opportunity, looking down the telescopic sight of a Gewehr 98 rifle, while his companion spots with field glasses.*

Snipers were also sent to the school from various parts of the army to improve their skills. These skills included compass and map work, crawling and the art of concealment.

STRATEGY AND TACTICS

By the beginning of World War I, it was generally accepted that soldiers should wear uniforms that blended in with their surroundings. The American sharpshooters of the Civil War, the British Rifle Brigade and the British Army of the Boer War had by now set the tone. There was, however, still a learning curve to be followed. The British in particular were slow on the uptake with regard to sniper tactics and it was only when a formal sniping school was set up that they began to realize the importance of sniper camouflage and concealment and to study it.

Camouflage and concealment

As Hesketh-Prichard says in his book *Sniping in France*: "The demonstrations showing the use of protective colouring and the choice of backgrounds always interested the classes very much. Often the whole class arrived within twenty yards of a man lying within full view without being able to spot him … in open warfare the observer and the scout have to obtain safety by concealment rather than by cover from fire."

As Hesketh-Prichard and others were to demonstrate, to camouflage a sniper effectively in the open a leap needed to be taken beyond the ordinary issue khaki uniform. The French contributed to the development of camouflage using their famous artistic skills. A jacket painted in 1915 by a French soldier called Guingot is thought to be one of the first examples of disruptive camouflage uniform. The French learned all too quickly that dressing their men in red trousers at the beginning of the war led directly to high casualty rates. The replacement light blue trousers were not ideal either but were at least an improvement. The gamekeepers or ghillies of the Scottish Highlands had learned to make a kind of portable hunting blind which provided three-dimensional camouflage and was designed to blend in with the surroundings. It was no point having a ghillie suit of bright green foliage if the setting was brown and autumnal. In World War I, much of the foliage was destroyed altogether so the sniper suit had to blend into the local mud and debris of the battlefield. If using real foliage from his surroundings, the sniper had to take into account that in due course it would start to wilt.

> *"Often the whole class arrived within twenty yards of a man lying within full view without being able to spot him … in open warfare the observer and the scout have to obtain safety by concealment rather than by cover from fire."*
>
> Sniping in France, *Hesketh-Prichard*

Turkish expertise

At Gallipoli, much to the discomfort of the Australians, the Turkish forces proved to be masters of disguise. Their snipers would not only conceal themselves effectively in their own lines but would also sometimes get behind the Australian lines, concealing themselves near oak trees and covering themselves in local foliage. Apart from camouflage that was worn, the sniper developed ways of concealing himself in trench lines and parapets so that his presence remained undetected even when the enemy were looking right in his direction. Part of the art of concealment lay in creating false holes and other ruses intended to distract the observer.

For example, the Germans often used steel sheets to protect their marksmen, with loopholes built in.

Above: A Turkish sniper captured by Australian forces at Gallipoli shows the high level of camouflage adopted by the Turks who sometimes operated behind Australian lines.

A canny sniper might set up a steel sheet with loopholes to attract attention while creating his real firing position and loophole behind some inconspicuous sandbags.

Other skills

Snipers had to learn to make the best use of the time of day or night, light conditions and so on. It was also important for the sniper to learn how to minimize movement so that he could lie in wait, take any necessary food and drink and get himself into the optimum firing position when the moment came. The Hawkins Position allowed the sniper to lie in wait for hours without undue fatigue while holding the weapon ready for use. This was a variation of the prone unsupported position with the upper sling swivel held by the non-firing hand, forming a fist to support the front of the weapon. The non-firing arm was locked straight. The butt of the weapon was rested on the ground and placed under the firing shoulder, minimizing the profile of the sniper while providing good stability and maximum concealment.

A good sniper is a creature of the shadows and always blends into his background. He never breaks the skyline, minimizes movement and sound proofs all his equipment. Hard edges, such as parts of the rifle, are broken up by the use of special camouflage bags or disruptive camouflage.

Early teamwork

Although the sniper is often thought of as working on his own, Hesketh-Prichard's school also taught the value of working with an observer equipped with a telescope. The pupils at the school were given training in deception techniques, which Hesketh-Prichard demonstrated in action when he set himself up as a dummy, having positioned a team of snipers in another place and told them to keep their heads down until the right moment.

Hesketh-Prichard deliberately attracted attention to himself by loosing random shots upon which the Germans let down their guard and revealed themselves. The sniping team thereupon accounted for them. The sniper school was used by Canadians, who proved to be very keen and adept snipers, and by other nationalities, including the Portuguese Army. British regiments with a particular talent for scouting included the Artists' Rifles and the Lovat Scouts.

In 1916, the Lovat Scouts (Sharpshooters) became the first official sniper unit in the British Army. Being formed largely of gamekeepers and ghillies from Scotland, they had a natural aptitude for concealment and stalking. The ghillie suit was named after them and is still used to describe a sniper camouflage suit. Lovat Scouts provided many of the trainers at the Sniping School and the unit was also deployed for sniping duties at Gallipoli.

CANADIAN SNIPERS

Canadians seemed to have a particular interest in and aptitude for sniping. An American serving in a Canadian regiment, Herbert McBride, also made a name for himself. Perhaps the most famous Canadian sniper was Corporal Francis Pegahmagabow (1891–1952), who had a tally of 378 enemies killed and 300 captured. "Peggy," as he was known, was a Native American of the Ojibwa tribe from Parry Island. He joined the 1st Canadian Infantry Battalion, which was the first Canadian battalion to be deployed to Europe. Peggy proved to be an extremely effective messenger and often got vital information through when under heavy fire. His real skill, however, was as a sniper. Either concealed in his own trenches or working his way unseen into No Man's Land, Peggy had a natural instinct for stealth and concealment and would lie patiently in wait for a target.

Peggy served at Ypres, on the Somme and at Passchendaele where he provided vital communications for the Canadians. He received the Military Medal for his work at Passchendaele, with a citation remarking on his skill as a scout:

> *"At Passchendaele November 6th/7th 1917, this NCO did excellent work. Before and after the attack he kept in touch with the flanks, advising the units he had seen, this information proving the success of the attack and saving valuable time in consolidating. He also guided the relief to its proper place after it had become mixed up."*
>
> *Official citation for Corporal Pegahmagabow*

Another Canadian sniper with a fearsome reputation was Henry Norwest. He was of Cree Indian stock and from his early years had developed the natural skills of a hunter, including stealth and patience. Norwest was also a master of camouflage.

He would often head out into No Man's Land or even behind enemy lines and lie undetected, sometimes for days, until he could be sure of his victim. Norwest used a rifle with a telescopic lens and his score is said to have been at least 115. These were kills confirmed by an independent observer. Norwest is likely to have made many more that were not officially confirmed. Due to his mastery of stealth and camouflage, Norwest was sometimes used by Canadian forces for observation missions. Unfortunately for Norwest, despite his skills, on a mission on August 18, 1918 a German sniper detected him and shot him through the head.

GALLIPOLI

Not only was sniping an important factor in the trenches of the Western Front, it was also practiced on both sides of the Gallipoli campaign, which was fought between April 1915 and January 1916. The aim of the British Commonwealth forces, including a large contingent of Australians and New Zealanders, supported by French forces, was to capture Istanbul and open a supply route to Russia.

The prelude to the Gallipoli landings was the naval Dardanelles campaign when the Royal Navy sent a significant fleet of about eighteen ships to batter Turkish gun emplacements along the coast. Turkish mines and shore-based artillery began to sow confusion among the Allied fleet and the focus was moved to a land operation so as to neutralize the Turkish artillery.

Below: Canadian officers are trained in the art of sniping during World War I. Many of the best Canadian marksmen were Native Americans well versed in the necessary hunting and tracking skills that made a good sniper.

BILLY SING AND ABDUL THE TERRIBLE

William Edward Sing (1886–1943), who was of mixed Chinese and English descent, joined the Australian 5th Light Horse Regiment and served in the Gallipoli Campaign of 1915–16. Between May and September 1915, Sing was credited with at least 150 Turkish casualties, for which he was awarded the British Distinguished Conduct Medal (DCM). Sing usually worked with a spotter, one of whom was Ion Idriess, who later became a well-known author.

Billy Sing's routine was to take up position with his observer before dawn. This was a time when the enemy would be least likely to detect any movement. Having moved inconspicuously into position, Sing and his observer would lie in wait. The challenge for the sniper is to be both motionless and alert and to maintain a monastic discipline with regard to food and water. Eventually, the target would fleetingly appear and Sing's finger would be ready to squeeze the trigger.

As the casualties mounted, the Turks came to the conclusion that the only way to deal with the Australian sniper was to pit an equally effective sniper against him. Cue "Abdul the Terrible," a German-trained Turkish sniper with a fearsome reputation. Being the expert that he

Below: *Billy Sing was the most famous and effective Australian sniper in the Gallipoli campaign. His reputation was such that the Turks deployed a super-sniper to neutralize him.*

was, Abdul went about his preparation with the forensic skill of a top detective. Each time a Turkish soldier was shot, Abdul would carefully analyze the corpse to work out the likely direction of the shot through following the angle of the entry and exit wounds. Gradually, Abdul narrowed down the area in the enemy front line from which the shot had come. Eventually, Abdul got a fix on a small rise near Chatham's Post. Having found his adversary's lair, Abdul set about building his own position and lying long hours in wait for his opportunity. He was too wise to shoot at other soldiers who occasionally presented themselves as targets, lest he should give away his position.

As Sing and his observer set about their daily observation routine one morning, the observer spotted Abdul with a powerful naval telescope. Sing looked down the telescope and found himself looking directly into the face and down the rifle barrel of Abdul the Terrible. What happened next was a matter of life and death for both snipers. Snipers know that the first shot must count – you do not normally get a second chance. That, however, is for a target that is unaware of the sniper's presence. In this case, both snipers would be aware of each other's presence and both would be almost staring down each other's rifle barrels. As Sing pushed back the loophole and pushed his rifle through, ready for firing, he knew that he would have to get it right the first time or be a dead man. Abdul noticed the movement and took aim. As Abdul squeezed the trigger a bullet from a Lee-Enfield traveled over the barrel of his rifle and hit him between the eyes.

Having failed to neutralize Sing, the Turks next tried to get him by plastering his post with artillery shells, and he again had a narrow escape.

It so happened that Australian and New Zealand infantry were training in Egypt prior to being sent to the Western Front. The Australian and New Zealand Army Corps (ANZAC) was formed and re-routed to Gallipoli. Once the ANZAC, British and French troops had landed, operations in the Gallipoli peninsula, despite a series of battles, often settled down into static trench warfare. Here the snipers on both sides kept careful watch for movements in enemy trenches and exacted a steady toll on anyone who was unwise enough to show their head above the parapet.

SNIPING AT THE END OF THE WAR

Richard Travis VC, DCM, MM, Croix de Guerre, served in the New Zealand Expeditionary Force in World War I, as part of the 2nd Battalion Otago Regiment. When the regiment was posted to Flanders, Travis organized the sniping and observation section and went out on night patrols in No Man's Land.

By the time the British had caught up with the Germans and established regular training for snipers, the two sides had roughly an equal number of snipers pitted against each other along the various fronts. About ten British snipers might be facing about ten German snipers and there would probably be one sniper and one observer for every twenty or so yards of the front line. Taking into account the observers, scouts and other specialists to back up the snipers, this meant that, despite its characteristically solitary nature, sniping was in fact carried out in considerable density. It also showed why the smallest mistake by someone in the trenches could be immediately and ruthlessly punished.

By the end of World War I, therefore, the sniper had established himself as a force to be reckoned with. He had graduated from a co-opted gamekeeper with a borrowed rifle to a highly trained specialist for whom gunmakers and others would design evermore sophisticated weapons and sighting equipment. The sniper had truly arrived.

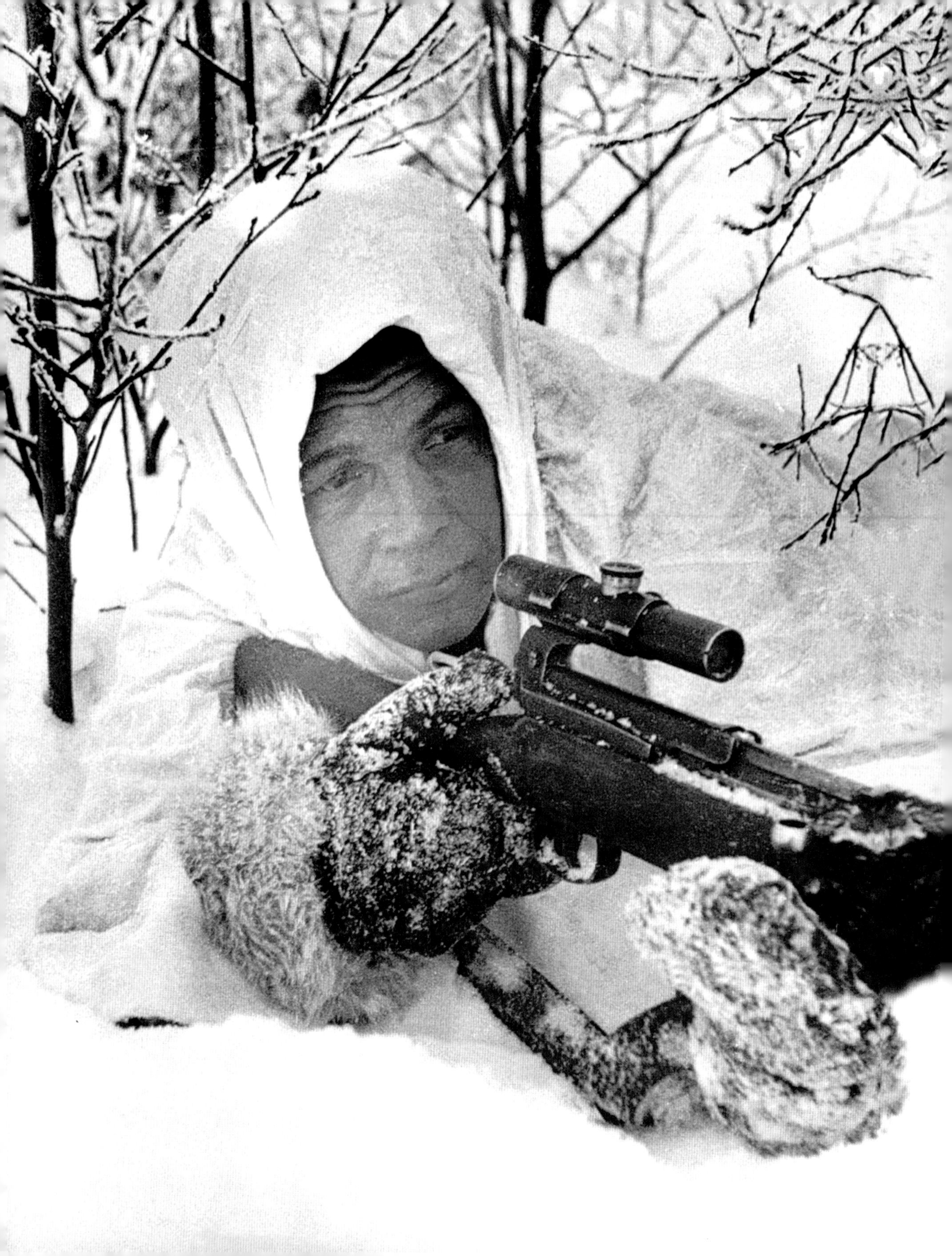

CHAPTER THREE

THE MARKSMAN AND MANEUVER WARFARE

Although the sniper had truly made his mark in World War I, in the intervening period until World War II sniper training waned in the German Army, such as it was under the constraints of the Treaty of Versailles, and did not receive much attention in the armies of other countries either. The exception that proved the rule was the Soviet Union. Arguably, however, it was the British who reminded the Germans of the effectiveness of a method of warfare that the Germans themselves had played such an important part in establishing during World War I.

Opposite: *A Soviet sniper awaits his chance on the Kalinin Front in the winter of 1942. He is armed with a Tokarev SVT40 semi-automatic rifle with a 3.5 PV telescopic sight. The SVT40 was an effective rifle in the right hands, though it required greater maintenance than the Mosin-Nagant.*

It seems somehow appropriate that snipers came to the fore in World War II when the British Army was in danger of being wiped out altogether as it retreated to Dunkirk in May 1940. Once the British Army was safely back in Britain, the British set up a sniper school at Bisley – The Small Arms School, Sniping Wing – and also ones in Wales and Scotland. The purpose of the school was not merely to teach good shooting but also all the skills concomitant with sniping, including fieldcraft, stalking and camouflage.

Sniping was proving to be a particularly useful tool for an army in retreat for slowing down a pursuing army. The Soviets would learn this lesson quickly during the German advance into their homeland in Operation "Barbarossa." So important was sniping in the Soviet Army that both men and women were trained for the task.

THE WINTER WAR, 1939–40
In the Winter War against Finland, the Soviet Army discovered to its cost how effective sniping could be in holding down large bodies of infantry. They would put this lesson into practice when it was their turn to face an invading army – the Germans.

The Soviet Army invaded Finland on November 30, 1939. The pretext for the invasion was that the Soviet Union wanted to take over part of the Karelian Isthmus to protect Leningrad, to establish a naval base at Hanko and also to take over some strategically important islands in the Gulf of Finland. Not unnaturally, the Finns refused.

It should have been a walkover for the Red Army. The Soviet Union had an estimated nineteen rifle (infantry) divisions and five tank brigades. The Finns, under the command of Marshal Karl Gustav Mannerheim, had only nine divisions. Approximately a hundred and twenty thousand Finnish troops faced four hundred and twenty thousand Soviet troops supported by 800 aircraft. The Finns, however, had a major ally – their knowledge of their own landscape. Well-placed snipers drawn from men who knew the country well wrought havoc among the Soviets and

Opposite: A Finnish sniper works the bolt of his Mosin-Nagant M28 sniper rifle. Finnish snipers such as Simo Häyhä made full use of their hunting experience in their work as snipers.

forced them to withdraw. In the first offensive the Soviets lost 27,500 dead against 2700 Finnish casualties. The Soviets returned in February 1940 with forces of overwhelming superiority, estimated at over three to one across the board, and, despite losing many more casualties, with sheer weight of numbers and firepower they eventually prevailed, and the Finns capitulated on March 12.

SIMO HÄYHÄ (1905–2002)

During the Winter War, the Finns distinguished themselves by their extraordinary fieldcraft and fighting skills against overwhelming odds. Finnish marksman Simo Häyhä was one of the best-known snipers of World War II because of his extraordinary record during the Winter War. He is reputed to have killed more than 700 enemy soldiers in less than four months – a feat not matched elsewhere in the history of sniping. Remarkably, Häyhä's record was achieved at a time of year when daylight was limited to just a few hours a day.

"White Death"
Nicknamed "Belaya Smert" (White Death) by the Soviet Army, Simo Häyhä was born in the town of Rautjarn in either 1905 or 1906. He joined the Finnish Army in 1925 and rose to the rank of corporal in a bicycle unit. After a year, he moved to the Civil Guard reserve where he remained until the outbreak of war in late 1939. Häyhä, whose abilities as a marksman had already been recognized, was assigned to *Jaeger* Regiment 34, which was deployed on the Kollaa River. In this sector Häyhä certainly had no shortage of targets, for the Soviets outnumbered the Finns by a hundred to one!

It was no surprise that before the war Häyhä had been a farmer and hunter with a reputation for

THE MARKSMAN AND MANEUVER WARFARE

marksmanship. He was a master of camouflage and concealment, in snowy conditions dressing in a white camouflage overall and took special care not to give away his presence.

He would operate in temperatures ranging between -20 and -40 degrees Celsius (-4 to -40 °F) and used techniques such as putting snow in his mouth to prevent his breath condensing in the cold air and giving his position away. To add insult to injury, Häyhä used a Finnish adaptation of a Russian rifle, the Mosin-Nagant M28. This rugged 7.62mm (0.3in) caliber rifle was designed for general infantry use but it was also adopted by snipers, both in Finland and later in the Soviet Union. In order to keep as low as possible against the ground Häyhä preferred to use open iron sights on his rifle as opposed to a telescopic sight. This testifies to his remarkable shooting skills, achieved without the advantage of telescopic magnification.

Hit and run at the Battle of Kollaa

The Battle of Kollaa was fought along the Kollaa River between December 7, 1939 and March 13, 1940. The invading Soviet troops had to contend with extensive man-made fortifications on the Mannerheim Line as well as thick forests and lakes. The Finnish winter brought thick carpets of snow, making movement even more difficult. It is not surprising, therefore, that the Soviets chose, where possible, to move by road. This, however, made them vulnerable to ambush tactics. The Finns developed a special tactic known as "Motti" by which they cut the Soviet forces on the narrow roads through the forests and isolated them in manageable chunks. The Soviet columns gradually became strung out as some vehicles failed to keep up with others or when obstacles in the road slowed them down.

Once the trapped Soviet units were considered to be weakened enough, the Finns would carry out lightning raids on skis, with sub-machine guns and grenades. If the Soviets tried to escape, snipers such

Below: Soviet troops man their trenches during the Winter War, January 1940. Ordinary Red Army soldiers were little match for expert marksmen like Simo Häyhä. Soviet casualties during the short campaign numbered more than 250,000 killed or wounded.

Right: A rare photograph of Simo Häyhä armed with his cherished Mosin-Nagant M28 rifle. Häyhä was just 1.6 meters (5ft 3in) tall, and preferred the slightly more compact M28 model because it was less cumbersome for his small physique.

as Häyhä would cut them down. Häyhä was also adept in the use of the sub-machine gun if the situation warranted. Large numbers of Soviet soldiers floundering in the snow would have been dealt with more quickly with the use of a sub-machine gun. The conditions of the Winter War and the tactics employed by both the Soviets and Finns were ideal for a sniper such as Häyhä.

Hunter is the hunted

Häyhä possessed all the skills of the good sniper: superb natural marksmanship backed by hours of practice; the hunter's instinct for use of ground and camouflage and the patience and endurance to remain concealed for long periods in extreme temperatures. These skills enabled him to achieve 505 confirmed kills with a sniper rifle. Häyhä was also handy with the Suomi KP/-31 sub-machine gun and his score rises to over 700 if his use of this weapon is also taken into account. Like any good Special Forces soldier, Häyhä was a one-man army.

On one occasion Simo Häyhä set out to track down a particular sniper from the Soviet 56th Infantry Division. This man had been responsible for killing a number of Finnish soldiers, including three officers. On this particular day, the Russian sniper had claimed yet another Finnish victim but unfortunately for him he now had one of the most skillful snipers in the world on his trail.

An experienced hunter, Simo Häyhä was a patient man. He had to wait a long time for his opportunity but he was well equipped with a warm winter uniform, mittens and enough food and sugar to keep up his energy levels. He also had a knife and some hand grenades for emergencies.

The Soviet sniper had been in action for many days and, as the sun set, with no further targets in prospect, he rose slightly from his prone position. Little did he know that Häyhä was scanning the snowy landscape. As he caught the glint of the Russian's telescopic sight, he fired and the bullet crashed through the forest and found its target.

Wounded

Not surprisingly, the Soviets did their best to get rid of Häyhä. They tried artillery strikes and counter-sniper operations involving teams of Soviet snipers. Eventually a Soviet sniper did manage to get a bead on him: he was shot in the face on March 6, 1941. He spent the next nine days in a coma. By the time Häyhä had regained conciousness, peace had been declared. Although his jaw was crushed and his left cheek blown away, Häyhä recovered and was promoted from a lowly corporal to a second lieutenant. He went on to live as a hunter and national hero until the age of ninety-six.

OPERATION "BARBAROSSA"

On June 22, 1941, Germany and its Axis allies began the largest offensive in military history. The German General Franz Ritter von Halder observed with some satisfaction in his diary that not only had the Soviets been caught by surprise but their defending forces were too widely dispersed along the 2900km (1800-mile) front. "The enemy has been taken unawares by our attack. His forces were not tactically in position for defense." General Heinz Guderian, mastermind of the *Blitzkrieg* that had taken Europe by storm, commented: "Detailed study of the behaviour of the Russians convinced me that they knew nothing of our intentions."

Although things would now go well for the Germans in high summer as they made huge inroads into Soviet territory, they would have done well to take note of the significant timing of their invasion. It was only two days away from the anniversary of Napoleon's invasion of Russia on June 24, 1812. Then, as now, never had so large an army been assembled for an invasion. Then, as now, the opposition seemed to crumble before the swift and glorious advance.

Although the Soviets had been taken by surprise, their resistance was both stubborn and skillfull. General Guderian commented, "the enemy continued, as always, to resist stubbornly. His battle technique, particularly his camouflage, was excellent."

Another German commentator wrote: "The Russians again proved their mastery in forest fighting. With sure instinct they moved among the impenetrable undergrowth. Their positions, not on the forest edge but deep inside, were superbly camouflaged. Their dugouts and foxholes were established with diabolical cunning, providing field of fire only to the rear. From the front and from above they were invisible. The German infantryman passed them unsuspecting, and were picked off from behind." If there was ever a testament to the advances made by the Red Army in formal sniper training and practice, this was it.

When the German 465th Infantry Regiment attacked a densely wooded area in September 1941, they suffered casualties of seventy-five dead and twenty-five missing due to the skilled work of Red Army "tree snipers" who carefully selected their targets before moving back to a new firing position.

Specialist snipers

In the Soviet forces, the distinction between snipers and more general sharpshooters was sometimes blurred but their policy of training up to six million soldiers because the Voroshilov Sharpshooter Badge bore fruit for, whether they were sharpshooters or snipers, their tactics were extremely effective. The adaptability of the Soviet snipers and sharpshooters in many ways represented the adaptability of the Soviet forces as a whole to the invasion. It was this ability to take body blows and yet still survive and come back for more that drew the German forces inexorably into the grasp of another ally that had helped to defeat Napoleon – the Russian winter. From October 20, the good weather gave way to rain and the German advance was held up by a sea of mud.

The Germans might have taken heart when the mud froze but the weather was far colder than they had ever imagined and the Germans did not have enough warm clothing. Not only did the Germans have to cope with the effects of the Russian winter on their own bodies, it also seriously affected their telescopic sights. When taken from the relative warmth of their quarters to the sub-zero temperatures prevailing outside, the lenses would almost invariably cloud and become opaque.

On top of this, lubricants such as grease for the precise working parts would become glutinous and the adjustment mechanisms would seize. Although the Germans tried a number of methods to overcome these challenges, it made their task against the highly skilled Soviet snipers even more difficult. By December the pendulum had swung. Soviet forces, well clothed in fur-lined and quilted uniforms, started to counter-attack.

THE MARKSMAN AND MANEUVER WARFARE

STALINGRAD

The struggle in the Soviet Union went on for many months, the advantage sometimes swaying this way and sometimes that way. On November 23, 1942, however, five German corps were surrounded in the Stalingrad pocket. It was the prelude to one of the

Above: *A German sniper of the SS* Totenkopf *division on the Eastern Front fires from a standing supported position. He is armed with a Mauser Karabiner 98K with a Zeiss ZF42 telescopic sight. The sight is mounted high to allow movement of the bolt. The Karabiner 98k rifle had an effective range up to 800 meters (875 yards) when used by a skilled sniper.*

MOSIN-NAGANT 1891/30

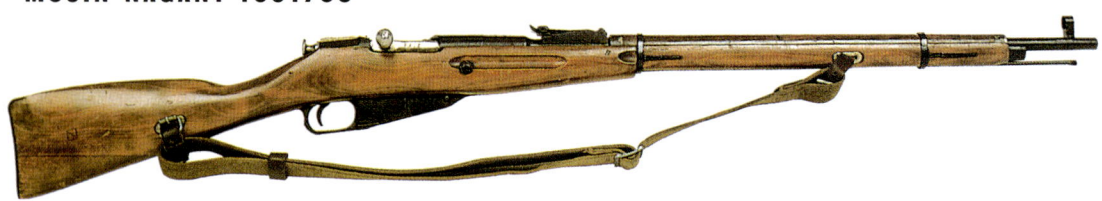

This rifle, sometimes described in Russia as the Vintovka Mosina rifle, was first adopted in Russia in 1891. Its double-barrelled name is derived from its development from two different and competing designs, one a Russian design by Colonel Sergei Ivanovich Mosin and the other a Belgian design by Emile Nagant.

Although the Mosin design was ultimately selected in competition, some aspects of the Nagant design, including the magazine and feed mechanism, were also incorporated. Large numbers were produced. They were used by Finnish forces during the Winter War and by anti-Franco forces in the Spanish Civil War. The rifle was standard issue to the Imperial Russian Army during World War I. The sniper version of the rifle was based on the Model 1891/30.

The telescopic sights fitted to this version were usually either 4x magnification PE or PEM or 3.5x magnification PU. The bolt was also adapted so that it would not interfere with the telescopic sight.

Country of Origin	Russia/Soviet Union
Caliber	7.62mm (0.3in)
Overall length	1287mm (50.7in)
Barrel length	730mm (28.7in)
Weight	4kg (8.8lbs)

---

greatest battles in history. The Germans had already underestimated what it would take to subdue the city of Stalingrad. One of their commanders commented: "In the town itself progress is desperately slow. The Sixth Army will never finish the job at this rate. … We have to fight endless engagements, taking one cellar after another in order to gain any ground at all."

The Soviet Marshal Chuikov wrote that success "did not depend on strength, but on ability, skill, daring, guile." The streets and buildings of Stalingrad were reduced to a maze of rubble and concrete blocks by bombing. This was a place where neither traditional infantry tactics nor tank tactics could be used. It was the home of the sniper.

By January 1943, it was clearly all over for the German Sixth Army trapped in Stalingrad but they had orders to resist to the bitter end. Eventually, the German commander, Field Marshal Paulus, bowed to the inevitable and surrendered. Over the entire campaign the Axis armies lost more than 800,000 personnel killed or captured, while Soviet losses were approximatley 1.1 million.

VASSIL ZAITSEV (1915–91)

Whereas Simo Häyhä had been the hero of Finnish forces during the Winter War, Vassil Zaitsev takes that honor for the Soviet forces during the German invasion of the Soviet Union and particularly during the Battle of Stalingrad. Not only did Zaitsev perform with devastating effect as a sniper himself, he is also said to have trained numerous other snipers whose cumulative effect on the German Army was prodigious. Stalingrad was a modern twentieth-

THE MARKSMAN AND MANEUVER WARFARE

century city with steel and concrete foundations. Many areas were reduced to rubble by German artillery and aerial bombardment and what ensued was what the Germans called "Rattenkrieg" – the War of the Rats. In this war, the sniper was king and Zaitsev was king of the snipers.

Like many good snipers, Zaitsev had been a hunter before joining the army. Brought up as a shepherd and backwoodsman, he had a natural sense of fieldcraft and the instinct for stalking his prey. It is said that in ten days Zaitsev killed forty Germans and as his score approached a hundred he became the hero that the struggling Soviet Union so desperately needed to build its morale and resilience.

Snipers' duel

As Zaitsev's tally of victims continued to rise, the story goes that the Germans plotted to get rid of him. This is not improbable as the Soviets had themselves tried to get rid of the famous Finnish sniper Simo Häyhä. Various identities have been put forward for the German sniper, one of them being Major König, an aristocrat who ran a sniping school in Germany. Although his identity has never been confirmed, an elite German sniper was brought in to Stalingrad and deployed on a mission specifically to neutralize the Red Army scourge. Zaitsev himself was aware of the presence of this super sniper and testifies to their duel

Below: Guards Sergeant A. M. Yaremchoock of the Kalininsky Front poses for the camera during the winter of 1942/43, a new recruit to the Red Army's rapidly growing sniper corps. He is camouflaged in a white winter smock and armed with a Mosin-Nagant M1891/30 fitted with a 4x RE telescopic sight.

in personal accounts. It was perhaps the most significant sniper duel in history and one where the hunter became the hunted.

Since there was no visual contact between snipers of opposing sides, how would Zaitsev know where and when the German was operating? After all, there were other good German snipers around. Zaitsev was aware of the difficulty. He tells the story:

"Then something happened. My good friend Morozov was killed, and Sheikin wounded, by a rifle with telescopic sights. Morozov and Sheikin were considered experienced snipers; they had often emerged victorious from the most difficult skirmishes with the enemy. Now there was no doubt. They had come up against the Nazi 'super-sniper' I was looking for."

There is no emotion in Zaitsev's words, despite the fact that his best friend had been killed. Snipers cannot afford emotion. Zaitsev knew that the battle was now on – sniper versus sniper – and that there could only be one winner.

One evening, when inspecting the German front line, Zaitsev noticed a German helmet moving along the trench line. He could tell by the way it was moving that it was being held up on a stick. This might have fooled a rookie sniper but it did not fool the master. It was obviously a ploy to get him to fire at the helmet and give away his position to the sniper concealed somewhere else and waiting for the shot. It was love-fifteen to the German sniper.

He had made his first mistake – underestimating his enemy.

Days passed and one morning Zaitsev took up position with an inexperienced colleague. As dawn broke, they lay motionless as the battle raged around them. Suddenly, Zaitsev's companion called out, "There he is!" and raised himself momentarily. A bullet winged in and hit him. He was fortunate to be only wounded. The German sniper had their position in his sights and was waiting for his moment. He had, however, made his second mistake: he had not made sure of his victim.

Zaitsev carefully examined the German front line to see where a sniper might be positioned. There were plenty of places an inexperienced sniper might take up position but he knew that this sniper would not pick anywhere obvious.

At last he spotted a piece of metal sheeting with a slight gap under it. Most people would not have given it a second glance in this debris-strewn landscape but Zaitsev had the experience to know what might lie behind the metal sheet. He could imagine a hide and a space for the sniper to lie. He knew instinctively that that was where his quarry was hiding.

Game of cat and mouse

To confirm his suspicions, Zaitsev raised a glove on a stick and a bullet immediately passed through it. Zaitsev studied the glove and the angle of the bullet holes. It confirmed that the shot must have come from the direction of the metal sheet. The German sniper had made his third mistake: firing at the slightest movement and giving away his position. There was no way that he could have killed his victim by firing at his hand. This was an elementary error.

Having confirmed the German's location, an inexperienced sniper might have been in a hurry to shoot at him there and then but Zaitsev knew better. He was not one for loosing off random shots in the hope that they might hit home. He silently

Above: *Vassil Zaitsev (left) directs two other Soviet snipers. Zaitsev made a particular impression at the Battle of Stalingrad. Although extremely effective as a sniper in his own right, he also knew how to work with a team and to train other snipers.*

withdrew from his position and planned to return another day.

A new day dawned and once again the battle began to rage around Zaitsev as he took up a new position. This time he had brought with him one of his most experienced companions – Kulikov. He knew that there was now no room for error. Showing their experience and expertise, they filtered out the raging battle and focused on their aim: to identify and shoot the German super-sniper. Most people would have been impatient to get on with the job in hand. After all, Zaitsev now knew where the German was located. However, the morning sun was shining on the Soviet lines and it could easily have reflected off Zaitsev's telescopic sights. Even a small glint of light would be enough for a sniper who was ready and waiting. Minutes turned into hours and still they waited. Gradually, the sun changed its position as the earth spun on its axis and the shadows moved over Zaitsev's position while the rays of sun played on the German front line and the steel sheet. The time had come.

As Zaitsev and Kulikov examined the ground in front of them, they noticed a glimmer of light reflecting off glass. It could of course be an old bottle or fragment of broken window. That is what most people would think, Alternatively, it could be the glass of a telescopic sight.

Kulikov took off his helmet and raised it very slowly, not in the clown-like way the Germans had raised the helmet days before, but the way someone

THE MARKSMAN AND MANEUVER WARFARE

carefully peering over the parapet would raise their head. The German sniper fired at the helmet and Kulikov feigned death by screaming and briefly rising and disappearing. It was a neat piece of acting and the ruse worked. Under the steel sheeting the German briefly raised his head to check he had got his victim. It was the last thing he ever did for at that moment Zaitsev squeezed his trigger. Although hailed as a

TEAMWORK

Although the sniper is often regarded as a solitary operator, and sometimes this is indeed the case, they often work in two-man teams, with one person responsible for the sniper rifle and delivering the shots and the other for a whole range of ancillary activities ranging from observation to camouflage and back-up fire support.

Vassil Zaitsev often worked with a companion and his famous defeat of an elite German sniper was partly due to the expert help of his companion, Kulikov. The German super-snipers Matthias Hetzenauer and Josef Allerberger also sometimes worked together as a team. In World

super-sniper, the German had made a series of errors that ultimately led to him losing the contest. He had been both impatient and trigger-happy and he had fatally underestimated his enemy. If the German had been the aristocratic Major König that some people think he was, perhaps he had fallen into the trap prevalent among the Germans at that time of thinking that the Russians were inferior.

LYUDMILA PAVLICHENKO (1916–74)

Born in the Ukraine, Lyudmila Pavlichenko was one of the Soviet Union's most famous female snipers during World War II. She quickly built up a formidable tally of 309 kills, which included 36 enemy snipers. Lyudmila Pavlichenko's combat career was impressive but actually quite short. Following the German invasion of June 1941, her initial attempt to join an infantry unit was stalled by a recruiter, who decided that she would be better employed as a nurse. Pavlichenko had other ideas. She had received basic military training at school in Kiev and was the holder of a Vorolshilov Sharpshooter Badge won in regional shooting matches, and she was not interested in nursing. She wanted to fight for her country.

Combat debut

Her shooting skills were quickly recognized and she became a sniper, initially using a Mosin-Nagant bolt-action rifle with a 4x magnification scope. Pavlichenko joined V.I. Chapayev's 25th Rifle Division, making her combat debut near Belyayevka, near Odessa, as part of a sniper platoon in the summer of 1941. There, she at first experienced great reluctance to take a life. Although she had been trained to kill, and thought she was ready, she found herself unable to shoot. Her hesitation vanished when a soldier near her was shot and killed. Pavlichenko knew the man only vaguely but he was likeable and cheerful and his death inspired a desire for revenge.

She soon began attracting the attention of her superiors with her skill and efficiency, frequently remaining in a camouflaged advanced position for eighteen hours at a stretch. For much of her career

---

War I, the British sniper trainer H. Hesketh-Prichard had often worked with an observer and developed diversionary tactics by team members to enable the sniper to get his shot on target.

As time went on, the concept of the sniper team solidified and snipers of the twenty-first century mostly operate as teams. Ultimately, the role of the non-sniping team member is to enable the sniper to focus as much as possible on the job at hand. The assistant will therefore take on a number of roles, including navigation to the target area, preparation of all necessary equipment, building hides, providing logistical support and communications and observing the target area with a telescope or any other relevant equipment.

Often the members of the sniper team will exchange roles. Both are likely to be fully trained snipers. A team member acting as observer may also be in contact with other units, such as artillery and aircraft, and be able to call in fire missions as appropriate.

If a sniper team is discovered by an enemy, the sniper rifle may not provide enough fire to enable the team to defend themselves and make an escape. The team member is likely therefore to be armed with an automatic weapon for intensive fire support.

Opposite: Moving like snow wraiths, two Russian snipers deploy into position. This image was most likely to have been posed as trained snipers would be unlikely to break a skyline and their weapons lack any form of camouflage.

Left: *A rare propoganda photograph of Lyudmila Pavlichenko posing from behind some foliage armed with a Tokarev SVT40 semi-automatic rifle.*

she employed classic sniper-and-observer tactics, selecting high-value targets such as officers and enemy snipers. Pavlichenko preferred to use the Tokarev SVT40 semi-automatic rifle, partly due to the fact that it had an easier cocking action than the Mosin-Nagant rifle. Her reputation quickly snowballed and soon she was being feted both in the Soviet Union and abroad.

Sniper leader

During August 1941, Pavlichenko, who had been promoted to sergeant, took part in the battle for Odessa, killing 187 enemy personnel over a period of ten weeks before the city fell to the Germans. Although wounded three times, she remained with her unit when it transferred to Sevastopol, in the Crimea. There, she served as a sniper leader and received a field promotion to lieutenant. By July she had been credited with some 309 confirmed kills, including more than 100 officers and a German sniper whose logbook listed over 500 kills.

In June 1942, she was wounded by mortar fire and was evacuated from Sevastopol by submarine. The city fell soon afterward and Pavlichenko's husband, who also served in the 25th Rifle Division, was killed. The decision to pull Lyudmila Pavlichenko out of the line may have been inspired partly by a desire to ensure her safety for propaganda purposes. She had become something of a national hero and her loss might have adversely affected morale. However, it is just as likely that the Soviet leadership thought that she could best aid the war effort by passing on her formidable skills to a new generation of male and female snipers.

On tour

Pavlichenko was sent on a tour of the United States and Canada, where she became the first Soviet citizen to be received by a U.S. president and was presented with a Winchester rifle and a Colt pistol as tokens of esteem. She returned to the Soviet Union as an instructor and for the remainder of the war she trained snipers and sharpshooters at the Central Women's Sniper Training School near Moscow.

In 1943, Lyudmila Pavlichenko was decorated for her achievements on the battlefield, being awarded the Gold Star of the Hero of the Soviet Union. She was also commemorated on a series of Soviet postage stamps. She ended the war as a Major and

SOVIET FEMALE SNIPERS

Because of chronic problems in finding the manpower to fulfill military and industrial tasks, the Soviet Government recruited some 7.75 million women, of whom 800,000 served in the military. Sniping was a precision role, which many women soldiers performed with expertise. It is estimated that in 1943 there were more than 2000 female snipers in the Soviet armed forces. Female snipers have been credited with more than 12,000 confirmed kills.

The Soviets found snipers were most effective during the defensive stages of the war (1941–43), after which the advantage of defense shifted to the Wehrmacht, and German snipers became a real danger to the advancing Red Army.

The illustration (right) shows a female sniper deployed around Kursk in July 1943. Soviet snipers were issued with one-piece specialist overalls to wear over their standard uniforms. However, during the war these uniforms were often camouflaged, especially for snipers. This overall was made using a khaki base with green foliage patterns. A large hood and soft cap would obscure the face in a position of hiding. Some overalls had strips of cloth sewn to the shoulders and sleeves to break up the silhouette. This sniper's killing tool is the 7.62mm (0.3in) Mosin-Nagant M1891/30 rifle, which served the Russian and Soviet military for almost fifty years.

Right: *This sniper is part of rifle battalion who fought at the Battle of Kursk, the great clash of armour and arms in July 1943.*

later served with the General Staff of the Soviet Navy. Many of the 1885 female snipers she helped train were not so fortunate or skilful; fewer than 500 survived the war.

JOSEF "SEPP" ALLERBERGER (1924–2010)

Born in Steiermark, Austria, Josef Allerberger served in the 3rd Mountain Division on the Eastern Front. He was credited with 257 kills. Allerberger was particularly adept at camouflage. One technique he used was to deploy an umbrella painted and covered with appropriate local foliage. The umbrella could be easily deployed and provided a light screen behind which he could conceal himself. Allerberger became a master of tactical sniping and could even stop a Soviet attack by the way in which he shot at the rear rank in order to wound them and moved on to the front rank. The sound of their wounded comrades behind them would almost invariably cause the front ranks of the attack to falter and lose confidence.

In action

After the defeat at Stalingrad in January 1943, it was mainly retreat for the Germans. Soviet snipers, who had been so effective amongst the ruins of Stalingrad, continued to harass the Germans as they retreated. Nowhere seemed safe and the Soviets would pick off green conscripts as well as more experienced NCOs and officers. It was almost impossible to track down the Red Army snipers and, once their locality was known, it required huge resources of mortars and machine guns to clear the area.

Raw recruit

The Germans realized that the best way of dealing with the Soviet sniper threat was to send out snipers of their own. An apprentice joiner from Bavaria, Josef "Sepp" Allerberger was conscripted into the Gebirgsjäger Regiment 144 of 3rd Mountain Division in February 1943, initially qualifying as a machine-gunner. In September 1943 he was posted to the Ukraine just as the Red Army was in midst of a massive offensive in the southern sector of the Eastern Front.

The intensity and ferocity of the frontline soon changed the callow youth into a determined fighter whose only philosophy was either to kill or be killed. As a machine-gunner, Allerberger realized very quickly that he was a number one target for the Russian snipers.

Almost inevitably, he was wounded and sent behind the lines to recuperate. During this period he came upon a captured Mosin-Nagant 91/30 sniper rifle and, intrigued, he asked for permission to practice with it. Allerberger both surprised and impressed not only himself but the armorer who was watching him, and it was soon arranged for him to change roles and become a sniper. He underwent formal sniper training at Seetaleralpe and was given a Kar 98K rifle with a 6x magnification scope.

Counter sniper action

When he returned to his unit, Sepp was greeted with considerable acclaim. Although snipers were frowned upon by some German commanders, Sepp's commander and fellow soldiers recognized their worth. Soon Sepp was being urged to deal with a Soviet sniper nearby who had been pestering the unit for days. Sepp duly got himself in position and tested the situation by raising a field cap above the parapet. The Soviet sniper showed his inexperience by putting a hole straight through it. It was a fatal mistake. Sepp was able to spot the gun flash and a slight reflection from a telescopic sight. He composed himself and carefully pushed his rifle barrel though a gap between some logs. Using the fixed iron sights, his task made even more difficult by a group of expectant fellow soldiers around him,

Opposite: A Red Army sniper armed with a Mosin-Nagant rifle stands guard wrapped in a captured German camouflage tent, summer 1942.

THE MARKSMAN AND MANEUVER WARFARE

he shot the Russian sniper. The euphoria created by his success spread through his company and soon an attack was launched, which cleared the Russians out of their forward trench positions.

Soon Sepp was notching up kills and every time he achieved ten confirmed kills he was given a silver stripe to put on his sleeve. The area in front of Sepp's company soon became clear of enemy snipers as they went off to seek easier pickings in safer areas where the enemy did not shoot back so effectively.

Fighting retreat

Soviet reinforcements built up inexorably and soon the Germans were on the retreat. It was now that Sepp Allerberger showed his mettle as well as the ruthlessness he had acquired over months of hard fighting. Often hugely outnumbered, the German units were fighting for their very existence and Sepp ensured that each shot caused maximum disruption. This meant not quietly killing selected targets as the sniper usually did but deliberately aiming to wound and cause maximum pain, thus creating confusion and loss of morale amongst the enemy. Sepp was a sniper with the precision of a surgeon: choosing whichever body part to wound in order to create a particular effect.

Sepp did not confine himself to infantry. On one occasion a Soviet T-34 tank hove into view as the lead point for an attack. A hatch on the tank was lifted briefly as a commander carried out a personal reconnaissance. Such was the potential power of the

Below: *Working in tandem, a German sniper armed with a Kar 98K rifle and his observer, looking through binoculars, scan the horizon for targets, somewhere on the Eastern Front.*

MATTHIAS HETZENAUER (1924–2004)

Impressed by the effectiveness of Soviet snipers, the Germans did their best to train their own sniper squads. One of the pre-eminent German snipers was Matthias Hetzenauer, who would be credited with 345 kills. Hetzenauer used a K98 rifle with a 6x magnification scope or a Gewehr 43 rifle (below) with a 4x magnification scope.

He was deployed on a number of dangerous missions and was often sent behind enemy lines when the Germans were about to launch an attack. Here he would maximize the disruption caused by the initial artillery barrage by picking off gunners, commanders and other key personnel. The German snipers mostly operated in pairs and Hetzenauer sometimes worked with Josef Allerberger, another famous German sniper. In May 1945, Hetzenauer was captured and spent five years in a Soviet prison camp.

---

sniper that an accurate shot by Sepp at this point could disrupt an entire enemy attack plan. As ever, Sepp's shot was on target and the Soviets were thrown into confusion. Headless and rudderless, the Soviet attack faltered and then collapsed, giving the Germans time to consolidate their defense.

On another occasion, an event occurred that bears close similarity to other sniper accounts from different eras and wars. A young Soviet lieutenant led a patrol in the open on a clear autumn day. He knew there were no enemy positions in the immediate area, otherwise he would have been more cautious, but, like so many before and after him, he had forgotten about potential snipers. These were green soldiers, not yet hardened by war.

For Sepp Allerberger, it was like being served up a three-course meal and not knowing where to start. The inexperienced officer was soon looking in surprise at a hole that had suddenly appeared in his chest. The remainder of the patrol scattered, except for two who lost their lives thinking they could save their officer. Sepp then withdrew from his lair.

Fieldcraft

This kind of quiet operation against relatively easy pickings was not typical for Sepp. It was more usual for him to be in the thick of the battle, creating maximum disruption with his precise shooting. Also, Sepp was fully acquainted with infantry movements and he knew how to operate with his company as well as how to get himself out of trouble.

Too many snipers lost their lives because their field craft and infantry experience did not match their marksmanship. Sepp knew there was a price on his head and he knew how to get out of a tricky situation quickly.

Near miss

Despite his experience and expertise, it was almost inevitable that even Sepp would make a mistake. A burnt-out tank in No Man's Land provided an excellent hide but it was also a fairly obvious one. Perhaps due to fatigue, Sepp forgot to consider things from the enemy's perspective and he returned to the location once too often. He took an observer with him. By this time the Soviets had organized their own sniper to watch the tank.

Unfortunately for Sepp's observer, just as he spotted a movement in the enemy trenches it was the Soviet sniper firing at the glint of his binoculars. The bullet destroyed the observer's face.

Above: The Soviet Army deployed a considerable number of highly effective women snipers. This is Maria Lalkova, who was of Czech origin, armed with the Tokarev SVT40 semi-automatic sniper rifle.

Sepp had no choice but to wait and escape under the cover of night if he was to avoid a similar fate.

Sniper company

Sepp did not make the same mistake again. On another occasion he not only found himself up against an enemy sniper but a full Soviet sniper company. Sepp knew this would require careful planning. He set out a number of false targets consisting of helmets with faces painted on them, which he asked fellow soldiers to raise when he gave them a signal.

He then went off and hid himself out of the immediate line of fire, using an old umbrella frame with foliage on it for camouflage. Apart from the soldiers behind the targets, he also arranged for machine-gunners to fire at the Soviets to disguise his own shots so they would not detect him.

Sure enough, when the helmet was raised, one of the snipers located in trees opposite fired upon it. Sepp identified the movement but waited for his team to open up with machine guns. Then he fired and hit the Soviet sniper. It did not end there. Sepp was in for a busy day: he and his team repeated the process, and it was not long before he had scored eighteen hits and the German commander decided to storm the woods. There, they discovered the bodies of the enemy snipers, all of whom were women.

Sepp and his comrades had plenty of time to marvel at the efficiency of Soviet sniper organization. They realized the devastating effect that the Soviet snipers had across the Eastern Front and were amazed at how the German Army had allowed their mastery of the art of sniping, developed before World War I, to lapse. Allerberger survived the war and returned to his native Austria to work as a carpenter until his death in 2010.

WAR IN THE WEST

In 1941 a revised British training manual was produced entitled *Notes on the Training of Snipers*. The full range of sniper training was introduced and careful selection procedures ensured that suitable snipers were chosen not just for their marksmanship skills but for their grasp of the full range of sniping techniques, which covered a wide range of fieldcraft.

The Lovat Scouts remained at the forefront of sniper training, as Captain C. Shore testifies:

"I was trained by NCOs of the Lovat Scouts. These men in their distinctive bonnets bearing the large silver badge with the stag's head and simple inscription "Je suis prest" ("I am ready") and their almost uncanny prowess in observation, stalking and shooting, earned my greatest admiration. They were quiet and restrained, not so eloquent maybe as the average Army instructor, but easily forceful. In their eyes lurked the quiet shadows of hillside forests; they were not loquacious, but in later months when we hunted together in German forests, the contents of my flask and the leaping flames of our camp-fires unloosened tongues and I was content to sit drowsily before the fire and listen to stories of Highland stalks, of great kills, and of their regard

GEWEHR 43 SNIPER RIFLE

German experiments with self-loading rifles began with the Gewehr 41(W), first trialed in 1940. This 7.92x57mm Walther design used a gas system of operation. However, the rifle's frontline reliability proved to be poor and in 1943 it was superceded by the Gewehr 43. The Gewehr 43 was heavily influenced by the gas-operated system and design of the Tokarev SVT40, used by many Soviet snipers. The simpler mechanism of the Gewehr 43 made it lighter, easier to mass produce and far more reliable. The addition of a ten-round detachable box magazine also solved the slow reloading problem of the bolt action sniper rifles.

The Gewehr 43 soon emerged as a successful battlefield weapon – more than fifty thousand Gewehr 41 and 43 sniper rifles were produced during the war. It was one of the most accurate sniper weapons of World War II, especially when fitted with the Zielfernrohr 43 (ZF 4) telescopic sight with 4x magnification.

Country of Origin	Germany
Caliber	7.92mm (0.312in)
Overall length	1124mm (44.25in)
Barrel length	546mm (21.5in)
Weight	5.03kg (11.09lbs)

ALFRED HULME (1911–82)

Alfred Clive Hulme VC was a New Zealand recipient of the Victoria Cross, the highest medal for gallantry awarded to British and Commonwealth forces. He is credited with stalking and killing thirty-three enemy soldiers in the Battle of Crete in just ten days.

On May 20, 1941, German *Fallschirmjäger* (paratroops) landed on the island of Crete, which was then held by Commonwealth forces commanded by Major-General Bernard Freyberg. The Allied forces included the New Zealand 2nd Division and some elements of the Greek Army. Although the large German paratroop force initially failed to take the island, they eventually captured Maleme airfield, which allowed them to fly in supplies and achieve victory.

Alfred Hulme, a sergeant in the 23rd Battalion, the Canterbury Regiment, was involved in a number of actions throughout the battle, and he took the initiative of disguising himself in a German Fallschirmjäger combat jacket in order to operate behind enemy lines. At Maleme airfield, Hulme led attacks against enemy forward positions. At Galatos he carried out a daring attack with grenades, destroying a planned enemy counter-attack. Near Suda Bay, Hulme, armed with an SMLE Mk III rifle, set out to stalk a number of enemy snipers, killing each one in turn. His meteoric sniper career was covered by the *London Gazette*:

> *"Sergeant Hulme exhibited most outstanding and inspiring qualities of leadership, initiative, skill, endurance, and most conspicuous gallantry and devotion to duty from the commencement of the heavy fighting in Crete on 20 May 1941, until he was*

Below: *Commonwealth troops are taken prisoner by German paratroopers after the fall of Crete. Over seventeen thousand Allied soldiers were captured during the two-week campaign.*

wounded in action 28 May 1941. On ground overlooking Maleme Aerodrome on 20 and 21 May he personally led parties of his men from the area held by the forward position and destroyed enemy organised parties who had established themselves out in front of our position, from which they brought heavy rifle, machine-gun and mortar fire to bear on our defensive posts. Numerous snipers in the area were dealt with by Sergeant Hulme personally; 130 dead were counted here. On 22, 23 and 24 May, Sergeant Hulme was continuously going out alone or with one or two men and destroying enemy snipers....

On Tuesday, 27 May, when our troops were holding a defensive line in Suda Bay during the final retirement, five enemy snipers had worked into position on the hillside overlooking the flank of the battalion line. Sergeant Hulme volunteered to deal with the situation and stalked and killed the snipers in turn. He continued similar work successfully through the day.

On 28 May at Stylos, when an enemy heavy mortar was bombing a very important ridge held by the battalion rearguard troops, inflicting severe casualties, Sergeant Hulme, on his own initiative, penetrated the enemy lines, killed the mortar crew of four, put the mortar out of action, and thus very materially assisted the withdrawal of the main body through Stylos. From the enemy mortar position he then worked onto the left flank and killed three snipers who were causing concern to the rearguard. This made his score of enemy snipers 33 stalked and shot. Shortly afterwards Sergeant Hulme was severely wounded in the shoulder while stalking another sniper. When ordered to the rear, in spite of his wound, he ... organised stragglers of various units into section groups."

for the chief of the Fraser clan, Lord Lovat, Commando Brigadier, who was badly wounded in the early Normandy campaign."

However, the British remained conservative in their allocation of equipment to snipers, as opposed to the Germans. Official camouflage uniforms for snipers were only issued in 1944, though the ghillie suit had been known about and worn since World War I.

The Enfield No.4 Mk1 (T) rifle fitted with the No.32 Mk 1 telescopic sight was distinguished not just by the scope but by the cheek rest on the buttstock. Mostly due to the design of the telescopic sight, this rifle proved to be more accurate at longer ranges than shorter ones but, nevertheless, it gained a reputation as one of the most reliable sniper rifles of its generation.

Canadian forces were sometimes issued with a limited number of home-grown variants of this weapon. Research Enterprises Limited (REL) provided a 3.5x magnification telescopic sight and the rifle received an improved cheek guard and shoulder shock-absorber.

In the early stages of the war, the British had no formal sniper training, though there would have been marksmen scattered in various regiments doing their best with standard-issue rifles with iron sights. Some training took place for snipers in France before Dunkirk, which may have enhanced the ability of the British sharpshooters to keep the Germans at bay when retreating to the beaches.

21 Army Group Sniper School

It was not until 1944 and the Normandy landings in June of that year that the British developed an effective sniping school, that was near the frontline and that could therefore provide the training and support that was required on operations. This was the 21 Army Group Sniping School, which started first in Courselles in Normandy and then moved with the advancing Allied armies to near Nijmegen, in the Netherlands.

As part of his training, the sniper's equipment was formalized. This included the Enfield No.4 rifle, two No. 36 grenades; 50 rounds of 7.7mm (0.303in) ball ammunition slung in a bandolier over the shoulder; five rounds of tracer ammunition (which was rarely if ever used as it was likely to give the sniper's position away); five rounds of armor-piercing ammunition (used for destroying machine guns and any other hard targets); binoculars (usually carried by the sniper himself around the neck); a prismatic compass (used for finding the sniping position and for additional observation reports); a watch that was used for sighting reports in addition to the compass (the watch was carried in a top pocket and not on the wrist as there was danger that the watch face would reflect light); British paratroop camouflage Denison smock; at least one camouflage face veil, sometimes two (which could be dropped over the face or used in other ways to disguise the sniper's position); camouflage cream; and emergency rations.

At the school the budding snipers were taught the usual range of sniping skills, which included zeroing the rifle and making adjustments for both wind and movement. Fieldcraft training included the usual mix of movement, positioning and camouflage that would help the sniper to conceal himself in whatever area he found himself.

Stalker training

As part of movement training, the art of the stalker was taught, whether it was walking in such a way as to minimize sound underfoot and retaining balance or learning to crawl on hands and knees without dragging the rifle or getting it dirty or crawling on the stomach. Stalking was an art in itself and was a lot more complicated than it sounds. If the stalker does not know the ground thoroughly, he is in danger of becoming the prey. The students were taught how to map and plan the ground and use the compass to work out their current position and route.

LEE-ENFIELD NO.4 MK I

SHORT MAGAZINE LEE-ENFIELD (SMLE) MK III

Country of Origin	United Kingdom
Caliber	.303in (7.7mm)
Overall length	1129mm (44.45in)
Barrel length	640mm (25.2in)
Weight	4.11kg (9lb)

Country of Origin	United Kingdom
Caliber	.303in (7.7mm)
Overall length	1130mm (44.5in)
Barrel length	635mm (25in)
Weight	4kg (8.8lb)

THE MARKSMAN AND MANEUVER WARFARE

Right: *Early model sniper camouflage suits, dating from 1941. In a training exercise somewhere in England, a scout sniper helps his observer into his camouflage gear, ready for a demonstration of counter sniper tactics.*

The students were taught how to build hides for longer periods and in such a way as to provide maximum protection in difficult weather conditions and to provide the opportunity for storage of backup equipment and a certain level of movement. The snipers were taught to observe as a hunter would observe, where the slightest movement is of significance. Training in the outdoors has the effect of heightening the senses, which are often dulled by comfortable urban living. Such skills came more naturally to those snipers who had a rural background and were used to hunting game. Related to this was the knowledge of and sensitivity to animal life. Animals could sometimes give clues to an enemy sniper's position by their movements or warning cries and the sniper had to be aware of not startling animals or birds and give away his own position.

MONTE CASSINO

Before D-Day, however, came the Italian campaign. The Allies had fought their way through North Africa, taken Sicily in July 1943 and made various landings in Italy, including at Anzio and Salerno from September. The campaign in Italy proved to be both painful and slow and was already being overshadowed by planning for the bigger invasion of France from England – Operation "Overlord."

There were many problems to be faced in Italy. Apart from the dogged German resistance, the landscape with high mountains and defiles was difficult to traverse with armored vehicles and seemed to have been designed for the benefit of defenders. The campaign soon developed into a battle of attrition. Snipers tend to thrive in attrtitional warfare. Whether it was in the steep defiles or narrow roads filled with obstructions or in towns turned to rubble, the sniper could all too easily rule and create confusion.

The Allies were held up on the so-called Winter Line in October 1943, the western part of which was

63

FALLSCHIRMJÄGER SNIPERS

Among the troops who took advantage of the rubble-strewn mountain-top at Monte Cassino were German Fallschirmjäger snipers of the 1st Fallschirmjäger Division.

The word "Fallschirmjäger" in German literally means "parachute hunter." Due to their tenacity and effectiveness, and their characteristic camouflage uniform, Allied troops came to know them as the "Green Devils." The Fallschirmjäger were first officially created in 1936 as the concept of parachute troops rapidly developed. In the opening scenes of World War II, the Fallschirmjäger proved to be stunningly effective, their most famous operation being the capture of the "impregnable" Belgian fortress of Eben-Emael in May 1940. They later played a significant role in the capture of Crete from the British in 1941.

For sheer tenacity, staying power and fighting skill, however, the defense of Monte Cassino stands as one of the greatest battles fought by this famous unit. Refusing to occupy the Benedictine abbey itself, they nevertheless kept the Allied armies at bay for months on end, exacting a heavy toll on any unit that attempted to oust them.

A typical Fallschirmjäger company would consist of a headquarters unit of one officer and thirty-five men and three rifle platoons of one officer and thirty-eight enlisted men divided into three squads of twelve to thirteen men. The weaponry carried by the Fallschirmjäger would typically consist of the FG42 assault rifle (known as the Fallschirmjägergewehr 42). This was an advanced design, which helped to inspire the design of the modern assault rifle. They were also equipped with MP44/43 assault rifles, MG34 or MG42 machine-guns and Gewehr 33/40 sniper rifles. The Gewehr 33/40 was based on a Czech bolt-action rifle design, which in turn employed a Mauser-type action.

The FG42 could also be adapted for sniping duties. The Fallschirmjäger also used the Gewehr 43/K43, which was a specialist sniper rifle fitted with Zielfernrohr 43 telescopic sights with 4x magnification. It had an effective range of 800m (874 yards) with a scope.

Opposite: A German Fallschirmjäger aims a FG42 selective fire automatic rifle, which was developed specifically for use by the paratroopers. Here the sharpshooter uses the flip-up front post iron sight and folding rear dioptre sight. The weapon could also be fitted with a ZFG42 or ZF4 telescopic sight.

called the Gustav Line, which hinged on the almost impregnable strongpoint of Monte Cassino. It was vital for the Allies to overcome German resistance before they could successfully move on to Rome. The hold-up extended to May 1944 when twelve Allied divisions attacked six German divisions along the Gustav Line, including the slopes of Monte Cassino. When the attack went in at dawn on May 11, however, the results were not encouraging.

Snipers on the mountain

Tasked with capturing the sixth-century hill-top abbey of Monte Cassino, the Polish II Corps were almost decimated. The abbey became a focus for the battle and, despite the fact that the abbey was not occupied by the Germans (the local German commander was a Catholic), a decision was made by the Allies to bomb it. By bombing the monastery, the Allies turned a historic monument into a heap of rubble, which provided the Germans with first-class defenses and which became a haven for snipers.

Operation "Diadem," launched by the British General Alexander, was the final attempt to push the Germans off the mountain. It included the British XIII Corps, Americans, Free French forces as well as Polish and New Zealand forces. The Americans suffered about 3681 casualties while overall the British lost about 4400. The Poles lost 1100. Despite the fact that this was Italy in spring and not Russia in winter, the conditions were extremely unpleasant, including rain, mud, cold and even snow. The rain during 1943/44 was some of the heaviest ever recorded in Italy. A Canadian soldier observed:

> *The face of the opposing mountain mass was honeycombed with German gun positions. Their observers sat up there in fortified emplacements with field glasses and telescopic sights, where they could watch every movement our attacking force made. At the base and on the flat area just across the river from us were machine-gun positions expertly camouflaged and fortified. They had zeroed in all their guns on various terrain features*

in front of them so their fire was very accurate. The Germans always did this careful artillery registration as they retired or pulled back.

The sniping was not all one-way in Italy. British snipers were also positioned to watch movements in No Man's Land and to harass German sentries. Captain Shore relates one such incident:

One unit had advanced to the Senio River and was holding a sector in which improvement of positions was made during the hours of darkness. The forward platoon of the unit was in and around a cluster of smallish houses about 200 yards [183m] from the bank of the river. From the roof of one of these houses there was a good clear view of the top of the bank held by the Hun. Snipers watching this bank observed that the Germans changed their sentries every even hour with monotonous regularity. At first the Hun was cautious and our snipers withstood the temptation to shoot hoping that targets would become more favourable when the Jerries had lost some of their caution. Later in the day the hoped-for happened, and at 1200 hours six of the enemy could be seen from the waist upwards.

There were four of our snipers on duty and having set their plan of execution ready they each selected a Hun and fired. Three out of the four Huns aimed at fell, and shortly afterwards their bodies were carefully dragged from the top of the bank by their comrades concealed below. At the 1400 hours relief the sentries were again very cautious and the snipers did not get in a single shot. But at 1600 hours two more Huns were sent to their particular Valhalla. It was a long and tedious day for the snipers with only two volleys. But it was a good day's work, five Germans having been accounted for without loss to our men.

D-DAY

With everything planned for an assault on the coast of Normandy, there was only one hitch – the weather. Meteorological experts had, however, indicated that there might be a break in the weather on June 6, 1944. The decision was made to go in. So began the largest seaborne invasion of all time.

Roughly divided between the U.S. First Army to the west and the British Second Army, including Canadian forces, to the east, the assault beaches were codenamed, from west to east, Utah and Omaha for the Americans and Gold, Juno and Sword for the British and Canadians. Although the weather conditions to some extent played into Allied hands due to the element of surprise – the Germans did not believe anyone would be crazy enough to launch an invasion in such adverse conditions – it had the

Left: *A Canadian sniper prepares himself for a shot armed with a Lee-Enfield No.4 Mk I rifle. Many No.4 rifles were modified for sniper use by the addition of a wooden cheek piece and telescopic sight mounts designed to fit a No. 32 3.5x telescopic sight.*

SPRINGFIELD MODEL 1903

Having noted the effectiveness of the Mauser design of rifles, the United States set up the Springfield Armory in 1900 to develop the Springfield bolt-action rifle based on the Mauser bolt design. This rifle would be standard issue to American forces during World War I. Between the wars, the Springfield was replaced by the semi-automatic M1 Garand rifle but it remained in service as a sniper rifle, where rate of fire was not an issue. The specialized sniper version of the rifle, which later came to be manufactured by Remington, was the M1903A4. These rifles were fitted with an adapted pistol grip on the stock and carried a 330 2.2x magnification telescopic sight.

Country of Origin	United States
Caliber	7.62mm (0.3in)
Overall length	1140mm (44.9in)
Barrel length	610mm (24in)
Weight	3.9kg (8.65lbs)

effect of disrupting Allied paratroop drops and bombing missions aimed at neutralizing beach defenses, notably those on Omaha Beach.

Confused and disoriented as the Germans may have been about where and when the attack was coming, the shores of Omaha Beach were full of gun, machine-gun and sniper hides. The beach was strewn with obstacles, including barbed wire and mines. Some of the snipers were lodged in tunnels, others were concealed in woods and some were concealed in trees.

Snipers on the beaches

Once the seasick infantry had landed, they were still about 183m (200 yards) from the shore due to the sandbars. Some were up to their necks in water as they tried to wade in and by the time they reached the real shore they were barely able to do more than shuffle due to the weight of their waterlogged equipment and clothing. The 116th Regimental Combat Team of the battle-hardened U.S. 1st Infantry Division landed three of their boats too far west. These happened to include the vital headquarters and beachmaster groups. German snipers kept this group pinned down so that they could not move out for hours. The area, known as Dog Green, continued to be a lethal spot for anyone unlucky enough to land in it. Later on, two companies of U.S. Rangers landed on the edge of the Dog Green area. Although they eventually managed to reach the relative safety of the seawall, they lost half of their men to snipers and other enemy fire.

The main cause of casualties on Omaha Beach were the machine-gun nests. These were carefully sited and mutually protected so that an attack on one would attract fire from another, not to mention sniper fire. American units became mixed and lost their direction due to the loss of officers, which would have been targeted by the snipers. The snipers also had the advantage of a series of interlocking tunnels so that they could disappear and reappear at will. As the Americans eventually began to move inland, they

U.S. ARMY SNIPER TRAINING

American forces, having been equipped with the Springfield Model 1903 sniping rifle, were later issued the M1 Garand C with an M81 telescopic sight. The Garand had its faults, among which was a noisy ejection of the clip when the last round had been fired. This would spell almost certain death for a sniper and care had to be taken not to fire the last round.

Apart from a short course in Camp Perry, Ohio, there was not much in the way of sniper training for the American forces, but they learned quickly once they had been on the receiving end of German sniper tactics. The Americans noted how the Germans could cause mayhem by picking off a few selected targets, whether they be officers or key personnel or drivers of vehicles in key positions, such as in a convoy. Shooting the drivers of the first and last vehicles in a convoy could cause mayhem. In due course, the Americans began to give the Germans a taste of their own medicine, as U.S. Army Sergeant John Fulcher recounted:

We snipers adopted a tactic the Nazis sometimes used. Slipping from our lines before daylight, we located a hill or ridge within range of a road or trail inside enemy territory, divided it into sectors for each two-man team – sniper and spotter –
and then settled down to wait for whatever came along ...

I spotted troops coming at the end of the road where it hazed into the horizon. I nudged my partner and nodded in their direction. ... Through binoculars, I could tell they were green replacements. Their uniforms were still a crisp gray green; their jackboots kicking up little spurts of dust still shone. They left a cloud of dust hanging in their wake.

As cool as could be, I cross-haired the officer and shot him through the belly. He looked momentarily surprised. He plopped down on his butt in the middle of the road. The report of the shot reached him as he fell over onto his back. He was dead by the time I brought my rifle down out of recoil and picked him up again in my scope. His legs were drumming on the road, but he was dead. His body just didn't know it yet.

The other krauts were so green they didn't know enough to scatter for cover until my partner got in his licks by knocking down one more. Even then, they behaved more like quail than combat troops. They hid in the drainage ditches and in some shell craters, their heads bobbing up. ... I figured I could have drilled

Opposite: *U.S. soldiers take cover from a German sniper in a town in northern France following the Normandy landings, July 1944. A single sniper could hold up much larger units for many hours if not quickly located and dealt with.*

> *"Get around the sniper and machine gunner and wipe him out ... If you allow your unit to bunch up behind a hedgerow and wait for hours you are only playing into Jerry's hand. He will move round where he can enfilade you or drop artillery or mortar fire on you ... It is time to get over the jitters and fight like hell."*
>
> Colonel Canham, U.S. 115th Infantry Regiment

two or three more, but I held my fire. It wouldn't do to be pinpointed, even by green troops. ...

The company reorganized without making any attempt to find us. ... As soon as the Germans swept around a distant bend in the road, they were greeted by the twin Crack! Crack! of two more rifle shots as they entered another Yank team's sector.

This professionalism was not always matched by other rookie GI snipers who all too often were inadequately camouflaged or loosed off too many shots from the same location, thus giving away their positions. The Americans learned fast, however, and by the time of the D-Day invasion in 1944 they were able to field an elite band of snipers.

THE MARKSMAN AND MANEUVER WARFARE

found snipers positioned in village houses, which meant they had to conduct laborious house clearances. Companies B and C of 2nd Battalion Regimental Combat Team were held up for several hours as they tried to clear snipers from woods near Colleville.

The German snipers positioned themselves so that they had a good view of any gates or openings in the hedgerows.

The problems had not ended for American forces still coming through the beaches because where

German emplacements and resistance had supposedly been snuffed out, snipers then reappeared to occupy the same positions. As American engineers continued to try to remove obstacles on the beach, they were continually harassed by sniper fire.

The snipers of Point du Hoc

One of the key actions of U.S. forces on June 6, 1944 – D-Day – was an assault on German gun positions on the Point du Hoc, about 6km (4 miles) west of Omaha Beach and to the east of Utah Beach. The guns, 155mm (6.1in) howitzers, threatened both Utah and Omaha beaches as well as transport and attack craft for a considerable distance out to sea.

The attack was to be carried out by the 2nd Ranger Battalion commanded by Lt.-Colonel James E. Rudder and the follow up was by 5th Ranger Battalion commanded by Lt.-Colonel Max F. Schneider. The U.S. Rangers were named after Rogers' Rangers, a group of eighteenth-century colonial militia. Commanded initially by William Darby, they had been created to form a similar force to the British Commandos, with whom they carried out training in Scotland. Tasked with attacking the key German batteries at Point du Hoc, the Rangers trained with scaling ladders on cliffs at the Isle of Wight. Three companies of 2nd Rangers were to carry out the initial assault, while the rest of the force would follow through and push inland.

Not surprisingly, the Germans regarded the position as impregnable. The beach was tiny and the cliffs at Point du Hoc were between 24–30m (80–100ft) high and either sheer or overhanging. Anyone contemplating an assault would need their head examined. The area was, however, covered with typical German efficiency by machine-guns and there were also snipers about.

Up the cliffs

Once the Rangers reached the cratered beach, they went straight into action. The Rangers fired rope rockets up the cliffs and began to scramble up. Some of these were cut by the Germans but some Rangers

Left: A U.S. infantryman tries to tempt a sniper to fire and reveal his position in the Normandy bocage, the network of small fields and thick hedgerows that proved to be a sniper's haven. Units could be held down for hours by a single sniper.

began to make it to the top. After about thirty minutes, about forty Rangers had reached the top of the cliffs. They discovered that the first gun emplacements were empty and that the guns must have been moved around the time of the aerial bombardments. German units in the area began to wake up and the Rangers found themselves under fire. Opposition proved to be particularly stiff near to an anti-aircraft position and, due to the maze of interconnecting tunnels the Germans had built, it was difficult to know where they might spring up next. German snipers were located in a group of ruined farm buildings. From here they had targeted any Rangers that came into their sights but they melted away when a group of Rangers moved towards the buildings. The Rangers at last found the missing guns and promptly destroyed them.

Although their mission had been accomplished, the Rangers were still coming under sniper fire and taking casualties. Their attempts to silence a German machine-gun resulted in further casualties as snipers picked off anyone who raised their heads. Although naval gunfire was successfully used to destroy a machine-gun nest due to some adept forward observation by a spotter team, snipers continued to operate. By this time the Rangers were beginning to tire of the constant presence of the German snipers and they took steps to try to eradicate them. But how do you find a sniper? Not only did the German snipers have the advantage of a maze of tunnels, which they knew as well as a rabbit knows its warren, they also had the advantage of a landscape that was filled with craters made by bombs and naval shells.

It was perfect sniper country and, although the Rangers found them as annoying as insects in a jungle, despite thorough patrolling, they never succeeded in finding them. Well trained as they were, even some of the Rangers fell for German ruses. When the Germans showed a white flag of surrender over a gun emplacement, two Rangers stood up in the open and were instantly killed. As the Rangers withdrew from the area of the anti-aircraft emplacement after a hail of artillery fire, German snipers killed two more of them.

Having suffered another night attack by the Germans in force, the Rangers, having hung on tenaciously for two days, eventually withdrew from the area, having accomplished their mission, though some took a leaf out of the German snipers' book and remained concealed in the thick bocage, waiting until the Germans were pushed out of the area by advancing friendly forces.

OPERATION "MARKET GARDEN" AND THE BATTLE OF THE SCHELDT

In the heroically fought but ill-fated Operation "Market Garden," the Allied attempt to use airborne forces to seize key Dutch bridges, there was effective sniping on both sides. British and Polish paratroopers were targeted by snipers, sometimes as they landed or as they moved towards their objectives. On the British side, Anthony Crane of 21st Independent Parachute Pathfinder Company, took up a sniping position at 34 Pieterbergseweg, Oosterbeck, when he began to take a toll of unsuspecting Germans who came into his telescopic sights. On one occasion he shot two Germans simultaneously and, after this loss of innocence, his score began to mount. He scratched his "score" on to the wallpaper of the house, which has been preserved for posterity in the Hartenstein Airborne Museum.

Some battles deservedly retain a prominent place in history, like D-Day or "Market Garden" (popularly known by the title of Cornelius Ryan's book and the blockbuster movie *A Bridge Too Far*). Others undeservedly receive little coverage. One such battle was the Battle of the Scheldt (October 1–November 8, 1944). The river Scheldt flows into the sea near the three islands of South Beveland, North Beveland and Walcheren. It is a typical Belgian-Dutch low-lying area characterized by dykes, canals and marshes. It is totally flat and it goes without saying that any soldier or vehicle can be seen from miles away.

Above: *British soldiers deploy in the streets of a Dutch town in late 1944 with standard Lee-Enfield rifles. Snipers made the advance through Belgium and Holland a slow business for the Allied armies.*

The Allies had taken the vital port of Antwerp in September but their hold on the port remained tenuous so long as German forces continued to hold positions in the Scheldt estuary. The First Canadian Army was given the task of removing the threat.

Among the Royal Hamilton Light Infantry, Company Sergeant-Major R. Morgan of C Company had a narrow escape when his helmet was pierced by a sniper bullet. The bullet failed to penetrate his skull. Company Sergeant-Major K.C. Lingen of D Company was less fortunate, being killed by a sniper near his headquarters. There is no coincidence that both men were the same senior NCO rank. It was the mark of a trained sniper that he would pick off key men in command.

Counter sniper action

When soldiers were tied down by a sniper who had shot one or more of their group, a trained sniper would be brought forward to seek him out and eliminate him. One such was U.S. Army Sergeant William E. Jones who served in I Company, 8th

Infantry Regiment, 4th Division. Jones carried a 1903 Springfield sniper rifle with a 10x magnification telescopic sight. This enabled him on occasion to spot enemy snipers who were invisible to the naked eye.

Even so, the enemy snipers were often so well concealed it was difficult to positively identify them and Jones was experienced enough to be aware of the dangers of loosing off a shot at an unconfirmed target and to give away his position. On one occasion, after two men of the company had been shot, Jones came forward and scanned the hedgerows and trees through his sight. There seemed to be nothing obvious until he noticed a slight movement in a tree. He scanned the tree again but all he could see was a large knot. Tree knots do not move. Jones waited rather than take a chance shot. Sure enough, the tree knot moved again. The enemy sniper's fate was sealed.

THE PACIFIC

The Japanese had many fighting qualities, which included high levels of discipline and obedience, fanatical tenacity supported by a Samurai warrior code, a mastery of ingenious tactics and, last but not least, a natural instinct for jungle warfare and use of camouflage.

The Japanese were masters of infiltration and of envelopment, often getting behind their opponents and catching them unawares. In this style of warfare, the sniper was an essential tool and Japanese snipers would often conceal themselves either in the ground or in the jungle canopy, sometimes firing at their enemy once they had passed through. Adrian Gilbert describes Japanese tactics in *Sniper*:

> *A distinctive feature of Japanese sniping was the use of trees as firing platforms. In some cases small tree chairs would be hauled up into the higher branches; in others the sniper would be tied into position, which prevented him from falling out of the tree if shot, thus informing the counter-sniper team that they had scored a hit. As an aid to*

CANADIAN SCOUT SNIPERS

The 1st Battalion, the Royal Winnipeg Rifles also experienced snipers first hand. As they relate in their diary of October 8, 1944:

Prolonged exposure to wet and cold still had to be endured in flooded slit trenches or smashed buildings as unusually bold enemy snipers and machine-gunners were on the lookout continuously and often succeeded in infiltrating between companies and platoons. Few of these lived to tell their story as the Royal Winnipeg Rifles were no less aggressive.

During an attack on the village of Graaf Jan, it was the turn of the Canadian snipers to move in and kill any Germans who exposed themselves to view. The diary for Friday October 13, once again bears testimony to the continuing ruthless activity of German snipers.

Some of the key scouting and sniper work carried out by the Canadians was performed by the Scout and Sniper Platoon of the Calgary Highlanders. A typical member of this platoon was Sergeant Harold A. Marshall, who was equipped with an Enfield No. 4 Mk 1(r) rifle with telescopic sight. Other equipment carried by Marshall included a machete, binoculars and a Mills grenade for close-quarters protection.

Opposite: Canadian snipers deploy through the rubble-strewn streets of Falaise in August 1944. They wear the Denison smock, also issued to British paratroopers, and, characteristic of Canadian snipers of the era, a camouflage face veil worn as a head cover. The Canadian snipers were armed with the Lee-Enfield No.4 Mk 1 (T) rifle.

The Canadian scouts wore camouflage veils, which were often tied around their heads when not in use and pulled down over their faces when in a camouflaged firing position. They wore British-issue Denison camouflage smocks, which were also worn by paratroopers.

clambering up and down the trees, the sniper was issued with climbing spikes. To Allied and German snipers the use of trees was discouraged (although observers used them regularly and were often mistaken for snipers) because they became a death trap if the sniper was discovered.

The Japanese were also masters of concealment on the ground. Their hides were sometimes connected to small trenches and they had the reputation of being able to wait there patiently for long periods.

U.S. Marine snipers
The sniper training in the U.S. armed forces at the start of the Pacific war was indifferent. The best prepared force in this regard was the U.S. Marine Corps, though the training, such as it was, had an emphasis on marksmanship and little on fieldcraft. Due to some enthusiastic campaigning by certain officers who recognized the value of sniping, a revised and more elaborate training program was set up at Camp Lejeune, Camp Pendleton and Green's Farm in California. The course lasted about five weeks and included fieldcraft, observation, camouflage, wind judgement and range estimation.

The Marines were notable for their long-range shooting and the candidates were taught to shoot up to 923m (1000 yards). However, long-range shooting was not always a requirement in the jungle, where distances were often comparatively short. As the war developed in the Pacific, the Marine Corps created sniper teams comprising three men – the sniper himself, an observer and a team protector who armed with either a rifle or sub-machine gun.

As U.S. Marine Private Daniel Webster Cass Junior discovered as he went in for the attack on Okinawa in 1945, the snipers at least did not have to go in with the first wave on the beaches. They followed behind the initial attack, along with the headquarters company. Despite the fact that the beaches and surrounding area had been plastered with naval shells and aircraft attacks, the Marines knew

Opposite: *A tree that had been used by a Japanese sniper somewhere in the Pacific shows how the thick jungle vegetation provided excellent camouflage and how difficult it was to spot a sniper. A figure standing to the left of the base of the tree is difficult to spot even though he is standing in the open.*

that the Japanese would still be lurking in wait. The 1st and 6th Marine Division went in along with five divisions of the U.S. Tenth Army. To Cass's surprise, after all the sound and fury of the softening-up attacks by Allied ships and planes, resistance seemed negligible. By the time Cass had reached the Katchin Peninsula, he was positively relaxed and even put his rifle to bed in its case. He would not have been so relaxed if he had known that this battle would later be known as the "Typhoon of Steel" due to the ferocity of the fighting.

Sure enough, this 1st Division was called into the Shuin Line where the Japanese, always tenacious fighters, were fighting even more tenaciously than ever. After all, this was their home territory. Cass was called in to clear machine-gun nests from a ridge. The cry was "Sniper up!" He and his spotter moved up to a ridge from where they could see the devastation caused by the Japanese machine guns but, at a range of 1097m (1200 yards) through fog and drizzle, they had difficulty spotting the source of the fire.

At last the spotter located a cave where he could see a thin trail of gun smoke. Then they saw the small telltale bursts of muzzle flash. At that range, if sniping were in the Olympics, Cass would be assured of a gold medal if he got a shot on target. There was no option. Marines were dying in the valley below and there was no way of getting closer without revealing their position. Cass slowly placed the crosshairs of the telescope against what he could see of a patch of uniform as the Japanese leaned forward to fire down the valley. Calling on all his training at Camp Pendleton, he took a deep breath, let half of it out and squeezed the trigger. The shot hit the area the Japanese were firing from. Cass was more or less on

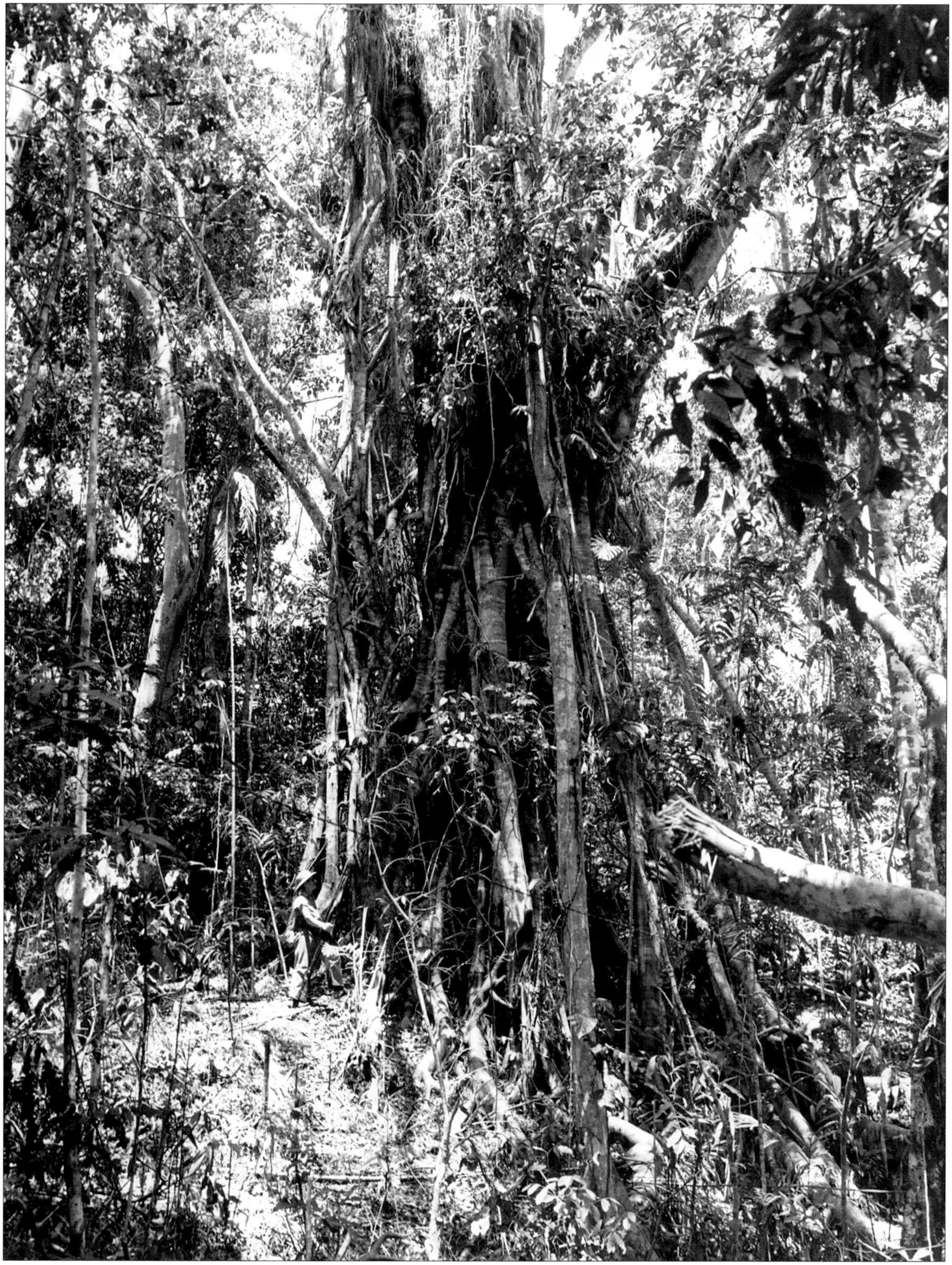

target and he kept on firing. From somewhere 7.62mm (0.3in) rounds were coming in and hitting home. The long-range sniper training of the U.S. Marine Corps had certainly paid off.

Guadalcanal

The first major offensive by Allied forces in the Pacific was at Guadalcanal. Here, 6000 U.S. Marines landed on August 7, 1942, catching the Japanese, who were building an airfield, by surprise. The Japanese, however, began to bring in reinforcements and the fighting in the jungle was intense and bitter, despite light opposition to the first landings. A U.S. correspondent accompanied the Marines on Guadalcanal and wrote an account of the battle that was to become a classic of war reporting. Some of his experiences with the fighting men included encounters with Japanese snipers:

> More Jap .25s opened up ahead; a storm of fire broke and filled the jungle. I dived for the nearest tree, which unfortunately stood somewhat alone and was not surrounded by deep foliage. While the firing continued and I could hear the occasional impact of a bullet hitting a nearby tree or snapping off a twig, I debated whether it would be wiser to stay in my exposed spot or to run for a better 'ole and risk being hit by a sniper en route. I was still debating the question when I heard a bullet whirr very close to my left shoulder, heard it thud into the ground and then heard the crack of the rifle which had fired it. That was bad. Two Marines on the ground ten or fifteen feet [3–4.5m] ahead of me turned and looked to see if I had been hit. They had evidently heard the bullet passing. That made up my mind. I jumped up and made for a big bush. … The sniper who had fired at me was still on my track. He had evidently spotted my field-glasses and taken me for a regular officer.
>
> I searched the nearby trees, but could see nothing moving, no smoke, no signs of any sniper. Then a .25 cracked again and I heard the bullet pass – fortunately not so close as before. I jumped for better cover, behind two close trees which were surrounded by ferns, small pineapple plants and saplings. Here I began to wish I had a rifle. I should like to find that sniper, I thought. I had made an ignominious retreat. My dignity had been offended.

The Japanese lost twenty-four thousand men in the battle while the Americans had sixteen hundred killed and four thousand two hundred wounded.

New Guinea

Although the Australian and New Zealand Commonwealth forces received little formal training

TYPE 99 RIFLE

Country of Origin	Japan
Caliber	7.7mm (0.3in) Arisaka
Overall length	1120mm (44.1in)
Barrel length	657mm (25.87in)
Weight	3.7kg (8.16lb)

JAPANESE SNIPERS

The Japanese wore a green uniform that was often supplemented by a sniper cloak and camouflage netting. They often painted any exposed parts of the body. The Japanese sniper rifle had initially been a modified Type 38 infantry rifle fitted with a 4x magnification scope.

This was followed by the Type 97 rifle, with 6.6mm (0.25in) caliber. By 1932 they had graduated to a Type 99 rifle with a 7.7mm (0.303in) caliber and 4x magnification scope.

The Japanese telescopic sights were fixed and came with no adjustments for windage or elevation, which Allied servicemen were accustomed to. The sniper was expected to make the necessary adjustment by aiming off as far as was necessary. Some rifles had open iron sights that still allowed some Japanese snipers to shoot with remarkable accuracy. The advantage of the fixed telescopic sight with no adjustment was that it would remain stable despite rough handling and, if the sniper knew his rifle well, he could aim off as required and allow the accuracy of the rifle to do the rest.

Right: A U.S. serviceman stands over the body of a dead Japanese sniper. Sometimes snipers were brought down by machine-gun fire or by shotgun-style barrages into the tree tops.

in sniper work, their experience grew as the threat to their homelands increased.

The Australians used either the Lithgow Short Magazine Lee-Enfield (SMLE) No.1 Mk.III rifle with the 1918 pattern telescope or the Enfield No.3 Mk.1* (T) rifle with the same scope. Both were highly effective weapons.

Despite the lack of formal training, many Australians selected to do sniper work had natural hunting experience gained in the outback and some were even kangaroo hunters. It did not take much to tidy up their skills with additional fieldcraft training and target practice to make them as effective, if not better, as snipers from other Allied nations. On Timor, an Australian sniper was said to have hit twelve advancing Japanese with twelve shots.

In their whirlwind expansion, the Japanese also attacked New Guinea to the north of Australia.

THE MARKSMAN AND MANEUVER WARFARE

This was part of a plan to isolate Australia by also capturing Samoa, Fiji and New Guinea. When the Japanese tried to invade Port Moresby on May 4, their plans were scuppered by the U.S. Navy in the Battle of the Coral Sea.

From July, the Japanese landed on the northeast coast from where they planned to move to Kokoda and down a jungle path to attack Port Moresby. The track itself was only a few feet wide and crossed some of the most remote jungle areas in the world for about 97km (60 miles). The Australians, who were massively outnumbered, put up a sterling defense but the Japanese managed to take the airfield at Kokoda.

Allied reinforcements arrived in Port Moresby and began moving up the track to confront the Japanese. Although the Australians initially retook Kokoda, they had to deal with a series of severe Japanese counter-attacks, which threatened to overwhelm them. As the situation became desperate, Private Bruce Kingsbury of the 2/14th Battalion launched a heroic lone attack intoethe Japanese lines, firing a Bren gun from the hip. He managed to kill several of the enemy but he was eventually shot by a Japanese

Below: An Australian sniper of Third Landing Group on New Caledonia in 1942. He has a Lithgow SMLE No.1 Mk III rifle with a 1918 pattern telescopic sight. Wearing a scrim face veil helps to break up the contours of his face.

M1 GARAND RIFLE

Country of Origin	United States
Caliber	.30in (7.62mm)
Overall length	1103mm (43.5in)
Barrel length	610mm (24in)
Weight	4.37kg (9.5lb)

The M1 Garand was the first self-loading rifle to ever be adopted as a standard military firearm. First introduced to U.S. forces during World War I, the M1 remained in frontline service into the 1950s. More than six million weapons had been produced by the end of production in 1959.

---

sniper. His actions had the effect of turning the battle at a critical moment and saved battalion headquarters from being overwhelmed by the enemy. Kingsbury was posthumously awarded the Victoria Cross. The Australians were also aware of the danger of Japanese snipers and where they were able to bring Stuart tanks into the battle, they fitted them with an upward-firing machine gun that would rake the tree tops.

U.S. counter-sniper tactics

U.S. forces also developed painstaking tactics to counter snipers in New Guinea and elsewhere. Hargis Westerfield, divisional historian of the 163rd Infantry Regiment of the U.S. Army's 41st Division, describes some of the counter-sniper tactics that were developed:

Our basic tactics consisted of three main steps – and a fourth which AT 163 [anti-tank troop] added with at least three 37s [37mm (1.45in) cannon]. First we began to deal with Jap Perimeters Q-R which lurked in holes 20–30 yards [18–27m] before us. We set up two-man counter-sniper teams in slit trenches on the forward edge of the Musket perimeter. While one man quietly scanned the opaque jungle with field glasses ... the other man cuddled his well cleaned rifle and waited. When the Jap shots rang out, the observer carefully spotted the green area where the shots came from. He pointed out the direction of the fire, let the rifleman observe through his glasses. The rifleman fired – until the Jap was silent – or Jap fire retaliated close enough to make him lie prone. Thus he secured our forward area.

Second, we sent counter-sniping teams into the trees on the flank and rear of Musket perimeter. To lessen the drudgery and danger of climbing among the dead branches in jungle sweat we set up homemade ladders. Usually we made them of telephone wire with stout wooden rungs. Once the two-man tree teams were aloft, we got to work. We shot at all trees which seemed to harbour Nippo rifles. When Japs fired, we followed our standing order. All teams returned fire. If unsure of the target, we engaged probable Jap trees in the general direction of the popping fire. With our M1s and 1903 rifles, we shot 200–400 yards [182–366m] ...

Third, we still needed another measure, because manning forward slit trenches with two-man counter-sniping teams was not enough. As soon as we posted sniper teams in trees, we could take the offensive. We could use these teams to guide attack patrols on the ground. We sent out small foot

VETERAN MARKSMEN

On June 15, 1944 two U.S. Marine Divisions went ashore on the island of Saipan in the Marianas against thirty thousand Japanese defenders. Once again, Japanese resistance was several times fiercer than even the worst estimates and an Army division had to be called in to reinforce the Marines. Once again, the advancing U.S. forces found themselves held up by cleverly situated Japanese machine-gun nests.

Adrian Gilbert includes a Marine's account of such an experience in his book *Stalk and Kill – The Sniper Experience*. The Marine in question was surprised to see two unorthodox figures coming to the rescue as they kept their heads down under the hail of Japanese lead. However he may have been comforted by their folksy appearance, he may not have been so confident that these veterans could do the job in the face of Japanese fanaticism. He was wrong.

THE MARKSMAN AND MANEUVER WARFARE

We were pinned down on the beach at Saipan by a machine-gun bunker. The pill-box commanded a sweeping view of the area and there was just no way he could get at it. Plenty of our boys had died trying.

Finally one of our ninety-day wonders got on the horn and requested a sniper. A few minutes later, I saw two old gunnery sergeants sashaying towards us, wearing shooting jackets and campaign hats! As soon as I saw these Smokey Bears bobbing over to us, I figured this could be some show. And it was.

These two old sergeants skinnied up to the lieutenant and just asked him to point out the bunkers. Then they unfolded two shooting mats, took off their Smokey Bears and settled down to business. One manned a spotter scope while the other fired a 1903 Springfield with a telescopic sight rig.

That bunker must have been 1,100 or 1,200 yards [1005–1097m] away, but in just a few minutes, with three or four sporting rounds, this old gunny on the Springfield slipped a round right into the bunker's firing slit. One dead machine-gunner. But their commander just stuck another man on that gun. Our sniper shot him, too.

After the fourth man bit a slug, I think they got the idea. We moved up on their flank and destroyed the bunker while our snipers kept the machine-gun silent. Then the two gunnys dusted themselves off, rolled up their mats and settled their Smokey Bears on their heads. And just moseyed away.

Opposite: *A U.S. Marine aims a Springfield Model 1903 in the Pacific jungle. The Springfield rifle proved to be both reliable and rugged in the difficult combat environment of the jungle.*

patrols of two–three men. Under direction from tree observers, our patrols shot down snipers or slashed other targets on the flanks of Jap Perimeters Q and R. And the ground troops set booby traps – grenades tied to two separate trees and connected by a trip-cord attached to the loosened firing pins. These booby traps caused Jap casualties, and once definitely affected our capture of a Jap Bren gun. Evidently the Japs had dropped the Bren gun when they fled from a grenade blast.

When we counter-sniped in these three steps, we carefully secured ourselves from accidentally shooting our 163 men. We briefed all our men on our methods. We located our own sniper trees so that nobody thought we were firing on him. Most important of all, we made it clear that nobody could fire on Jap snipers – except regularly designated counter-snipers.

Fourth, with the arrival of AT 163's 37mm cannon (at least three) we took another step against these hidden Jap killers. ... Methodically, AT's carefully aimed 37s were topping the jungle trees around Musket perimeter. For without tree cover, no snipers could operate. In BAR-man Fallstick's opinion, the number of trees made the task hopeless, but he admitted that he saw a tremendous number of mangled trees on the horizon. Thus did 163 Inf's 1/Bn counter-snipe the Nip snipers who took sight pictures on us from above Musket perimeter.

The Americans also sometimes used British Boys 13.9mm (0.55in) anti-tank rifles to rip through tree trunks behind which snipers were concealed. Firing a weapon of this caliber proved to be something of a challenge, even though its effects were often conclusive. Russell Braddon, who served in the Australian artillery recalled one incident:

Since the sniper fired from behind the top of the tree trunk, he could be shot through it – a Boys rifle was therefore essential for the job. With the barrel resting on my shoulder and the butt

CANINE COMPANIONS

In the Makin operation of November 1943, H. Hallas relates in his book, *The Devil's Anvil*, how the 5th Marines employed an innovative new anti-sniper weapon – dogs.

The dog platoons included Doberman Pinschers and on one occasion a dog called Boy saved a whole company of Marines from the prospect of walking into an ambush when he detected a Japanese unit armed with two machine guns and several other weapons.

The Dobermans did not just alert the Marines to the presence of the enemy, they also actively engaged them. Hallas wrote: "Similarly, on 20 September, the 4th War Dog Platoon reported that one of its dogs 'alerted a Jap sniper at about fifty yards [45m] distance and killed him.' The following day a dog by the name of Pardner was reported to have 'chased a Jap sniper approximately 150 yards [137m] before the sniper was killed.'" On the whole, however, conditions on the island were not right for the dogs. Apart from cutting their paws on the coral, the dogs also began to suffer from shellshock and became unmanageable. The dog platoons served successfully in the island campaigns, including Guam, Saipan, Iwo Jima and Okinawa. The dog handlers were awarded five Silver Stars and seven Bronze Stars for heroism in action and more than 40 Purple Hearts for wounds received in battle. Although several dog handlers were killed in action, a dog platoon was never caught out in an ambush.

Below: *U.S. Marine "Raiders" and their dogs head off to the frontline in Bougainville. Dogs such as these could be an effective tool in finding snipers and in some cases killing them. Dogs could be adversely affected by the noise of war, however, and become too dangerous to handle.*

against his arm, Harry took a long aim, apparently quite undeterred by the bursts of fire from all sides ... in fact as we stood there our feet spread wide apart to take some of the shock I was very deterred indeed. Then Harry fired and I was crushed to the ground ... and the sniper toppled gracelessly out from behind his tree ... I left Harry, still swearing volubly and rubbing his shoulder.

Otherwise, the Australians improvised with a Bren gun, discovering that it was sometimes a weakness of Japanese snipers to be drawn into firing at exposed objects, such as a piece of cloth or a helmet, at which someone would return fire with a Bren gun.

THE KOREAN WAR

The world may have thought it had had enough of major conflicts following the end of World War II but in June 1950 the Democratic People's Republic of Korea (North Korea) invaded the Republic of Korea (South Korea) with the backing of the Soviet Union. The new world order was that the United States and the Soviet Union were the two superpowers and, since direct conflict between them was likely to be too costly for both sides, they backed proxies who represented their conflicting ideologies.

President Truman had designated the 38th Parallel as the line that separated the interests of the Soviet Union and the United States in Korea and persuaded the United Nations to take responsibility for the country in 1948. In this case it was not just the United States that came to the aid of South Korea but the United Nations. In a diplomatic coup, the United States was thus able to pursue its aims with the backing of the international community.

The opposing forces consisted of South Korea's Republic of Korea Army (ROKA) and the North Korea People's Army (KPA). Communists in South Korea drew in the resources of ROKA, which was also watching the border area. By 1950, the Soviet Union was ready to approve an invasion of the south by the KPA, which was relatively well trained and also supported by Chinese soldiers. On June 25, 1950 the KPA rolled over the 38th Parallel and the Imjin River, heading towards Seoul. On June 28, the KPA entered Seoul and the ROKA, on the back foot but not in disorder, knew that its only chance was assistance from the United States and its allies. Existing U.S. forces in the country were reinforced by U.S. Army and Marine units and a British Commonwealth brigade. The United Nations forces were under the command of General MacArthur.

After an amphibious landing at Inch'on, MacArthur's forces pushed through and liberated Seoul. Allied forces continued to push the KPA north beyond the 38th Parallel but the advance of U.S.-backed democratic forces proved to be too much for the communist powers, the Soviet Union and China.

The Chinese People's Volunteer Force came over the border and attacked Allied forces. The tide of advance was turned. Soviet pilots in MiGs provided air cover and by January 1951 Seoul had once again fallen to the communists. By May 1951, the ROKA had pushed the Chinese and KPA back over the 38th Parallel with significant U.S. and other Allied assistance. The huge Chinese expeditionary force, however, eventually pushed back in 1952, carrying out a series of infiltration attacks.

Infiltration and attrition

In this war of attrition, with both sides first advancing and then retreating and with Chinese attacks in particular involving infiltration and attrition, there were plenty of opportunities for snipers to do their work. The Chinese sniper Zhang Taofang was accredited with over two hundred hits, firing a Mosin-Nagant 7.62mm (0.3in) rifle. This score was said to have been achieved without the use of a telescopic sight.

Otherwise, the UN-sponsored forces that arrived in Korea had little by way of sniper training and equipment to begin with. As so often before, the lessons had to be relearned through bitter experience.

As snipers such as Zhang Taofang began to pick off Allied troops one by one, various commanders began to search around for their own snipers and, finding them lacking, asked for marksmen to be trained. It was as if both World War I and World War II had never happened. As the Germans and British had done in World War I, sniping rifles with telescopic sights were requisitioned wherever they were available and these included Springfield 1903-A4 rifles. Other rifles included the Garand M1-C and the Winchester M70 target rifle.

WILLIAM S. BROPHY

Among the precious sniping talent that arrived in Korea was Ordnance Captain William Brophy. Brophy had led a company in battle in the Philippines during World War II for which he had been awarded the Bronze Star Medal and the Combat Infantryman's Badge, among other awards. In civilian life he worked as a gunsmith. Brophy was to prove a very useful man to have around because, when he arrived in Korea, he discovered that the soldiers had no idea how to maintain their specialized Garand M1-D sniping rifles. There was also an inadequate supply of spare parts or even the correct ammunition.

Although the Winchester 70 was a fine rifle, due to the long ranges found in the area of the 38th Parallel and elsewhere, the rifle was not reliably accurate above ranges of 914m (1000 yards). Brophy had a solution for this: the use of a 12.7mm (0.5in) machine gun, which could comfortably achieve ranges of around 1372m (1500 yards). The machine gun was also a stable platform from which to fire and could be finely adjusted. The problem with the 12.7mm (0.5in) machine gun, however, was that it was not easy to conceal or carry about. Since Brophy was a gunsmith by trade, he knew how to play about with weapons.

One solution he came up with was a Soviet PTRD 14.5mm (0.57in) anti-tank rifle fitted with a 12.7mm (0.5in) machine-gun barrel. American troops were lucky to have someone who both knew about firearms as well as what it was like to fight on the frontline. Servicemen needed weapons that worked when the chips were down, when it was freezing, when the trench was full of mud and water or when there was a sandstorm.

Despite his recommendations, neither the U.S. Army or Marine Corps agreed to take on a specialized sniper rifle and instead continued with modified infantry rifles. Brophy was ahead of his time. The proof that he knew what he was talking about lies in the fact that most modern armies are now issued with specialized sniping rifles. Also, his idea of using a 12.7mm (0.5in) machine gun for sniping was occasionally replicated in Vietnam when conditions allowed.

"CHET" HAMILTON

Chester F. "Chet" Hamilton joined the U.S. Army at the age of seventeen and served in the 1st Infantry Division. Chet had exceptional shooting skills and, apart from his active military service, he would also go on to win medals in many shooting competitions. By the time he was twenty, he found himself in another war at a time when the scarcity of snipers on the U.S. side was a cause for concern.

Having already established himself as something of a marksman, Chet found himself unexpectedly popular. He was soon assigned the position of company sniper. Posted up to the frontline, all Chet could see was a maze of barbed wire and trenches with no distinguishing features or aiming points. If he had served in the Pacific, this might have reminded him of Japanese positions – the featureless facade disguising a maze of tunnels where the enemy were present in large numbers. Search as he might for targets of opportunity, he found the Chinese forces were too well disciplined to stick their heads above the parapet. Things changed, however, when the Americans put in a frontal attack supported by

THE MARKSMAN AND MANEUVER WARFARE

artillery. As the GIs clambered up the hill towards them, the Chinese had no choice but to shoot down at them. Suddenly Chet was presented with a shooting gallery of Chinese soldiers, all of them fully occupied with the targets in front of them. Chet set about his work and, after a period of about two hours that the U.S. attack lasted, he knocked down about forty Chinese defenders. In the heat of battle, the Chinese must have assumed they were being hit by the attacking forces. Little did they know that a prize-winning U.S. marksman had them one by one looming large in his telescopic sights.

On another occasion, Chet, now a platoon sergeant, took his men out on a probing patrol. They were uncomfortably close to the enemy and in constant fear of being cut off. As they waited for reinforcements, some Chinese soldiers who had become isolated from their own lines due to artillery shelling tried to make a break back to safety. They would probably have made

Below: *Two scout snipers of 1st Division, U.S. Marines, aim a Springfield 1903 rifle (foreground) and an M1 sniper rifle. Although the Marine in the foreground wears white camouflage overalls, he has not broken up the shape of the rifle with camouflage.*

THE MARKSMAN AND MANEUVER WARFARE

it if it were not for the fact that a U.S. marksman was in the vicinity. Despite the fact that Chet was not on this occasion carrying his sniper rifle as he was not on official sniper duty, he picked off the Chinese whenever they tried to make the dash.

Rookie sniper

U.S. Marine Corporal Ernest R. Fish found himself in a similar position to Chet Hamilton. Having achieved high scores at Camp Pendleton, he was dragged out of the frontline and given some

THE MARKSMAN AND MANEUVER WARFARE

Above: A U.S. sniper team undergo training during 1952, wearing somewhat rudimentary helmet camouflage. The sniper is armed with an M1 Garand rifle with an M82 telescopic sight.

Opposite: A sniper and spotter of U.S. 1st Marine Division look out for enemy targets in Korea in January 1950. The sniper is armed with an M1 Garand rifle.

rudimentary sniper training with an M1 rifle and a 2x magnification telescopic sight. This was hardly an ideal weapon for the purpose and not comparable to the Springfield rifles and Winchesters made available to the army. However, a well-zeroed rifle in the hands of someone as gifted as Corporal Fish was a dangerous weapon.

Back in the frontlines and with snow camouflage overalls, Fish found himself out on patrol looking for targets. Unfortunately, the North Koreans were as circumspect as their Chinese allies and Fish found himself staring at a lot of snow and a lot of empty trenches. Eventually, a North Korean was unwise enough to stand up in his trench and gaze in Fish's direction. You do not gaze at snipers.

In Korea, apart from a few honorable exceptions, sniping was a do-it-yourself job in response to an emergency. It was as if sniping were a lost art or that military forces were in denial about its importance, not only as a support in both defense and attack, but as a means of keeping enemy snipers at bay.

The Korean War proved again that sniping was not just some bad dream from World War II but an essential part of infantry tactics, especially in more static tactical situations. Those armies that did not train snipers did so at their peril.

ZHANG TAOFANG (1931–2007)

Zhang Taofang was a Chinese soldier during the Korean War who is credited with seventy-one confirmed kills in thirty-two days without using a magnifying scope.

The Korean War began as an invasion of South Korea by North Korea, leading to intervention by the forces of many nations under the United Nations banner. This in turn resulted in China joining the conflict to prevent the defeat of its neighbor and ally, North Korea. The war gradually settled down into a grim stalemate along the "main line of resistance." This created ideal conditions for sniping, with both sides occupying static positions.

By January 1953, Zhang Taofang had been in the Chinese People's Liberation Army for under two years. He was assigned to 8th Company, 214th Regiment, XXIV Corps, holding positions on the main line of resistance around Triangle Hill. This position was flanked by high ground, creating ideal sniper positions, and thus inevitably became known as Sniper Ridge. A system of trenches protected these positions, with tunnels constructed through the upper part of the ridge to allow snipers to move into firing positions on the forward slopes and retire in the face of artillery or heavy enemy fire.

These heavily fortified positions had been the scene of bitter fighting the previous year. Indeed, the losses incurred around Triangle Hill were a major factor in the decision by UN commanders not to launch more large-scale attacks against Communist positions. This in turn resulted in a stalemate that lasted until the end of the war.

First contact

Zhang Taofang joined the fighting around Triangle Hill on January 11, 1953. He was assigned to a sniper team and issued an elderly Mosin-Nagant rifle, which had only iron sights (considered accurate at ranges of up to 400 metres [438 yards]) rather than a magnifying telescopic scope. With this distinctly inadequate weapon he joined the snipers harassing UN positions, and waited for a suitable target to present itself.

After eighteen fruitless days of waiting Zhang Taofang got what he wanted, and opened fire on his target. His shooting was poor but persistent, two serious errors for a sniper, since every shot gives the enemy an opportunity to zero his position. After twelve missed shots Zhang Taofang attracted a huge volume of return fire and narrowly escaped being killed.

Realizing that he needed to improve his shooting, Zhang Taofang worked out how to

Opposite: U.S. infantry work their way through hilly territory north of Seoul, winter 1951. Craggy, mountainous terrain made up much of the main line of resistance and was consequently ideal country for snipers, with good viewing points and clear fields of fire.

> *"That's when my buddy got killed. We were bringing up the rear. There was a road that cut into the mountains. He darted across and hit the ditch. I darted right behind him. A sniper got him. He was lying dead in the ditch. I was left by myself."*
>
> Pvte. Eugene Sutherland,
> U.S. 7th Infantry Division

make better use of his basic iron sights, and claimed his first victim the next day. He also developed his sniper craft, no longer brazenly blasting away at the enemy, and rapidly became a deadly effective marksman.

His skills improved so quickly that on February 15, 1953 he scored seven confirmed kills with nine shots, still without using a scope. According to Chinese records, he made seventy-one successful kills with two hundred and forty shots during a forty-day period. Other claims put his tally in the hundreds.

There have been suggestions that Zhang Taofang's record is dubious, given the weapon he was using at the time. His success is possibly attributable to an intimate knowledge of static enemy positions gained from long hours of observation. With enemy targets liable to present themselves in predictable locations, which he might have already fired on, it is not implausible that Zhang Taofang could have learned to gauge distance and bullet drop based on previous shots taken in the same area.

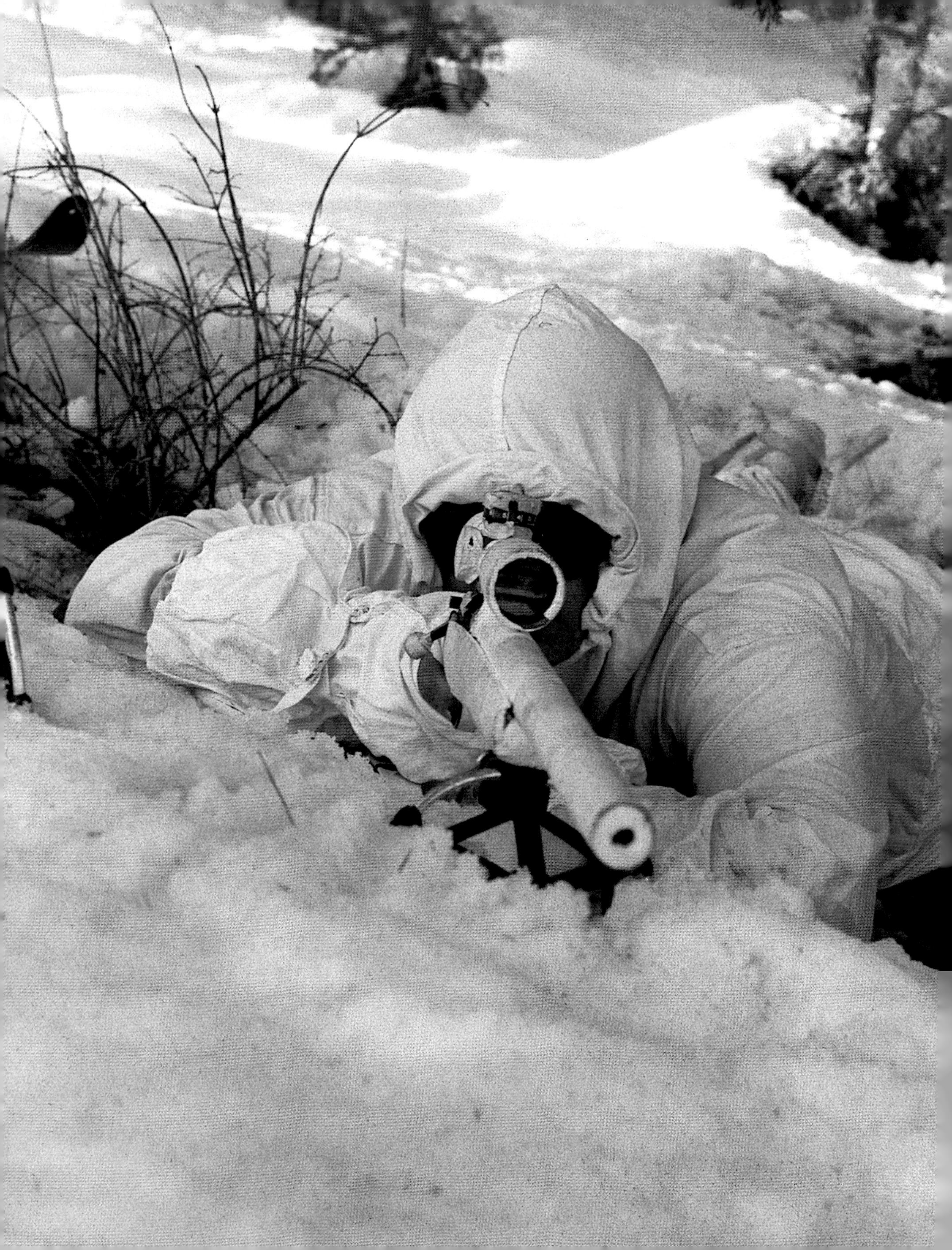

CHAPTER FOUR

COLD WAR CONFLICTS

In Vietnam, as in Korea, the United States found itself embroiled in a conflict where it tried to prevent the democratic south of a nation being overrun by the communist north. To make matters more complicated, communist sympathizers called the Viet Cong also operated in the south. As in Korea, the communists were backed by the Soviet Union and China and the U.S. became evermore deeply committed as it pursued its policy of containment.

Opposite: *Corporal Scott C. Anderson, a scout/sniper with the 23rd Marines, 5th Marines Division, takes aim on a training exercise in 1986. He has an M40A1 rifle with a Unertl 10x magnification telescopic sight. Note the comprehensive snow camouflage, including overalls, mittens and rifle camouflage.*

Above: *A U.S. Marine aims an M40A1 rifle on the Que Son mountains in Vietnam in 1969. The Marine has made little attempt at camouflage, showing bare arms and a spotless rifle.*

From 1961, the number of U.S. "advisers" were increased exponentially and by 1965 there were active combat units on the ground. By 1969, these had risen to five hundred thousand men. Not only did American forces have to cope with the complexities of jungle warfare, including extreme heat and difficult terrain, but their enemies also proved to be elusive, capable of sustaining large casualties and of running an open-ended war of attrition.

This was not a force that was prepared to fight decisive pitched battles. Although they might appear to have been defeated in one engagement, they would always reappear for another. The Viet Cong's People's Liberation Forces (PLAF) were ordinary villagers who took up arms on a part-time basis before returning to their daily lives. Local organized forces of Viet Cong (VC) remained in hiding in swamps, mountains or other remote areas. These forces were supplied from the north via the Ho Chi Minh Trail or, as an alternative, they either captured U.S. weapons or bought them from corrupt officials.

Attempts to segregate villagers from Viet Cong, in a similar way to which the British had separated Malayan villagers from communist guerrilla infiltration during the Malayan Emergency (1949–60), proved fruitless as the Viet Cong influence was too insidious and the cancer could not be isolated. The North Vietnamese leader Ho Chi

RECONNAISSANCE

The *Concise Oxford English Dictionary* definition of reconnaissance is "military observation of a region to locate an enemy or ascertain strategic features; preliminary surveying or research."

Reconnaissance can take many forms, depending on the unit that has responsibility for it in any particular armed force, and it may include working out the lie of the land or specifically identifying the type and movements of enemy formations. Reconnaissance is associated with the roles of specialist tasks such as forward observation and target acquisition and also with sniping. The U.S. Marine Corps took the logical step of formalizing this natural association and for this reason their snipers are known as scout/snipers and are trained to fulfill both reconnaissance and sniping duties. This should not be confused, however, with Marine Recon. There are separate Marine reconnaissance battalions that provide a proactive mix of intelligence gathering, reconnaissance and preparatory raiding. Marine Recon have responsibility for deep penetration and reconnaissance patrols and were active in Vietnam. A similar service is provided by the British Army by the Pathfinder Platoon, whose missions may include covert reconnaissance as well as direct action. Typically, the Pathfinders will prepare landing grounds and identify enemy positions ahead of the arrival of the main force. Members of the Brigade Patrol Group of the British Royal Marines also provide intelligence gathering and are trained as snipers. Special forces of many kinds are often involved in reconnaissance work, whether it be the British SAS or the U.S. Delta Force.

Below: *Soldiers of the U.S. 9th Division pause on patrol after a sniper bullet is fired. The Viet Cong and North Vietnamese PLA were fully aware of the value of snipers.*

Minh issued a statement that summarized effectively the nature of the insurgency. He said that if the Americans "want to make war for twenty years then we shall make war for twenty years."

NORTH VIETNAMESE SNIPERS

Not only did the North Vietnamese send arms and other supplies down the Ho Chi Minh trail, they also sent snipers. They were armed with the Mosin-Nagant Model 1891/30 rifle with telescopic sights and, like the Japanese in the jungles of the Pacific, they were capable of holding down units for hours as they lay concealed in thick jungle foliage. Such was the effect of the sniper that aerial assets could be called in and thousands of pounds of ordnance expended, sometimes to no avail.

The sniper therefore was a true emblem of the war of attrition that was taking place and he was also emblematic of how a vastly more powerful force, namely that of the United States, could be held at bay by vastly inferior but well-placed units. In one incident, a single North Vietnamese Army (NVA) sniper held down two Marine companies and required the involvement of six fighter-bombers. If this was what was needed to deal with one sniper, what would be required to deal with thousands?

Below: *A U.S. Marine sniper aims through an embrasure constructed from concrete blocks. He is using an M40A1 rifle with a Redfield telescopic sight and wears a body armor vest.*

Above: U.S. Marines undergo sniper training among rice paddy fields in Vietnam. The helmet is used as a support for the M40A1 sniper rifle and the spotter has also dispensed with head protection.

The U.S. military relied heavily on helicopters to move its troops around and to insert them for offensive missions. North Vietnamese snipers targeted helicopters and also selected targets once the troops were on the ground. They created maximum disruption by shooting key personnel such as officers, NCOs, radio operators and those carrying or operating vital equipment and weaponry.

The Battle of Ia Drang

In the fight at Ia Drang in October 1965, Captain Bennett, Commander of Company A, 2nd Battalion 5th Cavalry, was killed by a sniper and sniper activity proved to be an enduring feature of the battle. The official history of the battle records:

Still concerned with possible enemy intentions and capabilities and no doubt wary because of what had happened to Company C on the previous morning's sweep, Colonel Moore directed all companies to spray the trees, anthills, and bushes in front of their positions to kill any snipers or other infiltrators – a practice that the men called a "mad minute."

Seconds after the firing began, an enemy platoon-size force came into view 150 meters [164

U.S. MARINES SNIPER SCHOOL

The current U.S. Marine Corps sniper course is called the Scout/Sniper School. In Vietnam, Captain Robert E. Russell was given the task of establishing a sniper school in Phu Bai in 1965.

Russell was in the Marines 3rd Division and Captain Jim Land of 1st Marines Division was also enrolled in the task of gathering a team of expert marksmen to train snipers. As candidates came forward to the schools, they were assessed for a range of skills and about 25 percent were returned to their units as unsuitable.

After all the fits and starts in the previous three wars – World War I, World War II and the Korean War – it had now become clear to the authorities that sniping could no longer be treated like an optional extra, with marksmen being asked to perform on a freelance basis when occasion demanded. Snipers on both sides had proved that sniping was a skill that had an influence on the battlefield way out of proportion to the numbers involved. If you wanted to influence the battle, you required trained and organized snipers.

As time went on, the U.S. Marine Corps started to develop a course that set it apart from sniper training in the U.S. Army as well as the training in other countries. The U.S. Marine sniper would also be a scout, providing essential reconnaissance information for the infantry battalion in which they served. The scout/snipers would be attached to the team of specialists who also dealt with target acquisition and surveillance. They were, in short, an elite and they had to pass through a searchingly rigorous assessment and training course in order to achieve that elite status. A potential scout/sniper in the Marines volunteers from the ranks and is normally given an assessment that may include rigorous fitness tests and interviews. If successful, the Marine would be passed on to the Scout/Sniper Basic Course (SSBC), which could take place at a number of different U.S. Marines bases, including Camp Pendleton, Camp Lejeune,

Quantico or Hawaii. This comprises an eight-week course, the rigour of which can be measured by its failure rate of 60 percent. Once the course is under way, students are taught basic marksmanship, which includes precision shooting under pressure at a variety of different ranges. The students work in a team – one firing while another spots and then they change over. To make it more difficult, the tests are conducted in the form of a race, which has all sorts of implications for fitness and the ability to be steady for the next shot. The score has to be at least twenty-eight out of thirty-five rounds on the black part of the target.

Apart from marksmanship, students are also taught stalking, which means approaching an observation post (OP) undetected. The aim is for the student to get themselves into a good shooting position at the OP without being observed and to have their rifle adjusted for the shot. Other parts of the course cover camouflage and concealment, movement, observation and field sketches and weapons. Successful students can elect to specialize in other areas, such as urban sniping, mountain sniping and team leading or to carry on with a course at a foreign sniper school, such as the British Royal Marines sniping school or the Israeli Foreign Forces Snipers School.

The role of the trained scout/sniper is to provide accurate fire in support of combat operations; to establish hides from which to operate as a sniper and an observer; and to be able to use all necessary tools, whether weapons, navigational equipment or radios, in pursuit of these tasks.

Opposite: *A U.S. Marine instructor guides a student sniper using a Remington Model 700 rifle from which the U.S. Marines M40A1 sniper rifle was developed.*

yards] in front of Company A, 2nd Battalion, 7th Cavalry, and opened fire at the perimeter. An ideal artillery target, the attacking force was beaten off in twenty minutes by a heavy dose of high-explosive variable time fuse. The "mad minute" effort proved fruitful in other respects. During the firing one North Vietnamese soldier dropped from a tree, dead, immediately in front of Captain Herren's command post. The riddled body of another fell and hung upside down, swinging from the branch from which the man had tied himself in front of Diduryk's leftmost platoon. An hour later somebody picked off an enemy soldier as he attempted to climb down a tree and escape.
[Seven Firefights in Vietnam, *John A. Cash, John Albright and Allan W. Sandstrum*]

In this battle, therefore, the VC/NVA snipers did not have everything their own way.

In October 1967, 3rd Battalion, 12th Infantry were sent out to monitor possible enemy insurgents near Dak To in Kontum Province. In a firefight on a hill, they discovered NVA snipers once again in trees. Like the Japanese, the NVA lashed themselves into the trees from which they swayed grotesquely when shot.

The Tet Offensive

During the Tet Offensive, the U.S. 3rd Marine Division heading towards Hue in trucks discovered that NVA snipers were just as adept at hiding in buildings. As the task force closed in on the city, communist snipers opened fire on the Marines from dilapidated buildings and thatched huts that lined either side of the highway. The column drove on, spraying each suspected sniper position with a hail of bullets as it passed. For 2nd Battalion, 12th Cavalry, enemy snipers would also prove to be a significant obstacle. Moving south of Hue, they came to a small hamlet called Thon Que Chu, whereupon the inhabitants evaporated.

As the battalion reached the hamlet, snipers began firing at the Americans from the woods to the south where the villagers had fled. ... The colonel called for an artillery strike from two South Vietnamese 105-mm [4.1in] howitzers at Pk-17. Without interpreters on hand to adjust the fire, however, the shelling proved to be ineffectual. Although the low cloud ceiling ruled out any close air support missions from the U.S. Air Force, brigade headquarters sent gunship and aerial rocket artillery helicopters to soften up the enemy position. ... The preparatory bombardment had done little harm to the enemy, but General Tolson demanded that Sweet take Thon Que Chu without further delay. Colonel Sweet strongly recommended waiting until the artillery battery attached to his battalion became operational at Pk-17, but Tolson overruled him. Out of options, the colonel decided to take Thon Que Chu with a frontal assault.

In a scene reminiscent of a World War I infantry assault, around 150 troops from the unit charged across the open field separating them from Thon Que Chu, with the remainder of the battalion providing covering fire. North Vietnamese bullets and mortar fragments quickly took their toll on the advancing men, who had no cover other than a small cemetery in the middle of the field. Colonel Sweet fed more platoons into the attack, and helicopter scout ships reappeared to strafe the enemy positions. The attacking troops reached the tree line shortly after noon and drove the enemy deeper into Thon Que Chu. Nine soldiers had been killed, most from sniper rounds to the head, and another forty-eight had been wounded in the assault.

[The 1968 Tet Offensive Battles of Quang Tri City and Hue, *U.S. Army Center of Military History*]

This was not the end. On February 9, 2nd Battalion 12th Cavalry moved out towards Thon La Chu accompanied by a South Vietnamese platoon. They came across a squad of enemy snipers who were well camouflaged. Two Americans and twelve South Vietnamese were killed before a team could outflank the enemy and kill at least three of the snipers. Once they had reached Hue, U.S. and South Vietnamese forces were once again assailed by sniper bullets, some of them emanating from the Imperial Palace.

CARLOS HATHCOCK (1942–99)

U.S. Marine Sergeant Carlos Hathcock is one of the highest-scoring marksmen in the U.S. Army, with a service record of ninety-three confirmed kills. Hathcock normally operated with a spotter and he maintained a set of equipment and supplies so that they were ready to go at a moment's notice.

Hathcock preferred the Winchester Model 70 with telescopic sight but he also carried an 11mm (0.45in) pistol for close-quarters defense and the team also had an M14, since a rifle designed for long-range shooting was not ideal for dealing with surprises at close quarters in the jungle. They also took binoculars, a spotting telescope, a radio and a range of essential rations.

On one occasion Hathcock and his companion took up a position near the Cade River in the vicinity of Dong Den, Vietnam. They built a hide, which they carefully camouflaged at the edge of the forest and looked out over a series of rice paddy fields. They observed their usual discipline of total silence. It goes without saying that they showed no lights, did not smoke and took care not to wear scented anti-perspirants or aftershave.

The team may have expected a solitary target to appear somewhere along the ridge paths that separated the paddy fields but soon they heard a noise that indicated something very different was on the way. It was the tramp of a whole company of NVA, consisting of about eighty men. Hathcock and his partner may have had mixed feelings at this point. They were out on their own with no support. Snipers like to be able to select their targets and remain anonymous. It would be difficult to take on such a large body of men in such otherwise quiet surroundings without somebody identifying the direction of the shot.

Surprisingly, the company of men chose to take the central path across the fields, which was parallel to Hathcock's tree line and at about 700m (766 yards) range. They were like ducks waddling across a shooting gallery and there was no available cover, apart from the water and marsh of the paddy fields. Experienced soldiers do not walk across an open space in broad daylight in a war zone.

Hathcock had to make a decision. Normally he would be too prudent to take on such a large body of men, even with his partner to support him with the M14 but, staring through his binoculars, he could see that these troops were green. The likelihood was that when fired upon they would simply panic rather than organize a counter-attack, as more experienced troops would do.

Green target

Following the sniper's principle of selecting targets that would cause maximum confusion, Hathcock selected the officer at the front while his partner selected the one at the rear. The two rifles fired consecutively and the two officers dropped onto the path. Now there was mayhem. The remains of the company threw themselves over the side of the path into the paddy field, minus one who was not quick enough. The NVA company now had several problems. They were stuck out in the open and their only firm path to safety would expose them to certain death. Anyone who has ever seen a wet paddy field will know that it is difficult to move in the sucking mud.

It was broad daylight so it would be a long, wet wait before they had any chance of movement under cover of darkness. Any attempt to spot the mysterious enemy sniper by peering over the path was also certain death. A couple of them tried and it was the last thing they did. After that the remaining officer decided to make a dash for it and Hathcock accounted for him as well.

The NVA who survived had no choice but to remain lying in the mud and water as the temperature rose steadily with the sun. Hathcock and his partner changed their location and awaited developments. The hours passed and eventually one of the NVA decided that the mystery enemy must have moved on by now and raised his head above the parapet. As nothing happened, he gathered his courage and hauled himself up on to the path. The inevitable did happen and he flopped back into the paddy field, a dead man.

Above: *U.S. Marine Sergeant Carlos Hathcock, one of the most prolific snipers of the Vietnam era, shows off his Winchester Model 70 sniper rifle fitted with a silencer and a night-vision telescopic sight.*

Unfortunately for the NVA, darkness did not bring an end to their agony. Hathcock had sent a radio message back to base asking for a series of flares above the fields. One after the other, the flares illuminated the night like day until day itself came round again. In sheer desperation, eight NVA attempted to make an attack towards the tree line, blazing away with their AK47s. The only problem was they chose the wrong piece of jungle to attack. The other problem was that they had to run through 700m (766 yards) of sticky mud and water. Hathcock and his partner picked them all off, bar one who managed to make it back to the relative safety of the bank.

No escape

Hathcock and his partner changed position again and settled in for another night of illuminations. On the third day five more NVA attempted another charge, again in the wrong direction, and all of them died in the process. On day four, the NVA tried a more successful tactic. One group tried to escape while others watched for the muzzle flashes. This time they spotted the sniper hide and bullets started to crash through the foliage around Hathcock and his partner, who changed their location. Again, the NVA tried to make a break and all of them were shot. This was followed by another attack, with the same result. At this point Hathcock and his partner had had enough and they decided to pull out, leaving the artillery to finish the job. It had been a grisly display of the power of the sniper.

Game shooter

Carlos Hathcock's extraordinary career had its origins in his boyhood, long before he joined the Marine Corps. The young Hathcock helped out his hard-up grandmother, with whom he lived after his parents separated, by shooting game in the woods near his home. It was here that he honed his marksmanship skills to the point where he began to win shooting competitions. Most notably, he won

Above: *Carlos Hathcock and a colleague pose next to a sign reading "Viet-Nam Hunting Club" with M14 sniper rifles, both of which are fitted with telescopic sights and silencers.*

the Wimbledon Cup for long-range shooting at Camp Perry in 1965.

Hathcock hunted using a rifle brought home from World War II by his father, and in his imagination he did not only stalk animals. He also hunted and killed imaginary Nazi soldiers during his hunting expeditions, but when he joined the U.S. Marine Corps it was not as a sniper. At that time sniping was a largely forgotten art despite the lessons of World War II and the Korean War, and it was not until after Hathcock began his deployment to Vietnam in 1966 that a platoon of snipers was raised by the USMC. In the meantime he served as a military policeman.

COLD WAR CONFLICTS

Hathcock's impressive record as a marksman made him a natural choice for the new sniper unit. Once out in the field he embarked upon a remarkable career, both in terms of the shots he made and the effect he had upon the enemy. At some point he acquired the habit of wearing a white feather in his hat band, and it was by this trademark that he became known to, and feared by, the enemy.

"The White Feather"

A bounty of $30,000 was posted for the death of "The White Feather" by the Vietnamese, and a special unit of counter-snipers was raised to hunt him. A number of other USMC snipers began wearing white feathers to try to take some of the pressure off Hathcock, appreciating the morale effect that his death would have had on both sides.

It was while conducting counter-sniper (or possibly counter-counter-sniper) operations that Hathcock achieved one the most famous feats of sniping in history. He was at the time operating from a firebase on Hill 55. An enemy sniper was in the area and had killed several U.S. Marines. He may have been in the area specifically to hunt Hathcock, but in any case he was a threat that needed to be removed.

Hathcock and his spotter, John Roland Burke, were hunting this sniper when Hathcock noticed a glint of light through the jungle. Snipers occasionally give away their position this way, by sunlight reflecting off the front lens of their scope. Hathcock was so sure he had a target that he chose to fire at the glint, almost certainly saving his own life by doing so.

Stealthily working their way around to where the presumed enemy had been seen, Hathcock found a body armed with a sniper rifle. The sniper had been shot directly down his telescopic sight and into his eye, killing him instantly. The only possible way for this to happen was if his rifle was pointed directly at Carlos Hathcock at the moment the bullet arrived. Had Hathcock been a little slower or less sure of his target, the White Feather bounty might well have been collected.

M14 SNIPER WEAPON SYSTEM

Country of Origin	United States
Caliber	7.62mm (0.3in)
Overall length	1120mm (44.1in)
Barrel length	559mm (22in)
Weight	5.11kg (11.25lbs)

The M14 semi-automatic rifle was selected for its accuracy, reliability and reasonably fast action. The rifle was converted by Rock Island Arsenal, to include the Redfield/Leatherwood 3-9x Adjustable Ranging Telescope and National Match-grade ammunition, giving it an effective range of 690m (750 yards). The rifle remained in service as the sniper weapon of choice for the U.S. Army between 1975 and 1988, when it was replaced by the M24 Sniper Weapon System.

Fieldcraft

Hathcock's incredible ability to locate and hit a target stemmed from his intense awareness of his surroundings. His focus and concentration were complete. This instinctive understanding of wind, air temperature and the lay of the land contributed to accuracy over great distances as well as the ability to determine where an enemy might appear. He was also skilled at predicting the results of a shot; where hostiles might look for the source of the attack, what they might do in response and where individuals might take cover. This enabled him to decide whether a shot was too risky to take, and to gain the absolute maximum result out of any given mission.

Assassin

There is of course more to sniping than simply shooting. Getting into position and hiding or escaping from the enemy afterward is every bit as important as accuracy with a rifle. Hathcock was a master of the art of stealth, which enabled him to assassinate a North Vietnamese general in 1967. This audacious mission required Hathcock to crawl over 1500 meters (1640 yards) through enemy territory. It is not so much the distance that commands respect, but the time this act of evasion required – four days and three nights.

During his epic crawl Hathcock was camouflaged so well that an enemy soldier failed to spot the sniper despite almost stepping on him. After inching into position, Hathcock waited for his opportunity and fired a single shot, killing the general. He then had to crawl stealthily away while enemy troops searched for him.

It is not possible to precisely determine the results of killing a senior officer on enemy plans or morale, but it is likely that this single shot caused significant disruption to the enemy as well as a boost to friendly morale. Certainly, at least some U.S. soldiers thought that Hathcock had made a big difference. Jack Mergott wrote a poem, entitled "White Feather," in which he speaks of "a battle never fought" where young men would have died – including himself – and finishes with the lines "… but when the sniper drew his bead… the life he saved was mine."

Hathcock relished the hunt, but not the killing of men. That was just something that had to be done, and like all snipers he was able to do his job clinically, without letting emotion interfere. He was also willing to be compassionate, but only up to a point. While attempting to interrupt enemy supply operations, he found himself aiming at a young boy who was transporting weapons and ammunition on a bicycle. Hathcock decided to shoot the bicycle frame, disabling the vehicle and making it impossible to deliver the weapons. However, the young courier returned fire, so Hathcock shot and killed him.

Wounded in action

Carlos Hathcock was rotated home in 1967, but returned to Vietnam in 1969 to lead a sniper unit. It was during this second tour that he was badly injured, though not by direct fire. Hathcock was riding an Amtrack (Amphibious Tractor) light armored vehicle as part of a convoy when his vehicle was disabled and set on fire by a mine. Hathcock personally saved seven Marines from the flames before escaping himself.

Hathcock was severely burned and was forced to leave frontline service, but he continued to train Marine snipers in the United States until ill health forced him to retire. Even then he visited the sniper training school whenever he could. From 1984 until his death in 1999 he helped train law enforcement snipers.

Hathcock's career had a profound effect on the technology of sniping as well as its perceived importance. His success, and that of others, convinced the United States' military that sniping was a necessary part of modern warfare. Sniper training, neglected for many years, was based upon

Above: *Corporal F.S. Sanders (right) and Lance-Corporal J.W. Howell aim at and spot enemy positions during Operation "Swift" in September 1967. Sanders uses his helmet to support his M40A1 rifle.*

the experience and skills of men like Hathcock. He had showed what could be done, and then went on to teach others how.

Heavy caliber weapons

Hathcock's sniping career also paved the way for the modern generation of extremely heavy anti-materiel rifles such as the M107 (Barrett M82A1) long-range sniper rifle. The progenitor of this weapon was an adapted M2 .50 caliber (12.7mm) heavy machine-gun, which several snipers used in Vietnam. Carlos Hathcock contrived a bracket to fit a telescopic sight to his weapon, which was converted to semi-automatic for this application. With this weapon, Hathcock made the longest confirmed sniper kill of the twentieth century, shooting 2286 meters (2500 yards). It was with a specialist sniping rifle designed to fire the same .50 caliber machine gun cartridge that the first snipers to surpass this incredible shot made their own record-breaking kills in the twenty-first century. Although Hathcock was not the highest-scoring sniper of the Vietnam War, and his long-range shooting record has since been broken, his influence on sniper technology and doctrine is still felt today.

ADELBERT F. WALDRON (1933–95)

Although Carlos Hathcock is perhaps the best-known U.S. sniper from the Vietnam War, there were others serving in the U.S. forces who notched up comparable numbers of kills and, in the case of Waldron, even more than Hathcock.

FIELDCRAFT

Fieldcraft comprises the range of skills that are required to operate mostly in open country without being seen or otherwise identified. It incorporates camouflage, movement, stealth and similar skills.

The reason why many hunters of wild game have gone on to become successful snipers is due to their instinctive grasp of fieldcraft through long experience. The Scottish ghillies who formed part of the Lovat Scouts would have had plenty of experience of stalking deer in the highlands, requiring stealth, patience and the knowledge of weather conditions. A stag is even more observant than an enemy sentry, with better eyesight and more finely attuned senses of hearing and smell. For this reason, the early sniping pioneers used gamekeepers and hunters either as snipers or as trainers. In both the U.S. Army and Marines sniper courses, as well as the British Royal Marines, a high level of fieldcraft is required before a candidate can pass a course. There are certain accepted principles of fieldcraft, most of which are common sense and all of which are more or less instinctively understood by experienced hunters and those who are familiar with the countryside. The instinct of hunting and concealment is also ingrained

Below: *Soldiers apply face camouflage before going on operations. The key to effective camouflage is to break up shapes.*

Left: *Good fieldcraft involves making best use of the ground and local vegetation. This soldier is aiming an M24 sniper rifle fitted with both a night-vision sight and folded bipod.*

in the human psyche, which explains why young children get such a thrill out of games of hide and seek.

For the sniper, certain principles have either to be learned or practiced. These include blending with your surroundings so as to break up the recognizably human shape. This is where the ghillie suit, invented by Scottish gamekeepers, comes in so useful. The sniper also needs to be thoroughly aware of the movement of the sun. The Russian sniper Vassili Zaitsev waited for the sun to move into the right position before taking on the German super-sniper. The sun shining on glass may identify a sniper scope. Snipers also have to be aware of how the sun might throw their own shadow and to take advantage of the shadow of other large objects such as trees or buildings.

Basic military training is not to show a silhouette, for example on a ridge or other skyline or in a window or doorway. The sniper needs to be aware of their environment and wear suitable clothing. As British paratroopers moved from the fields around Arnhem into the town itself during Operation "Market Garden," Major John Frost is said to have commented on their green camouflage and foliage in their helmets. The U.S. Marines have worked both on urban camouflage and on equipment such as specialized boots and knee and elbow guards to optimize movement in urban terrain. A sure giveaway in an otherwise blank environment is movement and/or sound. The smallest movement of a branch or sound of a snapping twig could provide the essential clue to give away a sniper's position.

Credited with 109 confirmed kills, Staff Sergeant Waldron served in the U.S. Army's 9th Infantry Division. Born in New York, he had initially joined the U.S. Navy but left in 1965. He enlisted in the U.S. Army in 1968 and was attached to Company B, 3rd Battalion, 60th Infantry Regiment of the 9th Infantry Division. This division was part of the Mobile Riverine Force (MRF) that operated in the Mekong Valley. Like most U.S. Army snipers, he carried the new M21 rifle with the Redfield/Leatherwood 3-9x Adjustable Ranging Telescope (ART) sight.

Waterborne sniper

Waldron was often in a somewhat unusual position for a sniper, and an army sniper at that, as he often operated from a moving boat on a river. This might have caused an ordinary sniper to put a few shots wide but Waldron was no ordinary sniper. Riding on a Tango boat on the Mekong River one afternoon, an enemy sniper started to pepper the boat with long-range shots. Waldron identified the sniper in a coconut tree about 900m (984 yards) away. The only problem was that he was on a moving boat. Waldron took careful aim and fired. After that, the enemy sniper was in no position to fire at anything.

Waldron served with the 9th Infantry Division, which was the only major U.S. Army unit to be deployed to the Mekong Delta. As part of the MRF (Mobile Riverine Force), elements of the 9th Division operated aboard Navy-crewed "Tango Boats" in the waterways of the Delta, which was a difficult combat environment at the best of times.

Various expedients were tried to cope with the delta environment, including the experimental "Pinkeye" boats that swept rivers for enemy personnel at night. These boats were fitted with a powerful searchlight covered by a pink filter. This created light conditions highly suitable for the use of low-light or "starlight" scopes by snipers. Two to four snipers were stationed aboard the boat to engage enemy personnel illuminated by the light. The snipers could engage directly or use tracer rounds to indicate a target for a ship-board 105mm (4.1in) howitzer firing "beehive" anti-personnel rounds.

Controversial combat record

The 9th Infantry Division began training snipers late in 1968, at about the same time that Waldron enlisted. He was not a teenage recruit but was in his mid 30s, and had served with the Navy from 1956 to 1965. He was given the rank of sergeant, equivalent to his navy rank. Perhaps because of his experience, Waldron was selected for in-country sniper training soon after he deployed to Vietnam in 1968. The division began to be withdrawn in the summer of 1969, giving Waldron just a few months to prove his effectiveness.

Above: *Sniper in the shadows: Adelbert C. Waldron makes use of simple camouflage through which he aims his M21 rifle. Top snipers such as Waldron had a natural talent for fieldcraft as well as marksmanship.*

Above: *A sniper and spotter of B Company, 4th Marine Division work together on Operation "Nanking Scotland II" in October 1968.*

There is some controversy surrounding Waldron and his record, and details are hard to establish. It is alleged that he did not pass sniper training before beginning his active career, though whether or not this is the case really matters less than the results he achieved.

There are those who dispute these results, too. Waldron is sometimes cited with 113 confirmed kills. This arises from an offhand remark by Colonel Mitchell WerBell, who was asked how many kills Waldron had made and could not remember exactly. He mistakenly stated 113 rather than the officially recorded 109, and this erroneous figure found its way into common use.

However, 109 kills is still an incredible number and this figure, too, has been challenged. The 9th Infantry Division has been accused of exaggerating its body count for various reasons, notably because the number of weapons recovered from the combat area did not tally with the claimed enemy casualties. It has been claimed that, in order to make its sniper training program seem more effective, the 9th Division would add the kills scored by a sniper's accompanying security element to his own tally.

The truth of this is hard to discern, but personnel from the 9th Infantry Division who were interviewed spoke highly of Waldron's effectiveness as a sniper and a combat soldier. At least some of his actions have been independently corroborated, so it is probable that he was indeed an extremely skilled sniper whose reputation may have been used by others to further their agenda.

Highly effective sniper
Waldron is officially credited with 109 kills, of which 82 were made in the first five months of his deployment. For his actions he was awarded the Silver Star, Bronze Star and two Distinguished Service Crosses for his service in Vietnam. This included his exploits aboard Tango Boats and also in a more conventional sniping environment.

Waldron favored a suppressed rifle, making it difficult for hostiles to determine where a shot had come from. He often shot from relatively short distances, averaging about 400 meters (440 yards). He also made extensive use of a "starlight" low-light sight, which was at that time an emerging technology but which is today a standard piece of kit. His M21 rifle was also a relatively new weapon, but went on to become the standard U.S. sniping rifle until 1988.

One official report of Waldron's exploits describes the effectiveness of the night sight/suppressor combination in the right hands. Waldron and his spotter had set up a hide a little south of Ben Tre, in an area that his company had swept that day. This was a fairly common way to cover a sniper deployment; the sniper team would accompany a patrol and then quietly drop out of sight, remaining behind to ambush any hostiles who came along afterwards. Waldron's position covered a paddy field close to a wooded area, and in due course a small patrol of five Viet Cong insurgents appeared from the woods. Waldron shot one of them, causing the others to take cover. Apparently unable to determine where the threat originated or if it still existed, the enemy patrol resumed movement after a few minutes. As they left cover, the Viet Cong were engaged; all four were shot and killed. About half an hour later, another small patrol appeared. All four members of this group were also eliminated.

This action illustrates a different aspect of sniping. Rather than making long shots, Waldron picked off enemy personnel at fairly close ranges, making multiple kills in a single engagement. His use of a suppressed rifle was instrumental in concealing his location and the electronically conferred ability to see in the dark was certainly useful, but in the end it came down to a man and his rifle.

Later life
After leaving the army in 1970 Waldron worked as a marksmanship instructor for a private security organization and gradually faded into obscurity. He seems never to have been tempted to write a book or give interviews, so many aspects of his career remain vague or controversial. There is enough hard evidence, however, to suggest that whatever the exact truth may be, Adelbert Waldron was a highly effective sniper.

U.S. FIGHTBACK
After suffering so much at the hands of Vietnamese snipers, the Americans realized they needed their own snipers to counter the large number of VC/NVA snipers and in this sort of warfare snipers were an essential fighting arm.

There was only one problem. Neither the Army nor the Marines had an identifiable, up-to-date sniper rifle, short of rummaging around in stores for veteran World War II and Korean War weapons. As so often before, whether it be the U.S. armed forces or the British, it was not just the authorities that took the initiative in resolving the problems but also committed individuals.

The development of automatic rifles such as the M16 had led to a somewhat loose approach to

Above: A U.S. Marine aims his telescopically sighted M16 rifle on the training range. The M16 entered U.S. Army service in South Vietnam in 1963, replacing the M14 as the standard U.S. rifle of the Vietnam War by 1969.

marksmanship. It was thought better to spray an area with bullets, as if soaking it with a hose, than aim at individual targets. This was fair enough if under pressure of an attack at close range from large numbers of the enemy but it was of little use for accurate shooting at selected targets of opportunity. There was also a problem when the enemy were well out of range and were taking accurate shots at U.S. servicemen. Spraying bullets back wildly had little effect. As has been seen so often before, whether in the trenches of France or Belgium or the Normandy bocage, the sniper has an uncanny ability to take control of the situation.

New sight

Once the Army in Vietnam had woken up to the fact that their sniping tactics needed to change, Captain Jim Leatherwood set about designing a suitable telescopic sight. He came up with the Leatherwood ART 1 telescopic sight which had an ingenious adjustment to cope with the problem of bullet drop. The scope was fitted to an M14 rifle and the combination was officially approved as the XM21 system. By the end of 1969, the new system was being fielded in some quantity. The Army also instituted a formal training program and soon properly qualified snipers with a highly accurate weapon began to make an impact on the enemy in Vietnam.

The U.S. Marines were also aware that sniping needed to be taken out of the closet and dusted off. Captain Robert A. Russell established a school for the Marines 3rd Division in Vietnam while Captain Jim Land established an equivalent school for the 1st Marines. Soon sniper platoons were officially designated by the authorities and were formalized as three squads of five two-man teams with a squad leader, a senior NCO, armorer and officer, amounting to one officer and thirty-five enlisted men.

Now all they needed was a rifle. The Army had already selected the M21. The Marines tested this along with the Winchester Model 70 and the M16, which was chambered for the smaller 5.56mm (0.223in) bullet. In the event, the Marines found that none of these suited their particular requirements. After lengthy testing, they selected the Remington Model 40x, the target version of the Remington Model 700 bolt-action rifle. The rifle was fitted with a Redfield Accu-Range 3x9 magnification scope which had advanced moisture resistance.

Now that both the U.S. Army and U.S. Marine Corps had both trained snipers and highly accurate tools of the trade, it was time for the VC/NVA to keep their heads down.

CHUCK MAWHINNEY (1949–)

Chuck Mawhinney served in the U.S. Marine Corps and his record of 103 confirmed kills puts him in the same stratosphere as Hathcock and Waldron. Mawhinney had been a hunter in his youth and, like many good snipers, had an instinctive feel for the natural environment, the effects of sound and movement and of how weather conditions would affect a shot. Having been recognized as a marksman in his early days as a Marine, he moved to Camp Pendleton for sniper training.

M40A1 RIFLE

The M40A1 was a modified version of the Remington 700 Model 40x magnification bolt-action rifle, which was the target variant of the Remington 700. This rifle was selected by the U.S. Marine Corps as their sniper rifle of choice for the Vietnam War and in due course it received further modifications by U.S. Marine Corps armorers at Quantico. The M40A1 featured a fibreglass stock and a Unertl 10x magnification telescopic sight, and had an effective range of 800m (875 yards).

The M40A1 proved to be an extremely accurate and reliable weapon and is still preferred by some users over the later version of the rifle, the A3.

Country of Origin	United States
Caliber	7.62mm (0.3in)
Overall length	1117mm (43.97in)
Barrel length	610mm (24in)
Weight	6.57kg (14.48lbs)

Above: A U.S. Marine Corps scout/sniper surveys some open paddy fields as part of his reconnaissance duties somewhere in Vietnam. He appears to be armed with a M40A1 sniper rifle.

Mawhinney was posted to Vietnam in 1968 and proceeded to notch up a significant number of kills. Apart from 103 confirmed kills, there were 216 additional probable kills.

Headshots

On one occasion, he spotted a platoon of NVA soldiers crossing a stream. Using an M14 rifle, he killed sixteen of them with head shots. This was an extraordinary feat, in view of the fact that he was not even using his more accurate bolt-action sniper rifle. Mawhinney disappeared into relative obscurity after the war but his achievement came to light after the publication of a book that included some of his exploits.

Mawhinney might not have ever become a sniper but for his love of hunting. The connection is not the obvious one; he had planned to join the Navy but was offered a deal by a Marine Corps recruiter. If he joined the Marines, as his father had done, he could defer enlistment until after the hunting season. This was too good to pass up, so Chuck Mawhinney became a Marine and, soon afterward, deployed to Vietnam to hunt men rather than beasts.

Mawhinney arrived in-country in 1968, just after the Tet Offensive, and was thrust into a period of very heavy fighting. Over the next 16 months he achieved a record of over 100 confirmed kills and 216 "probables." At the time, the U.S. military required confirmation of a kill by an officer or by examination of the body. This was often not possible in a fluid combat environment, with the result that Mawhinney's incredible sequence of sixteen headshots – though witnessed by other soldiers – were listed only as probables since the bodies floated away downriver.

Mawhinney, like other snipers, had to come to terms with his profession. His philosophy held that by taking a few lives he saved many more. This is undoubtedly correct – the morale effect and disruption caused by a successful sniper will always weaken the enemy's ability to fight and thus hasten the end of the conflict. With one exception – a North Vietnamese Army paymaster – everyone Mawhinney shot was holding a weapon. This was his rule: anyone with a weapon was fair game.

Sniper mentor
One of Mawhinney's duties as a sniper was to train others. An experienced sniper was partnered up with a rookie – who might be a graduate of sniper training but who was not yet proved in combat – as his observer. Under Mawhinney's guidance a succession of young observers were coached in fieldcraft and the realities of combat sniping until he felt that they were ready for their first shot.

Mawhinney offered his trainees guidance as they prepared themselves to face the challenge of taking their first life. He stressed that this was an enemy who would kill both the sniper and his observer given the chance, and that botching the job could be fatal for the sniper or for someone else.

On one occasion Mawhinney did fail to kill an enemy. Spotting a rifle-armed man at about 300 meters (330 yards) distance, he aimed and fired what should have been an easy shot. To his astonishment the target did not go down but instead took off running. Mawhinney fired several more times, but he could not hit his target.

The man got away as a result, Mawhinney discovered later, of his scope being earlier adjusted by an armorer who had failed to tell him of the change. It was not disappointment at failing to hit his target that bothered the sniper; it was the question of how many of his fellow soldiers that rifleman killed because Mawhinney failed to stop him.

First kill
The new sniper's first kill was carefully selected as what Mawhinney called a "confidence shot" – an easy shot from a fairly short range. This was usually at a distance of around 300 meters (330 yards). Once the new sniper was ready to function alone, he would receive his own rookie observer and both he and Mawhinney would become the senior members of two new partnerships.

Mawhinney had to be ruthless and be willing to kill, but wherever possible he did not leave his victims to suffer needlessly. He often put a second shot into a fatally injured target to end his misery. He also tried to preserve the lives of his own colleagues. Realizing that a competitive "kill-board" set up by a platoon leader was prompting the more reckless snipers to take needless risks in order to get ahead in the kill count, Mawhinney insisted that the offending board be taken down and the competition scrapped.

Withdrawal and discharge
Mawhinney became disillusioned with the war in Vietnam, and realized that there was little prospect of winning with the current strategy. Despite this he extended his tour twice, reasoning that he could keep more young Americans alive if he remained in the field. However, he was eventually suspected of suffering from combat stress and sent home to become an instructor.

Snipers are usually incredibly self-disciplined but they also tend to be highly individualistic. Mawhinney was no exception; he did not take well to the parade-ground atmosphere of a training camp and left the army to take a job with the United States Forest Service.

For many years Mawhinney was a forgotten figure, which he preferred. However, eventually his story emerged and he was forced to admit publicly

COLD WAR CONFLICTS

Above: *U.S. Army specialist marksman Joh Rice uses the scope of his M14 rifle to scan a section of high ground in this photo taken sometime in 1970.*

that he was indeed a sniper who had killed dozens of men. Examination of military records established his reputation as one of the top-scoring snipers of all time, a distinction that he never wanted. To him, sniping was simply a job that had to be done whatever he felt about it, and he had given his best.

EXIT STRATEGY

By March 29, 1973, the last U.S. military units had left Vietnam and all that was left was the final wrangling between North and South Vietnamese forces and the remaining U.S. advisers. Whatever the arguments for the strategy of the war in Vietnam, the sniper had proved his worth and was now established as a permanent and vital part of the fighting arms of the U.S. Army and Marine Corps.

SMALL WARS

The British fought an extended war against communist insurgents in the jungles of Malaya between 1948 and 1960. Here the British Special Air Service (SAS) as well as equivalent units from Australia and New Zealand developed jungle warfare skills and also carried out a successful "hearts and minds" operation that effectively isolated the communist insurgents. Special forces were also deployed in Borneo between 1963 and 1966 to prevent Indonesian raids from coming across the border into Sarawak. Due to the dense jungle, there was not much opportunity for sniper work.

In December 1963 the Aden Emergency began within the Crown colony and the Protectorate in the

COLD WAR CONFLICTS

south of the Arabian Peninsula. Two rival nationalist organizations were active, the Front for the Liberation of Occupied South Yemen (FLOSY), which was supported by Egypt, and the National Liberation Front (NLF), which had Marxist roots. In this protracted conflict, fought largely in rugged mountain terrain, there were snipers on both sides. Various British units were deployed to the area, including Royal Marine Commandos, the Parachute Regiment and the Argyll and Sutherland Highlanders. The major units were backed up by the SAS. In an area known as the Crater, in an extinct volcano, snipers from the Royal Marines watched for the opportunity to pick off Arab terrorists from their positions high up in the hills. Several terrorists were killed as they walked through the streets and alleyways, unaware that they were in the sights of a sniper. One Royal Marine, Mick Harrison, took up a position in a ruined Turkish fort. He would haul himself into his concealed position while it was still dark and be ready at dawn to watch for real targets.

Unusual for a sniper, Harrison would actually reveal himself to the enemy so that they would show themselves in turn. After this, he would have to move his position. Harrison was commended

Below: *British Royal Marine Lance-Corporal John Tilley scans the Crater area near Aden in June 1967 for insurgent activity. He is armed with an L42A1 rifle, the standard British Army issue sniper rifle of the 1960s era.*

L42A1 RIFLE

Country of Origin	United Kingdom
Caliber	7.62mm (0.3in)
Overall length	1181mm (46.5in)
Barrel length	700mm (27.5in)
Weight	4.43kg (9.76lbs)

for gallant and distinguished conduct in Aden, the citation reading (see right):

Unfortunately for the British, the communist guerrillas were adept snipers themselves and they targeted British officers and NCOs and commanders of armored vehicles. In one incident near Al-Mansoura, the commander of a Ferret armored car was hit between the eyes by a sniper's bullet as his vehicle emerged from a detention center. The local guerrilla forces were excellent marksmen and they were obviously also used to their native environment. It took the British some time to acclimate. A troop from A Squadron SAS were pinned down by enemy snipers on the Radfan in April 1964. They managed to get away after receiving support from RAF Hunter aircraft but it had demonstrated once again the effectiveness of local tribesmen in their own country.

ARAB-ISRAELI CONFLICTS

The current troubles in the Middle East starting with the creation of the state of Israel on May 14, 1948 and continuing to the time of writing have been one of the most protracted series of conflicts in history. In so far as they are centered around Jerusalem, they involve three of the major religions of the world – Judaism, Christianity and Islam – and can be said to be central to world history.

"He was in a position overlooking the Crater under sporadic small-arms fire and was the target of a blindicide [anti-tank grenade] attack. Over a period of four days, working with another sniper position, he systematically eliminated terrorist snipers opposing him so that all terrorist fire ceased during daylight hours."

Citation for Royal Marine Mick Harrison

In such a protracted conflict and in such an environment, the sniper has had an important role to play on both sides as he tries to dominate the battlefield or intimidate occupying forces, though the fast-paced style of Israeli maneuver warfare meant that in the earlier conflicts the sniper was mostly a mobile asset, supporting platoon movements and so on. During the Six-Day War, June 5–10, 1967, a battle was fought at Ammunition Hill in the

Jordanian-controlled part of East Jerusalem. The Israeli commander, General Uzi Narkis, decided to conduct a ground attack against Ammunition Hill using artillery and a paratroop company, 3rd Company 66th Battalion. Jordanian snipers took up a position in Antenna House and started to take a significant toll of the Israeli attackers. About twenty-four Israeli soldiers were killed and ninety wounded before the hill was taken.

During the Yom Kippur War, which started on October 6, 1973, Egyptian forces attacked Israel across the Suez Canal while Syria attacked across the Golan Heights in the north. During the tank battle against the Syrians, Syrian snipers using Soviet Dragunov rifles were deployed on the battlefield with the specific task of identifying and shooting Israeli tank commanders. The Israelis were using a version of the British Centurion tank, known as the Sho'ot, and when sitting out of the turret their silhouette was clear against the skyline. The tank battle was one of the most fiercely contested ever as the Israelis initially had only thirty-three tanks against nine hundred Syrian tanks. Although the Egyptian and Syrian armies had demonstrated their aggressive fighting qualities in the Yom Kippur War, Israeli forces pushed their way into Syria and also crossed the Suez Canal on to the West Bank and encircled the Egyptian Third Army. Due to the growing tension between the superpowers – the United States and the Soviet Union – a peace agreement was made and UN

Below: *Israeli paratroopers fire back after coming under fire from PLO snipers in the Israel-Lebanon border. The PLO were quick to realize the value of the sniper in their ongoing war of attrition.*

COLD WAR CONFLICTS

Above: *Dressed in bizarre camouflage, a group of guerrilla snipers of the Action Organization, Palestinian commandos pose for the camera on October 7, 1969. Their role was to intercept Israeli forces operating in the Jordan River valley.*

buffer forces were interposed between the combatants. A cease-fire agreement was signed in November between Israel and Egypt and peace agreements were signed on January 18, 1974. On May 31, 1974 Israel and Syria signed a cease-fire agreement. Although Israel and Egypt would formally end the state of war between them with the Camp David accords of March 26, 1979, Israel would continue to have problems with Palestinian separatists who had their main base in Lebanon. On June 14, 1982, Israel invaded Lebanon and started shelling Beirut. Israeli troops withdrew from Lebanon in June 1985.

The next challenge that arose for Israel was rioting by Palestinian Arabs in the Gaza Strip, the West Bank and parts of Jerusalem from December 1987. Known as the First Intifada, this involved a wide range of disturbances that resulted in the deaths of about 1100 Palestinians and 164 Israelis. The Israeli Defense Force (IDF) has a prescribed policy of "focused foiling" of terrorists, which involves assassinations. To carry out this strategy and in such conditions, the sniper is a useful tool.

Anti-terrorist unit

One of the units of the IDF is the Shimshon Battalion, which was established in 1997 primarily to conduct operations in the Gaza Strip. It is primarily an anti-terrorist unit tasked with identifying terrorist leaders and breaking up their structures. The units are trained specifically for urban warfare and target potential assailants armed with rocket-propelled grenades or missile launchers. The Shimshon Battalion is part of the Kfir Brigade, which also

U.S. MARINES IN LEBANON

On June 6, 1982, the Israelis invaded Lebanon, taking the opportunity to attack terrorist forces that had opposed them, including Abu Nidal, the PLO and Muslim Lebanese forces. A peacekeeping force was sent to the Lebanon, including eight hundred American, eight hundred French, four hundred Italian and ninety-nine British soldiers and Marines.

In 1983, however, Islamic Jihad drove two truck bombs into the barracks of American and French forces, killing 299 servicemen, including 241 U.S. Marines. Meanwhile, U.S. Marine sharpshooters engaged with snipers at Beirut airport. One Marine was killed and another wounded by snipers. The Marines returned fire and are said to have killed five snipers who were firing at them. When rescuers tried to clear the rubble and help those caught in the barracks bombings, they were fired on by snipers as they worked. The rules of engagement given to the U.S. Marines stationed in Beirut at the time contained the wisdom of experience: "If you receive hostile fire, direct your fire at the source. If possible, use friendly snipers."

In October, Marines came under sniper fire at a position near the university. The Marines promptly fired back but casualties began to mount and in some cases they had to move units away from key positions, such as guarding the airport, "because we

Below: U.S. Marine scout/snipers survey a built-up area in Lebanon in January 1983. An M40A1 sniper rifle lies between them. Smoke in the distance suggests the area is a combat zone.

COLD WAR CONFLICTS

Left: *A U.S. Marine sniper takes up a prone-supported position in the Marine compound close to the Beirut International Airport. He is armed with a camouflaged M40A1 rifle.*

were just taking too much sniper fire. It was no longer safe to walk out in the flight line. The snipers were there at the end of the runway, had [us] zeroed in and you just couldn't walk out there without drawing fire. So we had to close that area completely." [*U.S. Marines in Lebanon 1982–1984*, Benis M. Frank]. The Marines deployed a trained sniper against their enemies and succeeded in killing most of them but, despite this, most of the Marine detachment had to withdraw to the safety of their ships.

In Hay es Salaam, Marine companies sustained sniper fire on October 14, and they deployed their own sniper team to counter the enemy snipers. As so often in previous battles and wars, this tactic proved to be effective (see right):

After the major explosion at the Marines barracks, Marine units received 12.7mm (0.5in) sniper rifles and additional night-vision goggles. It was a sign that the time for just taking it was over. Having witnessed Amal militia ambush, Lebanese Armed Forces armored personnel carriers (APCs), capture the soldiers and then shoot them in cold blood with the 12.7mm (0.5in) machine gun mounted on the roof of the APC. U.S. Marine Corporal Rutter and his teammate Crumley felt an extra edge to their shooting skills when they were finally permitted to respond to the fire they were receiving from the Amal. Rutter put a bullet through the firing port of a bunker, silencing the gunner inside, while Crumley

> *"The team surveyed the area with sniper scopes for several hours, pinpointing the snipers actually firing at Marine positions. The team then opened fire with 18 rounds of match 7.62 ammunition at 14 targets. Their success was evident by the sudden silence from each hostile position."*
>
> U.S. Marines in Lebanon 1982–1984, Benis M. Frank

took aim at an Amal sniper who, while he thought he was doing the right thing by changing position after firing, did so with such predictable regularity that it was just a matter of time until he could change position no more.

This episode was proof again that trained military snipers could eliminate troublesome enemy snipers, machine-gunners and other elements without having to mount an infantry exercise or call in artillery with risk of collateral damage.

comprises the Nachson, Haruv, Duchifat, Lavi and Netzah Yehuda Battalions. There are other sniper units in the IDF, including the Givat Brigade. The Givati Reconnaissance Battalion also incorporates snipers. Israeli snipers used the M14 SWS rifle, which was adapted by Israeli Military Industries.

The Palestinian Liberation Organization (PLO) had a specific policy of using snipers in its ongoing conflict with the IDF. One of the tactics used by the Palestinians was to cover their snipers by having crowds throw rocks at Israeli troops, causing a distraction. The snipers would then fire upon the enemy under cover of the confusion that was caused. The Palestinians also used rocket-propelled grenades in similar circumstances.

In one incident, a PLO sniper positioned himself on a hilltop and fired at soldiers and civilians at a checkpoint in the Palestinian suburb of Silwad. The IDF soldiers who were present used a well-rehearsed drill to try to neutralize the sniper. This involved advancing up the hill towards the sniper during which seven IDF soldiers were killed. By the time the IDF soldiers reached the top of the hill, the sniper had vanished.

Sniper to sniper

Despite the fact that the IDF soldiers were using a formal battle drill to counter the sniper, their casualties mounted and the operation proved to be a failure. The alternative methods sometimes used in countering snipers are mortar or artillery fire but this can end up causing more damage to civilians in the area than it does to the sniper.

A well-trained sniper knows how to move position between shots and to disappear when his position is

Right: *Israeli Defense Force snipers use tripods to support their M24 sniper rifles during an operation in the West Bank town of Bethlehem on May 27, 2002. Note that both snipers also carry M4 carbines for close-quarter defense or assault should the need arise. The sniper on the left carries spare 7.62mm (0.3in) rounds slung around his wrist.*

COLD WAR CONFLICTS

identified. As occurred in the bocage of Normandy, the most effective way of engaging an enemy sniper can be through deploying a friendly sniper.

THE FALKLANDS WAR, 1982

Argentina had claimed sovereignty over the Falkland Islands, which it called the Islas Malvinas, in the South Atlantic since the beginning of the nineteenth century. The islands had been occupied by the British since 1833 and the population of the islands wanted to remain British.

The invasion of the Falkland Islands by the British was instigated both by the need of an unpopular Argentine ruling junta to distract attention from its economic mismanagement but also the pusillanimous attitude of the British towards the islands and their security. As the Argentine Government watched the British Government cut back the Royal Navy, they considered it was probably worth the risk. On April 2, 1982, the Argentines invaded the Falkland Islands with elite commandos and followed up the next day with the invasion of South Georgia, which was about 1600km (1000 miles) east of the Falklands.

The Argentines may have been correct in assuming the dice were loaded in their favor and that the British had been suffering from a post-imperial hangover. What they had not considered was that the British Prime Minister was Margaret Thatcher and that self-doubt was decidedly out of vogue.

The British responded by immediately declaring a 332km (200-mile) exclusion zone around the Falkland Islands and assembling a naval task force. The distance to the Falkland Islands was about 12,875km (8000 miles), which would test most people's determination, and therefore the Argentines had plenty of time to consider what was coming their way, namely 3 Commando Brigade Royal Marines, including 2 and 3 Parachute Battalions; the Royal Marines Special Boat Squadron and D and G Squadrons 22 SAS. The regular army element included 5 Brigade, comprising 1st Battalion Welsh Guards, 2nd Battalion Scots Guards, 1st Battalion 7th Duke of Edinburgh's Own Gurkha Rifles and a troop of the Blues and Royals.

Although the task force would take some time to travel 12,875km (8000 miles) by sea, Britain was also quick to move on the diplomatic front. Within days, Britain had gained the full support of the United Nations, the European Economic Community, NATO and the Commonwealth. Argentina, on the other hand, could not even get the support of the Organization of American States. The United States was helpful to the British cause.

On the Falkland Islands, after the initial landing by elite Argentinian commandos, the island was heavily reinforced by conscripts, bringing the Argentine garrison up to a strength of about ten thousand men. The Argentine forces, however, could not be

L1A1 RIFLE

Country of Origin	United Kingdom
Caliber	7.62mm (0.3in)
Overall length	1055mm (41.5in)
Barrel length	535mm (21in)
Weight	4.31kg (9.5lb)

Above: British Royal Marines pose after victory in the Falklands War of 1982. The Marine third from right kneeling carries an L1A1 self-loading rifle (SLR) with a telescopic sight.

underestimated. There were well-trained troops available, they often had more advanced equipment than the British and among them there were trained snipers who would cause the British a lot of problems. The first British landings were made at San Carlos on May 21. By May 25, three more Royal Navy ships had been lost and a transport ship carrying essential MH-47 Chinook helicopters was also sunk. British land forces divided, with 45 Commando and 3 Para heading eastwards and 2 Para south to Goose Green, which was taken by the British. While 45 Commando and 3 Para moved on foot towards Stanley, 5th Brigade landed at San Carlos and was then moved around by sea to Bluff Cove where landing crafts were attacked by Argentine aircrafts, causing many casualties, especially among the Welsh Guards.

Now, however, the British forces were poised to attack the high ground positions around Stanley, namely Mount Longdon, Two Sisters, Mount Harriet, Tumbledown Mountain and Wireless Ridge. Due to the loss of many of their transport helicopters, the British soldiers had just had to walk with all their equipment across extremely difficult terrain. Now they would have to attack well-prepared positions up several hills, where Argentine snipers, well trained and with good equipment, awaited them.

Mount Longdon

Between June 11 and 12, 1982 British forces consisting of 3 Paratroop Regiment supported by 29 Commando Regiment, Royal Artillery made an attack on Argentine positions on Mount Longdon.

D Company of 3 Para were tasked with sending out a probing platoon to capture an Argentine prisoner for questioning. The patrol included

COLD WAR CONFLICTS

COLD WAR CONFLICTS

specialist snipers who fired on an Argentine position, aiming at the officer. The Argentines responded by firing mortars, artillery, machine guns and small arms at the snipers.

As the British attack gathered pace, it was the turn of the Argentine snipers to make their presence felt. Private Nick Rose of 6 Platoon tells us what happened when the platoon tried to advance:

"Pete Gray stood up and went to throw a '42' Grenade and he was shot by a sniper in his right forearm. …. There's 'incoming' everywhere, loads of stuff going down the range and then 'bang' my pal 'Fester' [Tony Greenwood], gets it just above his left eye, only a yard away from me. That was a terrible thing. … Then it was 'Baz' Barratt. 'Baz' had gone to try to get field dressings for Pete and as he was coming back 'bang,' he got it in the back. This was when we just stalled as a platoon."

3 Para Mount Longdon: The Bloodiest Battle
by Jon Cooksey

Left: *A British sniper with an L1A1 self-loading rifle (SLR) and night-sight escorts Argentine prisoners. Note the difficult ground over which the British forces had to advance.*

SNIPERS ON MOUNT HARRIET

On the nights of June 11 and 12, 1982, 42 Commando Royal Marines made an attack on the vital high point of Mount Harriet. It was essential that this location was taken so that the route to Port Stanley could be cleared. The British were opposed by the Argentine 4th Infantry Regiment who were well dug in. At the same time, an attack would be made on Two Sisters by 45 Commando.

L Company Royal Marines soon found their progress held up by snipers who had the advantage of excellent positions in rocky outcrops. The advancing Marines, on the other hand, had to contend not only with freezing weather, but also minefields that were intermingled with ground that was boggy or covered in slippery lichen-covered rocks. As they struggled through, the Marines could be spotted by the Argentines who had more advanced night-vision equipment than the British.

The plan for 42 Commando was to assault the enemy from the rear. K Company would assault the eastern end and L Company would assault the western end. As K Company moved forward, they were engaged by and engaged with machine-gunners, snipers and riflemen. The members of 3 Troop were held up by

Left: *A sniper of the British Royal Marines during a break in the fighting during the Falklands War of 1982. He carries an L1A1 self-loading rifle (SLR) with a night vision scope. He wears a camouflage smock and non-issue walking boots.*

Argentine snipers. Corporal Newland of 1 Troop made a daring single-handed attack on the Argentine positions, climbing up a rocky crag and tossing in grenades before attacking the survivors with his self-loading rifle.

Adrian Gilbert in his book *Stalk and Kill*, includes Newland's personal account of the action:

> All the time we were lying there rounds were ricocheting off the rocks at us and the cold was freezing our bollocks off. On the radio I hear Sharkie [Corporal "Sharkie" Ward] talking to his boss. He said, "We're pinned down by a sniper and we can't move." I thought, "Right, someone's got to go for this bastard." So I took off my 66 Shells [for the 66mm light anti-tank weapon], got on the radio to our boss, and said, "Wait there and I'll see what I can do."
>
> I crawled around this mega-sized boulder, rolled into cover and looked around the corner of this rock, thinking that the sniper had to be there somewhere. There was more than a sniper – there was half a troop! About ten of them were lying on a nice flat, table-top rock, overlooking the positions. It was perfect for them. They had a machine-gun on the left and the rest of them were lined out with rifles. Every time one of ours tried to move forward, one of them would shoot at him, so it looked to us as if there was only one sniper who was keeping on the move. They were waiting for us to break cover and try and clear this one sniper – then they would just waste us with their machine-gun.
>
> I sat back behind this rock and whispered down my throat mike to Sharkie about what I'd found. I picked up my SLR, changed the magazine and put a fresh one on and slipped the safety catch. I then looped the pin off one grenade on to one finger on my left hand and did the same with another.
>
> I pulled one grenade, whack – straight into the machine gun. Pulled the other, whack – straight at the spics. I dodged back around the rock and heard the two bangs. As soon as they'd gone off I went in and everything that moved got three rounds. I don't know how many I shot, but they got a whole mag. I went back round the corner of the rock, changed the mag and I was about to go back and sort out anyone who was left when Sharkie called on the net: "Get out! We're putting two 66s in." I went up by a different route and as I rounded this rock, I saw one of the guys that I'd hit. I'd only got him in the shoulder but he'd gone down like the rest of them, and in the dark I'd automatically thought he was dead. But he was far from that, because as I came back round the corner he just squeezed off a burst from his automatic. He must have realized he was going to die unless he got me first. I felt the bullets go into both my legs. I thought, "Shit, the f***r's got me." I was so angry, I fired fifteen rounds into his head.

When L Company started moving, they came under both machine-gun fire and even fiercer sniper fire. L Company took three casualties almost immediately and had to fight their way toward to clear six machine-gun positions and at least four sniper teams. Their movement was so held up by the snipers that it took them about five hours to reach their objective. It required the use of Milan anti-tank missiles to remove the snipers before they could advance further.

The Argentines had positioned their machine guns and snipers well, as Rose's 6 Platoon had discovered to their cost and as other platoons were also discovering. The Argentines had a position that included about two 7.62mm (0.3in) FN MAG GPMGs, a 105mm (4.1in) recoilless rifle and a 12.7mm (0.5in) heavy machine gun. In addition to these, there were snipers with passive night sights.

At about this time, Sergeant McKay of 4 Platoon, B Company, realizing something had to be done to break the stalemate, made a heroic attack on the Argentine position, along with other members of his platoon, one of whom was killed and two wounded. This provided some relief for 4 Platoon and no doubt helped to maintain the forward momentum of the attack. B Company tried another attack and, sustaining casualties, A Company passed through to relieve them. Once again, the Paras felt the effects of accurate sniper fire in addition to machine-gun fire as they advanced. At one point A Company had to crawl on their stomachs in their attempt to keep below the enemy sniper fire. Eventually, after supporting fire ceased, the Company cleared the enemy positions with bayonets fixed.

The attack on Mount Longdon had been one of the bloodiest in the entire Falklands campaign, with eighteen British dead and forty wounded and over fifty Argentine dead. More casualties would follow as the Argentines wreaked vengeance on the British with artillery fire. The battle had shown the effectiveness of snipers equipped with night-vision sights, which had almost managed to stall one of Britain's elite regiments in its tracks. It was only because of extreme tenacity, determination and heroism that the Paras had managed to fight through the fire.

Once the high ground had been taken, the Argentine defenses effectively ceased to exist. With a demoralized army retreating before the British into Stanley, the Argentine commander on the islands, General Menendez, had little choice but to surrender. The Falklands War had cost the lives of 255 British servicemen and 700 Argentines.

OPERATION "URGENT FURY", GRENADA, 1983

Grenada was an independent country within the Commonwealth, and the British monarch was head of state, represented by a Governor-General. It was also in the backyard of the United States of America. A coup in 1979 resulted in a left-wing government under Maurice Bishop, who was a Marxist leader of the New Jewel Movement. He set up a People's Revolutionary Government (PRG), which was backed by Cuba. Not surprisingly, the United States did not welcome these developments. In 1982, a team of Cuban military advisers arrived on the island. Another coup in 1983 led to the establishment of a Revolutionary Military Council and Soviet and Cuban involvement on the island increased. There was now a substantial Cuban force on the island. With the spectre of the Cuban missile crisis in their minds, the U.S. decided to invade, with the support of the Organization of East Caribbean States (OECS).

Part of the invasion force was Task Force 123, including 1st Special Forces Operational Detachment-Delta (SFOD-D) SEAL Team 6, 160th Operational Detachment-Delta (SFOD-D) SEAL Team 6, 160th Special Operations Aviation Regiment (SOAR) and 1st and 2nd Battalions 75th Ranger Regiment. Also deployed was United States Army Reserve (USAR) 1st Special Operations Wing.

SEAL assault

One of the key objectives in the assault was the mansion of the Governor-General. U.S. Navy SEAL Team 6 were inserted by two UH-60 Black Hawk helicopters at 06:15 on the morning of October 25, 1983 under heavy fire. Security personnel left the compound and the SEALs got themselves into optimum positions for the inevitable counter-attack. One Black Hawk was hit by the sniper fire and a member of the SEAL team was wounded.

After bundling the Governor-General, Sir Paul Scoon, into a closet for his own safety, the SEAL team set about selecting suitable firing positions.

There was one sniper in the SEAL team and his position would prove critical to the operation. He went to the top of the mansion and did a quick reconnaissance of the upstairs windows. Having found a suitable position where he could see without being seen, the SEAL sniper adjusted his equipment and settled down with his G3 SG-1 sniper rifle.

He did not have long to wait. Soon a Soviet-made BTR-60 armored personnel carrier appeared, accompanied by a large body of soldiers. The soldiers attempted to advance towards the building through the eastern gates of the compound and the SEAL sniper took them in his sights. As they advanced, the sniper dropped one of them after another, until twenty of the enemy were dead. The enemy retreated, shocked by the accurate sniper fire in addition to conventional fire received from other members of the SEAL team. The SEALs were under extreme pressure due to the size of the opposition. A U.S. AC-130 Spectre gunship overflew the area in time to meet the second attack. The gunship succeeded in destroying the BTR-60 APC. The enemy retreated to safer positions where they could continue to fire at the mansion. The siege lasted about 24 hours until the SEAL team was relieved by U.S. Marines.

Sniper success

In view of the fact that Special Forces are not trained to fight long-running battles against large numbers of enemy troops – they are trained to do a job and extract themselves quickly – the defense of the mansion had been a remarkable feat. The reason for their success, however, was due in large part to the effectiveness of their sniper team who dominated the battlefield, making a considerable physical impact on the enemy by reducing their numbers significantly and also by creating a climate of fear and caution, which prevented the enemy from storming the mansion.

HECKLER & KOCH G3 SG-1

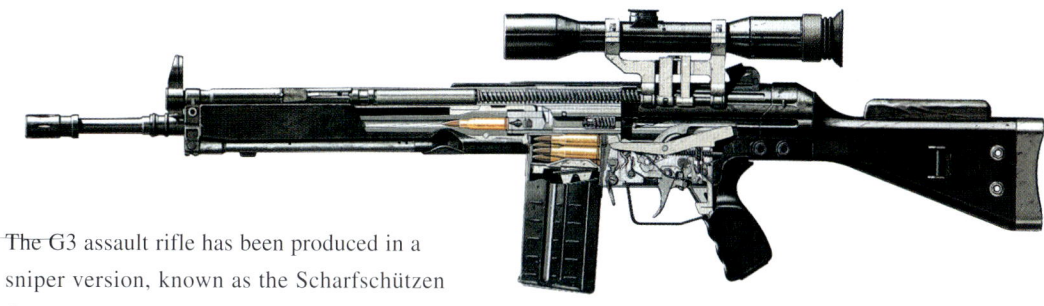

The G3 assault rifle has been produced in a sniper version, known as the Scharfschützen Gewehr, or SG-1. This was essentially a standard G3 rifle but featured a telescopic sight (usually a Schmidt & Bender) and also a more sensitive trigger unit and specially selected barrel. It has a lightweight bipod attached to the front of the foregrip. In this form the G3 entered service as a police weapon. It is also used by special forces around the world, specifically the U.S. Navy SEALS.

Country of Origin	Germany
Caliber	7.62mm (0.3in)
Overall length	1025mm (40.4in)
Barrel length	450mm (17.7in)
Weight	4.4kg (9.7lbs)

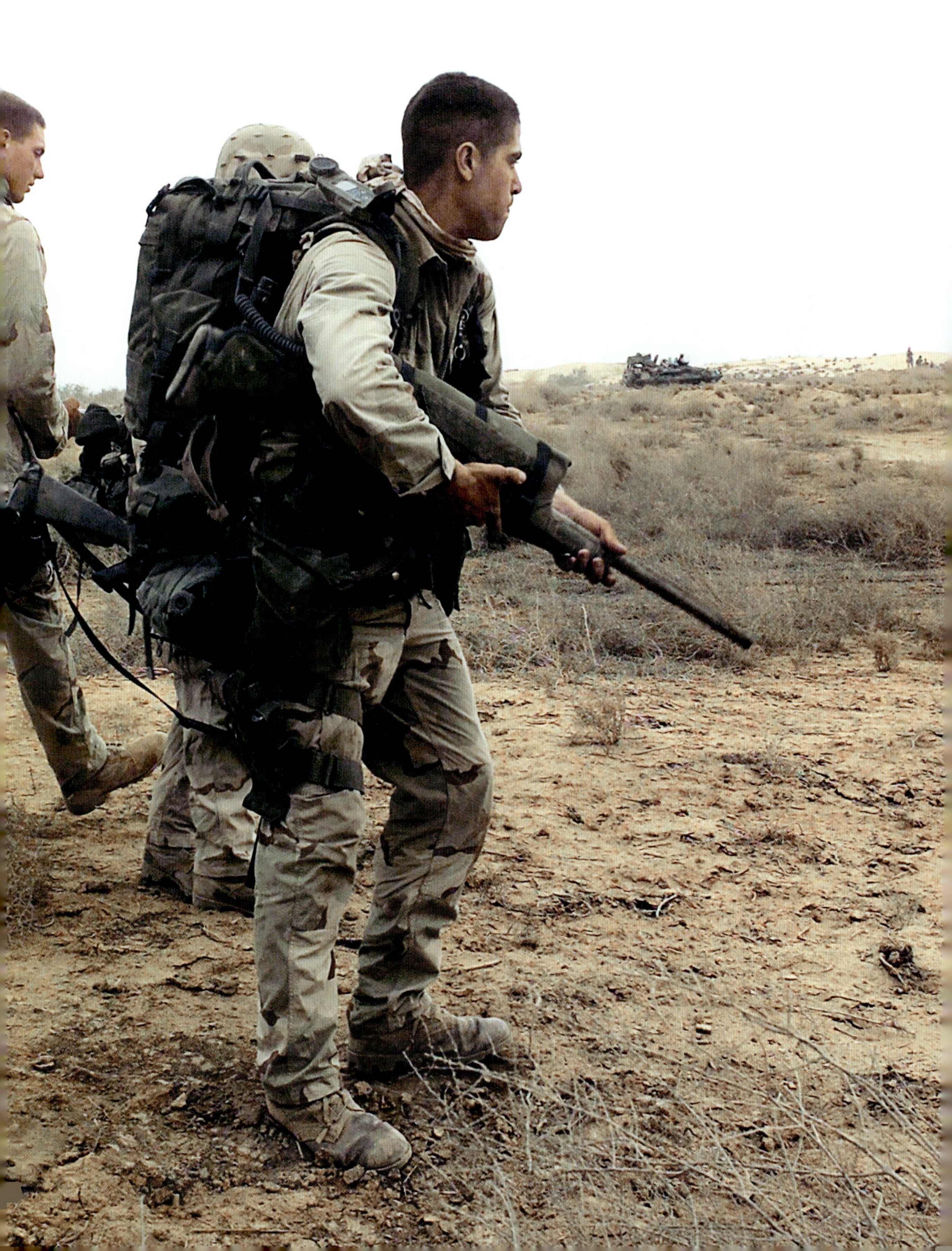

CHAPTER FIVE

THE MODERN SPECIALIST

In the wars of the end of the twentieth and the beginning of the twenty-first century, the sniper had become an essential fighting instrument for the modern battlefield. Training has been enhanced and new weapons have been developed to maximize the sniper's potential. Snipers operated across the battlefield spectrum, holding the key to both urban and wider battlefield tactics. Sniper teams were essential components of Special Forces and for regular army and Marine units. The importance of sniping was also fully recognized by insurgents.

Opposite: A *U.S. Marine Corps scout/sniper attached to 2nd Battalion, 5th Marines, carries his sniper rifle and field phone as his unit prepares to move out from a staging area in northern Iraq during Operation "Iraqi Freedom." The telescopic sight on his M24 rifle is covered to protect it against possible weather damage.*

"DESERT STORM" SNIPERS

While the Iraqi Army was swiftly defeated on the battlefield during Operation "Desert Storm," Coalition snipers were used in counter-sniper operations, maintaining security and the destruction of Iraqi weapons' caches.

The sniper with the highest number of confirmed kills in Operation "Desert Storm" was Frank Grieci of the U.S. Marine Corps with fifteen. The 1st Marine Division advanced into southern Kuwait on February 24, 1991 and the snipers moved with them. The U.S. Marines became involved in a series of "artillery raids, deception operations, combined arms raids and screening operations" according to Global Security.

Company K of the 3rd Battalion, 5th Marine Regiment, known as "Kilo 3/5," landed by ship and advanced inland only to find that a cease-fire had been declared before they could make contact with the enemy. Despite this, there were still many enemy soldiers in Iraq and Kilo 3/5 would see action of a type they did not expect.

Sure enough Kilo 3/5 were ordered to clear their sector of any remaining Iraqi units that may have been bypassed in the general advance. They were also tasked with clearing bunkers of Iraqi soldiers. After this, Kilo 3/5 set about clearing minefields. On the night of March 1, Kilo 3/5 was advised that another unit had been attacked with rocket-propelled grenades and was duly put on alert for combat operations the following day in the area of the Al Wafrah forest. This area of low trees and farms was adjacent to the Al Wafrah oil fields. During the night, the unit

Below: *Members of the U.S. Marine Corps carry out sniper training with an M40 rifle during Operation "Desert Shield" in Saudi Arabia in 1990.*

> "The Al Wafrah forest was an area of low trees, small farms, agriculture and livestock plots, homes, and a small town... The minefields had been under the watchful eyes of Marine snipers throughout the night. Every now and then the snipers would fire a round and take out an enemy soldier in one of the many bunkers...."
>
> *Mark Welch on Company K,*
> *3rd Battalion, 5th Marine Regiment*

snipers kept a close watch on the area of the minefields. Kilo 3/5 duly went about its business of conducting house, building and bunker clearance. Despite the use of Psychological Warfare operations (PSYOPS), the enemy showed no willingness to surrender and instead began sporadic firing at the Marines. Again, the Marine snipers quickly took control of the situation and eliminated the enemy gunmen, with no loss to the Marines.

This was by no means the end of the episode for Kilo 3/5 as they then moved into the oil field itself. Again they received small-arms fire and again they returned fire with small arms and sniper rifles. This time they had heavier support from the battalion as well as aerial support so it was not such a surgical sniper engagement as previously.

In 1990 the Iraqi dictator Saddam Hussein decided that the best way of overcoming his large financial debt to Kuwait for his war against Iran and at the same time gain oil fields and greater regional influence was to invade Kuwait. Like the Argentine junta at the time of the Falklands War, he estimated that the Western powers would not have the political determination to oppose him in force and his troops rolled into Kuwait on August 2.

Also like the Argentine junta, Saddam Hussein gravely miscalculated. By invading Kuwait he now posed a grave threat to Saudi Arabia, which had immeasurable strategic importance to the West. Arab nations were also disturbed by the regional implications of his actions as his abuse of an Arab neighbor suggested he might just as well do the same to them. Thus it was possible to put together a mixed coalition of Western and Arab powers to oppose Iraq. On November 29, the UN Security Council warned that if Iraq had not withdrawn its forces from Kuwait by January 15, 1991, coalition forces would be authorized to use "all necessary means" to expel them.

OPERATION "DESERT STORM," 1991

In January, the Coalition forces totaled about 700,000, including 540,000 U.S. troops. At 2.38 a.m. local time on January 17, 1991 U.S. Apache helicopters attacked Iraqi air defenses, paving the way for a massive aerial attack, including F-117A Stealth bombers. The aircraft attacks were supplemented by sea-launched cruise missiles. Both precision-guided and conventional munitions were dropped. On February 24, the land campaign began. The U.S. Marines, supplemented by Saudi task forces, attacked Kuwait from the south.

On February 25, the U.S. VII Corps, including the 1st British Armored Division, swung into action, outflanking Iraqi forces to the west, while the XVIII Airborne Corps, including the French 6th Light "Daguet" Division swung even wider to protect the left flank. Meanwhile, British and American Special

THE MODERN SPECIALIST

Forces had been engaged in a secret battle behind the lines to track down and destroy Iraqi "Scud" missile launchers.

"Scud" hunters

The neutralization of the "Scud" missiles was an essential component of the war, not just because the missiles, with a range of about 300km (186 miles), could carry either a conventional, chemical and biological or a nuclear warhead and could inflict considerable damage, but also because Iraq was using them against Israel in order to force Israeli retaliation and to break the delicate threads that held the Allied coalition together. The Allies had promised Israel that they would take effective action against the "Scuds" if Israel did not enter the fray.

On January 18, 1991, seven "Scud" missiles landed on Haifa and Tel Aviv and others followed. The coalition was on a precipice and Special Forces had their work cut out. Although satellites and ground surveillance aircrafts had some success in identifying fixed launching sites for "Scuds," the thirty-six or so mobile launchers could easily be concealed in the vast deserts of Iraq and would in any case be constantly on the move. U.S. Army Special Forces Operational Detachment-Delta (SFOD-D) (Delta Force) and the British 22 Special Air Service Regiment (22 SAS) were sent in to track down the mobile launchers and to either call in aerial bombardment or to attack the launchers and missiles with whatever weapons they had at their disposal.

The SAS were to cover a large area of Western Iraq, between Highway 10 and the Saudi Arabian border, known as "Scud Alley." The Delta teams were to cover an area northwest of Highway 10, known as "Scud Boulevard." The Delta teams carried with them long-range 12.7mm (0.5in) Barrett anti-materiel sniper rifles, which could be used either to disable or destroy the "Scuds."

After the Iraqi forces had been sent packing back towards Baghdad, suffering a disastrous "Falaise Gap" experience as Coalition aircrafts tore into their retreating columns, an uneasy peace settled over the region – Allied forces set up a watch and carried out aerial patrols. The stone in the shoe for the Allies was not just the incipient threat that Saddam Hussein's regime posed in the region but also the unresolved issue of weapons of mass destruction (WMDs).

Iraq continued to suffer economic sanctions and UN weapons inspectors made several visits to corroborate the destruction of Iraqi WMDs. As there was no certainty that this was indeed the case, the United States and Britain became more inclined to intervene militarily.

BARRETT M82A1 RIFLE

Country of Origin	United States
Caliber	.50 cal (12.7mm/0.5in)
Overall length	1450mm (57in)
Barrel length	737mm (29in)
Weight	14kg (30.9lbs)

CHECHNYA, 1995

The Russians had learned some painful lessons in Afghanistan in the 1980s and went about reorganizing both their sniper-training program as well as developing their sniping rifle. Although the Dragunov was an excellent rifle in many ways, it was also somewhat cumbersome and a more compact version with a folding stock was produced for airborne troops, designated the SVDS. The Russian sniper course was extended to a year, including both infantry and specialist training in marksmanship and fieldcraft. The new regime was not before time because, after the collapse of the Soviet Union, Russia was to face another significant challenge in the shape of the Chechen uprisings.

In December 1991 the head of the All-National Congress of the Chechen People, Dzhokhar Dudayev, staged a coup and declared Chechnya to be independent. After a period of aggressively anti-Russian policies, Russian troops invaded Chechnya on December 11, 1994 and took over the capital of Grozny in 1995. There followed a battle of attrition involving snipers on both sides. The Chechen rebels were equipped with Dragunov SVD rifles and went out in search of Russian snipers. One of the means they used to get around was the Grozny drainage system, which sometimes enabled them to get behind the Russians.

Martin Pegler relates the story of what happened when the Russian sniper team, believing they had searched the drains, invited a local general to come forward and inspect the area. The general approached the entrance and, as he did so, a Chechen sniper somewhere in the depths of the drain network, shot him through the neck.

This incident underlined the fact that the Chechens knew their own territory and had the patience to wait for targets of opportunity while the Russians were still working on the principle of snipers as part and parcel of maneuver warfare. In open ground, the Chechens

Above: *A Russian Special Forces sniper observes the area near the military commandant's office in the Leninsky district of Grozny after an attack by unidentified gunmen on March 14, 2005. The presence of snipers could be a powerful deterrent.*

would often use a sniper along with a support team. Should the sniper draw fire, the support team would then open up and engage the opposition.

Russian sniper rifles

In the operation by the Russian Federal Government to besiege Grozny in the Second Chechen War (1999–2000), a selection of sniper rifles were carried in assault detachments that carried a wide range of weapons, including Shmel infantry rocket flamethrowers and AGS-17 Kalashnikov assault rifles with GP-25 under-barrel grenade launchers. The snipers were armed with either Degtyaryov sniping rifles or Vintorez low-noise sniper rifles. The

RUSSIAN SNIPER TACTICS

By the time of the Second Chechen War (1999–2000), the Russians had done more work in training and reorganizing their sniper teams. They returned with only two or three-man units, which included a sniper armed with a Dragunov SVD, a machine-gunner and an RPG-gunner or a rifleman.

The Russians also deployed elite snipers in pairs who would take up positions in hours of darkness and set up ambushes. They would be accompanied by a support group who were at least 200m (219 yards) to the rear and 500m (547 yards) to the side. If the sniper got into trouble, the support group could normally be depended upon to provide enough covering fire for him to withdraw. If this should not be the case, the sniper could resort to calling in artillery on his position or using grenades. The priority was to evade capture at all costs. The Russian sniper carried a range of extra equipment with him, apart from his sniper rifle with telescopic sight, possibly including a machine pistol, a knife, entrenching tool, binoculars, radio, laser rangefinder and periscope.

Below: *A Georgian Army two-man sniper team take a break somewhere in South Ossetia, 2008. The sniper is armed with a Dragunov SVD sniper rifle, fitted with the PSO-1 optical sight.*

THE MODERN SPECIALIST

Russians encountered problems, however, in an urban environment at night due to the scarcity of night-vision optics and of night-vision telescopic sights for sniper rifles. There was also a lack of infra-red (IR) imagers. The Russians had some success with their 12.7mm (0.5in) V-94 semi-automatic sniper and anti-materiel rifle. Designed by the KBP instrument design bureau in Tula, this is a gas-operated, rotating-bolt semi-automatic rifle with a free-floating barrel. It is fitted with integral bipods and has both iron and telescopic sights. The later version of this rifle was known as the OSV-96. The advantage of the V-94 was that it could be used effectively as an anti-sniper weapon as its range was greater than that of the rebel sniper rifles. It was also quite effective against soft-skinned vehicles.

Vintorez special forces weapon

The Vintorez silenced sniper rifle was developed in the 1980s specifically for special operations personnel, including Spetsnaz units. The Vintorez was designed to penetrate most types of issue body armor and uses for this purpose a specially designed subsonic cartridge with a 9mm (0.35in) bullet in a 7.62mm (0.3in) case.

For a sniper rifle the Vintorez has a comparatively limited range at 300–400m (328–437 yards) but this is counter-balanced by its lethality. The range is not such an issue in an urban environment for which it was designed. The Vintorez is characterized by an integral silencer built around the barrel. The rifle carries a PSO-1 telescopic sight with 4x magnification but can also carry other sights, such as the PKS-07 collimated sight or PKN-03 night sight.

It is fitted with iron sights as a backup. It has a removable butt stock and can be easily transported in a briefcase. Part of the reason for the popularity of the Vintorez is that it can be used for either one-shot or automatic firing. It can be fitted with a twenty-round magazine for automatic roles. This means that

DRAGUNOV SVD

The Dragunov SVD is a semi-automatic sniper rifle designed by Evgeny Dragunov, which was accepted into Soviet service in 1963. For sniping duties, the rifle is supplied with special sniper cartridges. The rifle is also fitted with a detachable PSO-1 optical sight with 4x magnification. It has an effective range of 800m (875 yards). The Dragunov has proved to be an adaptable rifle that can be used by marksmen who do not have the specialist training of fully fledged snipers. The rifle can be used in automatic mode for shorter-range engagements when necessary.

Country of Origin	Soviet Union
Caliber	7.62mm (0.3in)
Overall length	1225mm (48.5in)
Barrel length	547mm (21.5in)
Weight	4.39kg (9.67lbs)

THE MODERN SPECIALIST

a sniper using a Vintorez has a rapid-fire weapon incorporated within his sniper weapon for emergencies.

The Russians also employed the 7.62mm (0.3in) SV-98 sniper rifle, developed by IZHMASH from a sporting rifle, the Record 300. It is a bolt-action rifle with a rotating bolt and a cold-hammer forged receiver and free-floating barrel. The rifle has both iron sights and a free-floating rail for a variety of telescopic sights, including the Russian PKS-07 7x magnification telescopic sight. It has an integral folding bipod. There was some criticism among military circles of the Russian-made telescopic sights as they had a tendency to become de-calibrated when the rifle was carried about. On some occasions, foreign telescopic sights were used in preference, manufactured by Zeiss, Schmidt & Bender and others.

Apart from equipment shortages and failings, including a lack of night-vision optics, the Russians encountered a number of tactical difficulties due to the command structures and lack of interoperability and coordination between different units. This resulted in a number of friendly fire incidents during the operations in the Caucasus. Having learned from their mistakes, by the end of the operations in the Caucasus the Russians had acquired a wide range of expertise and were sought after as advisers to sniping units in other countries.

THE BALKANS, 1992–95

The war in Bosnia and Herzegovina between 1992 and 1995 brought back to Europe a nightmare that

Below: *U.S. Army personnel of 10th Special Forces Group conduct training on the M24 7.62mm (0.3in) sniper rifle for a Georgian soldier (left) at a firing range on the Advance Operational Base (ABO) in support of Georgia Train and Equip Program (GTEP).*

THE MODERN SPECIALIST

Above: A sniper's eye view of Sarajevo. As the city was ringed by hills, it provided the perfect context for the sniper to work. Snipers had clear fields of view down the long roads, such as the infamous "Sniper Alley," or could pick civilians and soldiers off when crossing intersections.

many had thought had been left behind in World War II. The complexity of the conflict was such that no one could really agree whether it was a war of aggression, with one state invading another, or a civil war. Whatever it was, it was thoroughly unpleasant, involving ethnic cleansing, internal displacement of populations, open warfare, and all of this was carried out often under the noses of impotent United Nations forces who were often humiliated or severely constrained by their rules of engagement. Once Bosnia had declared its independence in 1991, the Serbian population called upon the support of forces from neighboring Serbia, which had retained most of the military hardware of the Former Republic of Yugoslavia. The Serbs besieged the city of Sarajevo between 1992 and 1996 and it became the scene of many atrocities, not least the terror tactics practiced by Serb snipers who intimidated both the military and civilian population by firing on them from the hills around the city or from apartment blocks.

Snipers in Sarajevo

General Sir Michael Rose was in command of the UN Protection Force (UNPROFOR) in Bosnia in 1994. He had commanded the SAS in the Falklands War and had also commanded the successful SAS hostage rescue at the Iranian Embassy in London. He now found himself in charge of one of the most challenging military missions of his life, for whereas the SAS had a characteristically decisive way of sorting out problems, in Bosnia his men had to keep their safety catches on and travel about in white-painted vehicles.

THE MODERN SPECIALIST

As he arrived in Sarajevo he was shocked by how a city of culture had been degraded into a place where death threatened at every moment. From the start of the war to his arrival about ten thousand people had been killed in the city, three thousand of them children. He talked to people hiding in bunkers to try to find out what was going on and suddenly understood what had happened to this place when he came across a sniper:

It was to be many weeks before I fully understood what they were saying. It happened when I saw a sniper carrying a Simonov rifle leave his position in a ruined block of flats. He was a good-looking boy, blond with blue eyes, in his late teens. But when he looked at me, his eyes were as dead as the small child he had almost

Below: *A sniper of the Serbian Volunteer Guard armed with a Kalashnikov AK47 rifle positioned behind a wall adjacent to the bridge across the river Drina prepares to fire at citizens of the town of Zvornik in Bosnia-Herzegovina, April 9, 1992. At least ten people were killed in Zvornik on this day.*

THE MODERN SPECIALIST

Above: *A French United Nations soldier and a woman give first aid to a Bosnian soldier shot by a sniper on "Sniper Alley" in Sarajevo. The Bosnian soldier died seconds later. The French soldier wears body armor that would provide some protection from the Serb tactic of shooting rescuers.*

certainly killed that day in a sniping attack on a Sarajevo street. It was not my war, but as a human being I was involved. I came to understand that this sniper represented as great a threat to civilization itself as he did to the citizens of Sarajevo. It took too long for the world outside to understand this simple fact, but at long last peacekeepers did come to the aid of the people of Sarajevo and Bosnia.

Violent and unpleasant as war is, it is governed by certain laws. It is one thing for two opposing armies to use snipers in pursuit of their military aims; it is quite another for a combatant to target innocent

143

URBAN COUNTER-SNIPING IN BOSNIA

The problem for counter-sniper operations in Bosnia was that it was difficult to locate the enemy snipers in the mix of urban and mountainous terrain and it was also difficult to avoid retaliation, which could make life even more uncomfortable for the unfortunate civilians.

Due to the covert nature of sniper movements, it is almost impossible to identify the presence of a sniper until he has fired and killed or wounded someone, at which point an experienced sniper will change location. He will also usually fire from within a room, if in an urban environment, thus providing no visible evidence of his presence and no visible trace such as a muzzle flash.

Experts have scratched their heads in an effort to resolve the problems posed by the skilled urban sniper and some technical advances have been made in creating equipment that can either detect the muzzle flash or the noise of a sniper rifle.

Another technological development is equipment that can scan the trajectory of the bullet through heat imaging. The problem with these solutions is that they depend on the sniper acting first which means that the "solution" will not help the first victim. Another highly sophisticated system

Below: *A French soldier armed with a McMillan Tac 50 sniper rifle on top of an armored vehicle, 24 June 1994. This was in response to three people being wounded and one killed at this Sarajevo intersection. The soldier is a potential target of a sniper hidden in buildings such as the ones behind him.*

can detect the laser optics in the sniper's telescopic sight. This is an ingenious solution that would enable the sniper to be intercepted before firing, but unfortunately it can easily be countered by placing a filter at the end of the telescopic sight.

Among the various regiments that toured Bosnia, whether under UNPROFOR or NATO mandate, was the 2nd Foreign Parachute Regiment of the French Foreign Legion. This regiment incorporated a sniper company. The 2nd Company of the 2e REP were specialized in mountain training and extreme weather conditions. The unit was equipped with a 12.7mm (0.5in) sniper rifle. The company was deployed in Bosnia and carried out ski patrols on Mount Igman.

Once NATO had intervened in Bosnia in an overtly fighting role, the snipers who thought they could continue firing in Sarajevo with impunity got a nasty shock. On January 9, 1996, a Bosnian Serb sniper shot a woman in Sarajevo and a French counter-sniper team immediately fired back at him. On February 1, 1996, a French counter-sniper team shot one sniper and captured another.

Security Council Resolution 1674 "On the protection of civilians in armed conflict" followed the Rwanda and Srebrenica disasters. Now "most multi-dimensional United Nations peacekeeping operations are … mandated by the Security Council to protect civilians under imminent threat of physical violence." Chapter VII UN missions are authorized to use "all necessary means" to fulfill a particular mandate. "The use of force by a United Nations peacekeeping operation should always be calibrated in a precise, proportional and appropriate manner, within the principle of the minimum force necessary to achieve the desired effect."

civilians. If snipers are going to kill women and children on the street, there is probably only one way to deal with them – deploy military snipers to take them on.

Sarajevo is situated in a long, narrow valley on the banks of the Miljack River. The river valley rises up to steep mountains and ridges that provide excellent cover for both snipers and enemy artillery. This was the position occupied by the Bosnian Serb Army, while the Bosniacs occupied the city itself. The peoples of the former Yugoslavia, not unlike the Afghans, knew how to maximize their rugged local landscape to maintain defensive positions against invading armies. Yugoslav partisans under Marshal Tito had kept two German divisions busy during World War II.

Not only did the Bosnia Serb Army (BSA) use sniper rifles, it also used anti-aircraft artillery in an anti-personnel role, firing down into the city, often at unarmed civilians. Another weapon of choice for the BSA snipers was the medium-to-heavy machine gun. One of their favorite techniques was to bring down a civilian victim at random. They would then wait for rescuers to arrive, including ambulances and UN vehicles. They would then fire on the rescuers.

This may have been an armed conflict but this sort of behavior broke just about every law of armed conflict, including the Hague and Geneva conventions and rules of customary law. "Military commanders are required to direct their operations against military objectives exclusively and, to the extent practicable, to avoid causing casualties or damage to civilian persons or objects." [Official UN report on the battle of Sarajevo.] The official UN report on the legality of the war in Sarajevo makes a particular point about snipers in the context of a discussion over collateral damage and casualties suffered by civilians:

The weapons systems being used by BSA forces in the Siege of Sarajevo, predominantly direct-fire weapons, and artillery at point-blank, frequently direct-fire, range, are systems which can be used with a high degree of accuracy. A sniper rifle is normally aimed at a particular person in view of the sniper. Mortars and guns used at short ranges normally fire projectiles which land quite close to where they are aimed. These are not inherently indiscriminate weapons, particularly in the case of sniper fire. If non-combatants are being killed or wounded, this occurs because the sniper intends to kill or wound them. ...

There is every indication that civilians have been deliberately targeted by snipers and by BSA artillery. As indicated in the discussion of BSA tactics, small arms and artillery have frequently been used as weapons of terror directed against the civilian population. ... As a general statement ... the rule of proportionality is not relevant to the sniping activities of the BSA forces and it is of questionable relevance to many of the artillery bombardments. BSA forces are deliberately targeting the civilian population of Sarajevo either as a measure of retaliation or to weaken their political resolve. Attacking the civilian population is a war crime.

[Final report of the United Nations Commission of Experts established pursuant to Security Council resolution 780 (1992)]

OPERATION "ANACONDA", AFGHANISTAN, 2001

In September 2001 an event occurred of such magnitude that it would alter all geopolitical and military decisions thereafter. At 8:46 a.m. on September 11, 2001 American Airlines Flight 11 was flown into the 96th floor of the North Tower of the World Trade Center in New York. Sixteen minutes later, Flight 175 flew into the 80th floor of the South Tower. At 9:59 a.m. the South Tower collapsed, followed by the North Tower at 10:30 a.m. At 9:38 a.m., American Airlines Flight 77 flew into the western side of the Pentagon. There were 246 people killed on the four hijacked airliners, one of which crashed before reaching its target. In the World Trade Center, 2602 people died, including 343 firefighters and 23 policemen who had come to the rescue. In the Pentagon, 125 people were killed. It was the greatest terrorist outrage in world history.

Al-Qaeda and Osama bin Laden were quickly identified as the perpetrators and they were known to be operating from terrorist bases deep in the mountains of Afghanistan. With public opinion behind them, the American authorities were not long in coming to the conclusion that they should strike at the terrorist cells and wipe out the Taliban regime in Afghanistan. The Taliban regime was given the opportunity to extradite Osama bin Laden and predictably refused. On October 7, 2001 American ships in the region and aerial forces began a campaign against the Taliban. It was the curtain raiser for Operation "Enduring Freedom." The operation involved twenty-five jets from two aircraft carriers, fifteen long-range bombers and fifty cruise missiles.

Special Forces snipers

The most effective component of the U.S. response, however, would be arrival in theater of teams from Special Forces Operational Attachment A of 5th Special Forces Group. These would be followed by B and C Teams to bring the Special Forces detachment up to about three hundred men.

Although relatively small in number, the U.S. Special Forces possessed skills, technology and weaponry that magnified their impact a hundredfold. They had laser designators, optics and global position system technology and were soon able to direct precision-guided munitions onto a selection of targets. They were an invaluable asset to the warlords and tribesmen of the Northern Alliance with whom they were allied against the common enemy, the Taliban. The Special Forces had access to a range of sniper rifles, which they used for occasional direct-fire support of the missions. These included the HK PSG-1, M40A1 and M24 standard sniper rifles and the 12.7mm (0.5in) Barrett M82A1 heavy sniper rifle. Apart from U.S. Special Forces in Afghanistan, other units began to be deployed, including the British SAS; Canadian Joint Task Force Two (JTF 2) and other conventional forces; Australian SASR; New Zealand SAS; French *1er Regiment de Parachutistes d'Infanterie de Marine* and *Detachment Alat des Operations Speciales*; German *Kommando Spezialkrafte* (KSK) and a variety of forces from other nations.

Canadian snipers

Another Canadian unit in the area was the 3rd Battalion, Princess Patricia's Canadian Light Infantry, which fought with the scout platoon of the U.S. Army's 187th "Rakkasan" Brigade. In the *National Post* it was reported:

> One member of the team, a corporal from Newfoundland, said on his first night in combat he and his partner got an Al-Qaeda machine-gun in their sights. … Crawling up into a good position, they set up their .50 caliber rifle – the MacMillan Tac-50, a weapon the corporal compares to having superhuman power in your hands. "Firing it feels like someone slashing you on the back of your hockey helmet with a hockey stick." When he hit his first target, an enemy gunman at a distance of 1700 meters [1859 yards], he said all that ran through his mind was locating his next target. A master corporal from Ontario, the lead sniper of his three-man team, said when they first landed in the combat zone "our spider senses were tingling … It was night and we didn't know what to expect." By daylight, after coming under enemy machine-gun fire, he managed to ease his rifle barrel between two rocks and quickly located an enemy sniper hiding behind a small piece of corrugated steel between two trees. He guessed the distance at 1700 meters [1859 yards] and fired one shot through the metal, killing the man instantly ….

Princess Patricia's Canadian Light Infantry (PPCLI) was formed in August 1914 and took the name of the youngest daughter of the then Governor-General of Canada, HRH the Duke of Connaught. With its first commander an officer of the British Coldstream Guards and in ability second only to the Royal Canadian Regiment, the PPCLI had a host of battle honors stretching through both World Wars I

HECKLER & KOCH PSG-1

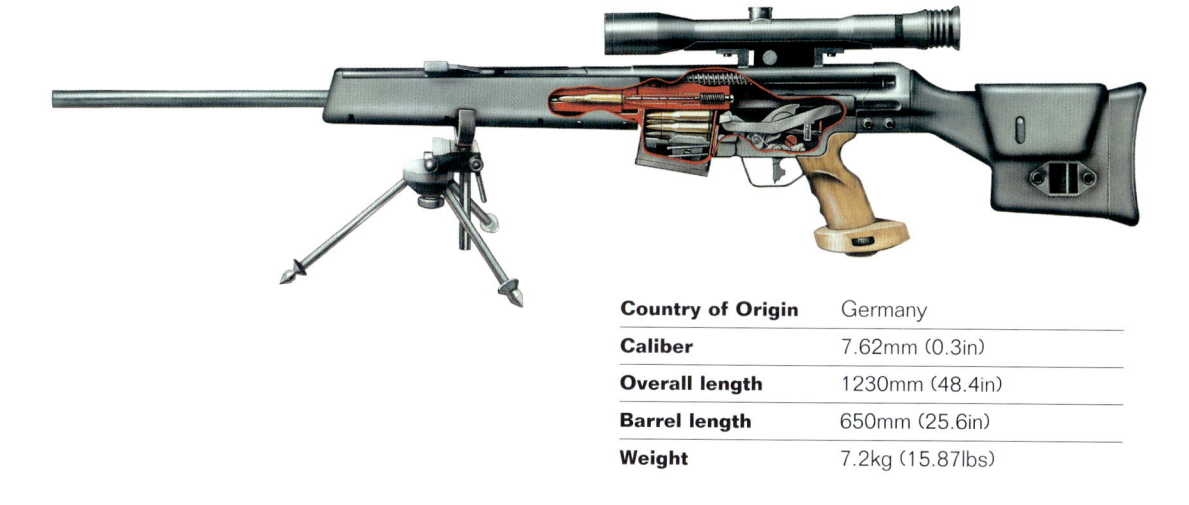

Country of Origin	Germany
Caliber	7.62mm (0.3in)
Overall length	1230mm (48.4in)
Barrel length	650mm (25.6in)
Weight	7.2kg (15.87lbs)

Above: A U.S. Special Forces sniper team with a Barrett M82 rifle on Shran Mountain outside Halabja on March 29, 2003. They worked alongside Peshmurga forces in a fight against Ansar al Islam, which had been terrorizing local people.

and II and the Korean War. The five-man sniper team of the PPCLI was led by Master Corporal Graham Ragsdale and it included Master Corporal Rob Furlong. During this mission, the team scored two record hits with the McMillan Tac-50 sniper rifle. One was at a distance of 2310m (2526 yards) and another at 2430m (2657 yards) – incredible ranges.

The five Canadian snipers operated as part of a six-man cell that also included one American sniper. The cell was divided into two three-man teams, each built around supporting a single heavy sniper rifle. Every team member was qualified to use the rifle, but one man would be the primary shooter. The others acted as spotters and security most of the time.

Master Corporal Aaron Perry was the primary shooter on his three-man team. He had previously served in Bosnia and Croatia and had an impressive record that included stints as an unarmed combat instructor and a paratrooper.

Record-breaking shot

In the early stages of Operation "Anaconda," Perry's team came under fire almost immediately after landing from their Chinook helicopter. Perry, a very large man, carried the rifle as the team sought high ground, then began to engage the enemy. Some of his targets were up to 1500m (1640 yards) away but he made such long shots, taken under fire and in difficult circumstances, look almost routine.

THE MODERN SPECIALIST

The second team, containing Furlong, was in a different Chinook that had been driven off by ground fire. Arriving later, the team found a situation that seemed to be under control. Their instinct that something was wrong proved correct near dusk as the position came under mortar and direct-fire attack. Everyone sought cover, except Master Corporal Tim McMeekin, who normally served as Furlong's spotter. McMeekin grabbed the rifle and began firing back, heedless of enemy fire. "The guy was an absolute machine," Furlong said later.

During the nine-day mission that followed, the sniper teams responded to requests for assistance from their fellow troops, lugging their heavy rifles up hills to engage enemy support weapon gunners, leaders and other high-value targets.

During this time Perry made a record-breaking 2310m (2526 yards) shot to eliminate an enemy forward observer, reducing the threat from enemy mortars. Furlong's 2430m (2657 yards) shot followed days later, killing an enemy machine-gunner. Upon their return to base, the snipers agreed never to reveal exactly how many lives they had taken during their mission. Thus far, the number remains unknown.

Previously, the Canadian sniper team, working with U.S. Special Forces, had helped to relieve a company of the U.S. 101st Airborne who were pinned down by enemy fire on the first day of Operation "Anaconda." The Canadians suppressed enemy mortars, heavy machine-gun positions and other enemy assets with telling accuracy. Apart from the obvious high level of training demonstrated by the PPCLI soldiers, the Americans were also impressed with the quality and power of the McMillan Tac-50, which mounted an even more powerful telescopic sight than was available to U.S. forces.

Their American allies were so impressed with the performance of the sniper team that they offered to

MCMILLAN TAC-50 LONG-RANGE SNIPER RIFLE

The McMillan Tac-50 is designed by the McMillan Brothers Rifle Company of Phoenix, Arizona. It is a rotary bolt-action rifle with dual front-locking lugs. It has a heavy match-grade barrel and a five-round detachable box magazine. In order to make the rifle easier to carry and handle, it has weight-saving design features such as a fluted barrel and fiberglass stock. The rifle is designed to be fired from a bipod. As the official Long Range Sniper Weapon (LRSW) of the Canadian Army, the rifle is paired with a Leupold Mark IV 16x40mm LR1T Riflescope optical sight. It is also used by the U.S. Navy SEALs, with the designation Mk 15.

Country of Origin	United States
Caliber	12.7mm (0.5in)
Overall length	1448mm (57in)
Barrel length	736mm (29in)
Weight	11.8kg (26lbs)

award them the Bronze Star for their actions. However, the offer was caught up in the mire of Canadian bureaucracy, with some speculating that the Canadian Government did not want to advertise the explicit nature of sniper work.

OPERATION "IRAQI FREEDOM", 2003

As part of the cease-fire arrangements with Iraq after Operation "Desert Storm" in 1991, the country had been ordered to destroy any weapons of mass destruction. Iraq, however, continued to play cat and mouse with UN weapons inspectors and by November 8, 2002 the UN expressed its impatience in Security Council Resolution 1441. It deplored "the fact that Iraq has not provided an accurate, full, final, and complete disclosure, as required by resolution 687 (1991), of all aspects of its programmes to develop weapons of mass destruction and ballistic missiles with a range greater than one hundred and fifty kilometers [932 miles], and of all holdings of such weapons." The resolution also deplored "that the Government of Iraq has failed to comply with its commitments ... with regard to terrorism ... to end repression of its civilian population and to provide access by international humanitarian organizations to all those in need of assistance in Iraq." The resolution also decided that "Iraq has been and remains in material breach of its obligations under relevant resolutions" and offered Iraq "a final opportunity to comply with its disarmament obligations under relevant resolutions of the Council." With no valid

Below: *A U.S. Marine Corps corporal sites through the AN/PVS-10 day+night-vision sniper scope fixed to his 7.62mm (0.3in) Harris M-86 sniper rifle, following an incident near Al Kut, Iraq, during Operation "Iraqi Freedom."*

THE MODERN SPECIALIST

Above: A U.S. Marine sets up his 7.62mm (0.3in) M-89 multi-barrel combo sniper rifle as members of his unit work to secure the town of Qalat Sukkar, Iraq, during Operation "Iraqi Freedom."

response forthcoming from Iraq, in March 2003 the United States and the United Kingdom declared the diplomatic process over.

Task Force 20

As the U.S. and UK built up their forces in the region, Special Forces from both countries went into Iraq on reconnaissance and search and destroy missions. They were accompanied by members of the Central Intelligence Agency's (CIA) paramilitary division. Task Force 20, as it was called, included snipers on the lookout for Saddam Hussein and for other leading members of the Ba'ath Party as well as senior army commanders. It will be noted that this set of priorities is very much the traditional set of priorities of the sniper. Snipers, like Special Forces operatives, magnify their power by taking out key personnel. The U.S. pinpoint attacks on certain key personnel, however, were not just limited to sniper rifles: they also used somewhat larger weapons, namely cruise missiles, targeted at palaces and headquarters where Saddam Hussein and his key officials might be residing. The only problem with this was that it did not have the endorsement of the United Nations and that, under International Law, the invasion was arguably illegal.

One of the operations performed by Task Force 20 was the attack on Saddam Hussein's sons, Uday and Qusay, who had taken shelter in a fortified villa in Mosul. The concrete-reinforced hideout was so impenetrable, however, that armored vehicles of 101st Airborne had to be called in to use artillery and TOW missiles against the building. As this was going on, and as Delta Force soldiers entered the building, Iraqi snipers fired on the Americans. One U.S. soldier was wounded before U.S. forces managed to drive the snipers away with return fire. Both Uday and Qusay were killed in the attack.

Snipers also provided a key element of the force tasked with the rescue of Private Jessica Lynch who had been captured after her convoy of vehicles had gone astray and run into an Iraqi ambush. Several of Lynch's fellow soldiers had been killed during the ambush. Task Force 20 was given the prisoner-of-war recovery mission backed up by up to three hundred Rangers. U.S. Marines conducted a deception operation to keep Iraqi forces busy.

The TF-20 sniper teams were inserted by MH-6 "Little Bird" helicopters and took up strategic positions around the hospital to provide essential fire support. After this, the assault teams were dropped on the roof and by the front door of the hospital. After about a quarter of an hour, the insertion team reappeared with Jessica Lynch on a stretcher. She was then loaded on to an MH-60K and extracted successfully to safety.

Snipers in Special Forces operations

Special operations in Iraq were carried out by Combined Joint Special Operations Task Force-West (CJSOTF-West). The core of this unit was U.S. 5th Special Task Forces Group, including SFOD Delta, and additional strength was provided by both the British Special Air Service (SAS) and the Australian Special Air Service Regiment (SASR). In addition,

Opposite: Quick Reaction Force soldiers of 4th Battalion, Royal Australian Regiment (Commando) on Operation "Bastille," Iraq, February 19, 2003. The soldier is carrying an M4 carbine fitted with an M203 grenade launcher, side-mounted AN-PEQ2 infra-red illuminator and AN/PVS-17A mini night-vision sight.

Australia provided 4th Battalion Royal Australian Regiment (Commando), which operated under the name of Task Force 64. Essential air support was provided by U.S. Air Force Special Operations Command and by U.S. Navy SEALs of Naval Special Warfare Command. Elite U.S. army backup was provided by the 75th Ranger Regiment.

There was speculation that a unit of the Polish Special Forces, *Grupa Reagowania Operacyjno-Manewrowego* (GROM), were also involved. GROM operatives were trained as elite snipers and had access to a range of sniper rifles, including Heckler & Koch PSG-1; Mauser 86 7.62mm (0.3in); KAC SR-25; SAKO TRG-22; Accuracy International AWM-F; and PGM 8.59mm (0.338in) standard sniper rifles and the CheyTac Intervention (.408 Cheyenne Tactical chambering) and Barrett M107 anti-materiel rifles.

As Bravo and Charlie Companies of 1st Battalion 5th Special Forces Group crossed over the Kuwaiti border into Iraq – part of the group headed towards Nukya, Habbaniya and Mudyasis – the teams began

MAUSER M86

Country of Origin	Germany
Caliber	7.62mm (0.3in)
Overall length	1120mm (44in)
Barrel length	730mm (28.75in)
Weight	6.12kg (13.5lb) empty with Zeiss scope

THE MODERN SPECIALIST

153

THE MODERN SPECIALIST

to spread out to clear a number of objectives, including the airfield at Ar Rutba, "Scud" storage facilities and so on. Outside Ar Rutba, one of the teams set up surveillance on the highways into the town but, in a similar incident to that which happened to the British SAS team Bravo Two Zero, they were compromised by Bedouins who then went off to warn the local Iraqi garrison.

The difference between the Bravo Two Zero and the U.S. Operational Detachment Alpha in this scenario was that the SAS were on foot while the Americans had Humvees with a considerable amount of punch. As the Iraqi Fedayeen trundled out in their

Above: *A U.S. Special Forces soldier trains with the Mk12 sniper rifle following the invasion of Iraq. The Mark 12 is widely used by U.S. Special Forces snipers, including the U.S. Navy SEALs and U.S. Army Rangers.*

vehicles mounted with DShK heavy machine guns, the U.S. Special Forces mounted an ambush, firing their 12.7mm (0.5in) M2 machine guns and 40mm (1.57in) Mk 19 automatic grenade launchers. The Iraqis temporarily withdrew but began to consolidate in prepared positions on the perimeter of the town. They also made a foray to threaten some Special Forces on a hill nearby.

There was now next to no time before the small group on the hill would be overrun by the Iraqis and the SF team leader had no choice but to use the extreme danger code word to call in close air support (CAS). Although this message was immediately relayed via AWACS to the fighter aircraft on call, it would still take time for them to arrive.

This was where the sniper rifle came in handy. Using the Mk12 Special Purpose Rifle, designed for and issued to U.S. Special Forces, the sniper teams suppressed the opposition so far as they could. Even when the aerial support finally arrived, the sniper with the Mk12 continued to take out targets with the sniper rifle, sowing enough confusion among the Fedayeen to enable the Special Forces unit to withdraw eventually.

Dam assault

On April 1, 2003 C Squadron 1st SFOD-Delta and 3/7th Rangers, assaulted the Haditha dam complex, the fear being that the Iraqis would open the dam to flood invading U.S. forces. Having seized the complex, they then had to contend with an Iraqi counter-attack, and a Ranger sniper managed to kill three Iraqis who were preparing to launch an attack with rocket-propelled grenades.

The Ranger snipers provided critical fire support in defeating further Iraqi attacks. The Delta squadron headed north in the search for high value targets but ran foul of about six Iraqi technicians where two Delta operatives were wounded. MH-60 helicopters were called in to pull out the two wounded men but as the Iraqis continued to fire at the helicopters, Delta snipers set to work to silence the opposition.

SEAL snipers were employed in the seizure of the Mukarayin dam, northeast of Baghdad. Six MH-53J 'Pave Low' helicopters were employed in the attack, with the snipers traveling in the lead helicopter. The operation was supported by Polish GROM Special Forces. The Pave Low helicopter carrying the SEAL snipers landed on the top of a three-story building and the snipers quickly deployed to cover the area. The remainder of the force deployed by fast-rope to secure both ends of the dam. The area was secured for five days pending the arrival of relief ground forces.

Objective Basra

The British operation to capture Basra, Operation "Telic," involved about forty-six thousand troops, including five thousand Royal Navy, four thousand Royal Marines, twenty-six thousand British Army and eight thousand one hundred Royal Air Force. British Royal Marines and the U.S. 1st Marine Division assaulted the southern port of Um Qasr, with initial reconnaissance carried out by U.S. Navy SEALs and Polish GROM Special Forces. After this, British forces advanced north towards Basra, with SAS and Special Boat Squadron (SBS) going ahead. The British 16th Air Assault Brigade occupied the Ramallah airfield north of Basra, confronting the Iraqi 6th Armored Division. The British 7th Armored Division advanced directly on Basra, meeting stiff opposition. Fourteen Challenger 2 tanks of the Royal Scots Dragoon Guards engaged with 14 Iraqi tanks. All of the Iraqi tanks were destroyed.

As the British approached Basra, the Special Forces in advance provided forward observation for artillery as well as providing sniper cover to target key Iraqi units, gun emplacements and so on that were trying to resist. Snipers were not confined to Special Forces, however. Accompanying units in the advance also had trained snipers with them. These included snipers from the Irish Guards and the Black Watch. As the Irish Guards moved towards and into the city itself, the use of snipers to keep the enemy at bay was a key component of their strategy. The commanding officer of 2 Company of 1st Battalion Irish Guards, Major Farrell, had a nine-man sniper team deployed in Basra. He knew that the presence of snipers among the British forces had an overwhelmingly negative influence on opposing Iraqi forces, including the local Fedayeen. Major Farrell said in an interview with the British *Daily Telegraph* newspaper:

"Our snipers are working in pairs, infiltrating the enemy's territory, to give us very good observation of what is going on inside Basra and to shoot the enemy as well when opportunity arises. They don't kill huge numbers, but the psychological effect and the denial of freedom of movement of the enemy is vast. Our snipers have done really well. What they do is very brave."

Street fighting

The way the Irish Guards snipers worked was to deploy in Warrior armored personnel carriers. At a given signal, the snipers would deploy out of the back of the vehicles while other troops provided covering fire with standard weapons. This initial phase would usually attract a range of enemy fire, including small arms and mortars. The idea was that, in the confusion of the battle, the enemy would not notice that not all of the British soldiers had pulled out. Once inside the buildings, however, the snipers would begin to dominate the situation, finding optimum positions from which to observe the area around them and to send back reports. The snipers, therefore, provide a useful dual role, capable of both acting as forward observers and calling in artillery or air strikes if necessary or using their sniper rifles to engage targets directly.

The snipers are confident in their training, knowing that in their concealed positions their only real threat would be a trained enemy sniper. The British snipers in Basra were equipped with the Accuracy International 7.62mm (0.3in) L96A1 bolt-action sniper rifle.

On one occasion, as reported by Sergeant Eddie Waring of the Irish Guards, the enemy were a little too close for comfort. The British snipers had installed themselves on a rooftop when they heard the Iraqis coming into the house below. The snipers had only three options: either to call in an Irish Guards rapid reaction squad, to fight their way out of the building or to remain completely still and hope the enemy would not notice them.

On this occasion the third option worked, though the snipers decided to wait in the building until a relief force from the SBS arrived to back up their withdrawal from the area. On another occasion Eddie Waring took out some Iraqi soldiers who were laying anti-tank mines. The sniping was not all one way, however, and two Irish Guardsmen were killed by insurgent snipers during the Basra occupation.

House-to-house

The Black Watch (Royal Highland Regiment) performed similar duties to the Irish Guards. The regiment was involved in the action to capture the city of Al Zubayr prior to the attack on Basra itself. In one incident, the Black Watch sniper team, while attempting to get themselves under cover in the usual way, found themselves in a street fight that was up close and personal. The sniper team had already killed a member of the Iraqi militia with a head shot. The remaining militiamen then disappeared into a house, with the snipers hot on their heels.

Lance-Corporal Pedro Laing reached the house first and kicked down the door. As he entered and shoved an old man safely out of the door, an insurgent inside the house threw a grenade at his head. Laing ducked and the grenade flew out into the street, where it exploded, wounding one of Laing's colleagues. Next, the insurgent picked up an AK47 and fired a burst at Laing, who again ducked. This was beginning to seem like some sort of computer game where the player randomly selects alternative weapons. Next on the menu was an RPG launcher, which the insurgent also fired at Laing. Again, Laing got out of the way in time and the grenade crossed the street before exploding, sending Corporal Harvey cartwheeling over a sandy bank. Harvey did not have time to worry about the damage he had sustained. He got up and fired at the insurgent in the doorway, killing him. Laing and his other companion then burst into the house and began to clear it with grenades and personal weapons while a Challenger tank nearby fired its machine gun into the top story. Soon all the insurgents were dead. This was not normal sniper work but it showed that snipers had to be ready for anything.

Otherwise, for sniper Vincent Polus of the Black Watch, sniping had been of the traditional variety. Vincent had spent hours in position watching a designated target area and over a period of eight days he recorded three kills. If a target appeared, Polus would radio his commander and ask for permission to fire. Then he would take two deep breaths before exhaling and squeezing the trigger. At one point Polus had spotted six men in civilian clothes walking towards a pickup truck, one of them a bodyguard carrying an AK47 assault rifle. Polus went through his routine, talking in a low voice through his radio mouthpiece to request permission to fire. Permission

Below: *An Iraqi Shiite sniper loyal to the radical cleric Moqtada al-Sadr fires at U.S. troops near the cemetery in Najaf, Iraq, on August 22, 2004. He is using a Dragunov SVD sniper rifle.*

AUSTRALIAN SASR

The operations of the Australian SASR began early in the war and before the main attack was mounted. The 1st Squadron Group Australian SASR, supported by 5th Aviation Regiment, was deployed to western Iraq from February 2003, part of their mission being to track down "Scud" and other Iraqi missile launchers.

This time, however, the Iraqis were wise to the presence of Allied Special Forces and sent out teams to intercept them. Sure enough, the Australians soon found themselves in contact with an Iraqi unit and, after an exchange of fire, some Iraqis were captured. More Iraqis were captured after a similar encounter and there was another incident where the SASR succeeded in destroying an Iraqi radio relay station. After this, a more powerful Iraqi unit comprising at least six vehicles attacked the SASR but the Australians were able to respond with long-range anti-materiel sniper rifles, Javelin anti-tank missiles and other weaponry. The Australian SASR moved on to a highway intersection at Highway 10 and Expressway 1 where they defeated local Iraqi forces. Here, they could watch the road, with snipers in position to intercept any Iraqi attempts at resupply. On April 16, 2003, the SASR moved on to their next objective, the Al Asad air base. Although they were outnumbered, the Australians managed to defeat an Iraqi pre-emptive strike mounted on sports utility vehicles and went on to take over the base.

Below: A sniper team from Australian Army Security Detachment Iraq (SECDET XIV). The Australian Army is issued with the Accuracy International SR-98 sniper rifle and the SR-25 sniper rifle.

given, he looked through the telescopic sight and adjusted his aim. He took his two deep breaths and then, while exhaling, squeezed the trigger. The bodyguard, who had climbed into the pickup, instantly fell out of it. The vehicle accelerated away and disappeared momentarily. Soon, however, it reappeared again and, once again Polus took careful aim. This time he hit the driver in the head, sending him reeling out of the vehicle and into a ditch. Not far away, a fellow sniper, Sergeant Mark Cameron, also had his sights on the vehicle. Firing twice, he killed two of the passengers while the remaining two ran away.

Special Forces snipers in northern Iraq

Operation "Iraqi Freedom" had begun with Tomahawk cruise missile strikes from ships and submarines that hit selected targets in Baghdad, the aim being to take out buildings where Saddam Hussein himself and his closest supporters might taking refuge.

In northern Iraq, however, the only option open to the Allied forces was to deploy Special Forces and other air-transportable units. The original intention had been to deploy the 4th Infantry Division via Turkey but Turkey was not prepared to allow military movements over its territory. It was decided, therefore, to deploy the 10th Special Forces Group in the region and for them to collaborate with local Kurdish forces who were hostile to the Iraqi regime. At the time, two-fifths of the available Iraqi military strength was allocated to the north and the object was to keep these units busy so that they did not have time to reinforce units in the south, who would suffer the impact of the

Below: *A sniper of Alpha Company, 1st Battalion, 6th Marine Regiment aims at insurgents in Helmand province, Afghanistan, with the new 7.62mm (0.3in) M110 semi-automatic sniper system with a Leupold 3.5–10x variable power daytime optic, January 2010. The new system was developed to replace the M24 rifle.*

main invasion. The U.S. operation was under the control of Combined Forces Special Operations Component Command (CFSOCC) and the Special Forces were reinforced by 173rd Airborne Brigade.

Joint Special Operations Task Force-North (JSOTF-North), apart from its task to engage with enemy units across a broad front, was also tasked with securing the oil-producing city of Kirkuk.

Inserting the Special Forces in the first place was no easy task. Flying in six Lockheed MC-130 Combat Talon aircrafts, they came under a hail of gunfire as they entered Iraqi airspace, one of the aircrafts being so badly damaged that it had to head back into Turkey and request special permission to land. The first objective for the U.S. Special Forces and their Kurdish allies was an Iraqi terrorist group known as Ansar al-Islam. The Special Forces divided themselves among the Kurds who were mostly armed with the rugged and reliable AK47 assault rifle. The Special Forces themselves had a range of weapons at their disposal, including 60mm (2.36in) mortars, 7.62mm (0.3in) M240 light machine guns, 40mm (1.57in) Mk 19 automatic grenade launchers, 12.7mm (0.5in) M2 machine guns and, of course, sniper rifles, which included the 12.7mm (0.5in) Barrett.

In the first attack against Ansar, although the Special Forces were able to call in initial air support from F/A-18s, once the planes left and the attack began, an Ansar machine gun opened up on the Kurds. The momentum of the attack could have stalled. It was vital to cut out the enemy fire. A Special Forces sergeant aimed his sniper rifle at the enemy gunmen and then took them out one by one. The enemy fire began to die down and the attack went through.

After defeating Ansar in this attack, the teams moved on to other objectives. Team ODA 081, comprising a captain, team sergeant, two medics, one weapons sergeant and a communications sergeant moved on with a team of Kurds towards Sargat. As they advanced, they came under Ansar fire from the mountains, including machine-gun fire and mortars.

Things became extremely dicey as the mortars crept closer to their cover positions. Reinforcements were not yet available but they had a weapons sergeant with an M21 sniper rifle who scanned the rocks for possible targets. As the team attempted to get closer to the Ansar position in order to counter-attack, a second weapons sergeant came to their aid from a ridge about a kilometer away. Using his sniper rifle, he began to take out one Ansar gunner after another until several were lying dead.

In view of the failure to get heavy reinforcements into position in time, it was the snipers who had saved the day. In order for the Special Forces to mesh effectively with the Peshmerga and other Kurd forces, a number of 10th Special Forces Group and personnel of the CIA Special Activities Division (SAD) had been infiltrated into Kurdistan as early as 2002.

SAS sniper operation

Once Allied forces had defeated the Iraqi Army and moved into Baghdad, there were numerous episodes of sniper activity involving both Special Forces and regular forces.

The British Special Air Service Regiment (22 SAS) ran a number of operations that included sniper operations. SAS training includes specialist sniper training for some soldiers and the SAS included some of the top snipers in the world. The SAS sniper armory includes the 7.62mm (0.3in) Accuracy International PM sniper rifle and the 12.7mm (0.5in) Barrett long-range sniper rifle. In July 2005, the SAS were called in to intercept three suspected suicide bombers who were planning a mission in Baghdad. The information was provided by an Iraqi agent working for the British Secret Intelligence Service (MI6). A sixteen-man SAS team was deployed along with U.S. Special Forces of 1st SFOD-D (Delta), comprising Task Force Black.

Opposite: Lance-Sergeant Chris Briggs of 1st Battalion Irish Guards keeps watch near the city of Basra, Iraq in April 2003 as Royal Engineers attempt to put out oil-well fires.

THE MODERN SPECIALIST

Before dawn, the SAS team took up positions with views of a particular house in Baghdad. The core team comprised snipers and spotters while the other Special Forces elements of Task Force Red provided perimeter security. Intelligence agents had positioned listening devices in the building so that the team had early warning of when the suicide bombers were likely to leave. The only problem with intercepting three targets once they had come out into the street is that if one of them was hit, the others would most probably set off their bombs, causing massive collateral damage and probable death to civilians nearby. In other words, all three targets had to be hit simultaneously and none of them could be allowed to get up again.

To make absolutely sure of their targets, the SAS were equipped with the newest and best sniper rifle available to the British Army, the Accuracy International L115A. Firing 8.59mm (0.338in) Lapua rounds, this was one of the most powerful and accurate rifles available. With intelligence coming through from the listening posts, the SAS snipers would have been able to get some idea of when their targets would appear on the street so as to make final checks and adjust their breathing pattern. Shortly after 8:00 a.m., the three terrorists opened the door and stepped out into the street. Three rifles fired simultaneously and the three terrorists collapsed with wounds to the head.

Sniper firefight

In April 2004 the 1st Battalion Princess of Wales's Royal Regiment arrived in Al Amarah. Among them was Sergeant Dan Mills who as part of a fifteen-man sniper squad was to find himself constantly close to the heart of the action. He would vividly record his exploits in his book *Sniper One: The Blistering True Story of a British Battle Group Under Siege*. Dan Mills and his unit got a warm reception from local Iraqi insurgents when they went on their first patrol in "Snatch" Land Rover Defenders, finding themselves in a firefight from which they managed to extract themselves through adroit use of battle drills and the SA-80 automatic rifle. Once they had recovered, Mills located optimum positions for his sniper team, including the top of an unused prison on the outskirts of the south of the city.

The unit was armed with the Accuracy International 7.62mm (0.3in) L96 sniper rifle. They were supplied with "green spot" ammunition, the green spot indicating that they were part of a batch of the first five thousand out of the mold. This meant that they were mostly untarnished. The L96 rifle was fitted with a Schmidt and Bender x12 magnification telescopic sight, which could also be fitted with a SIMRAD night filter. The sniper's number two had three sets of binoculars, one of which was thermal and could pick up the heat signature of the human body. The observer also had a laser range finder and a periscope of a type first used in World War II. This would allow him to see over a parapet without raising his head.

Apart from the sniper rifles and their personal weapons, if things got really nasty and they were assaulted by a large body of insurgents, the snipers kept an L7 General Purpose Machine Gun as a standby. The "Gimpy," as it had been called by British soldiers since the 1960s, could put down 750 rounds of 7.62mm (0.3in) a minute, making any assailant wish he had planned something else for the day.

However, the snipers were not always in static positions. Sometimes they were called out to rescue soldiers on patrol who were trapped by enemy gunfire. On one occasion, members of a mortar platoon were trapped at a road junction, with a wounded man and no escape options due to the weight of fire. There were probably only two available options in this scenario: for a Warrior armored vehicle to come to the rescue; or for a sniper team to take out the gunmen.

As it happened, it turned out to be a mixture of both. British snipers were immediately deployed to a rooftop from where they could scan the area where the

IMPROVED BRITISH SNIPER TRAINING

The requirement for snipers in both Afghanistan and Iraq was growing exponentially and the British decided to step up their sniper program. Regiments such as the Irish Guards and Black Watch arrived in Iraq with their own sniper units and they were soon extremely busy.

Having been regarded as something of an optional extra in previous conflicts of the twentieth century, snipers found themselves overbooked. In view of this, the British extended sniper training in order to bring regular army snipers closer to the levels of excellence of Special Forces snipers. Part of the training would incorporate the L115A1 rifle, which up to 2007 had been restricted to Special Forces use. The course also marked the doubling of snipers in the British Army, totalling around three hundred. Protracted warfare in Afghanistan and Iraq had revealed that the sniping rifle was often the ideal weapon to counter insurgents who often protected themselves by mixing among the civilian population, thus creating a situation where attacking them by conventional means would risk serious collateral damage. The presence of a devastatingly powerful sniper rifle such as an L115A1 or a 12.7mm (0.5in) Barrett acted as a powerful deterrent because the insurgents never knew where the bullet might come from. The course set up in the Brecon Beacons in Wales echoed the course set up by Hesketh-Prichard in World War I as it taught snipers not only how to shoot but to infiltrate into enemy territory without being detected and to exfiltrate successfully when the job was done.

Below: *A British soldier fires the new L115A3 Accuracy International .338 Lapua sniper rifle in Warminster, England. The rifle was brought in as part of the Sniper System Improvement Program in 2008 and replaced the previous L96 sniper rifle. The rifle has a 5–25 x 56 Schmidt & Bender sight and spotting scope. It is fitted with a noise and flash suppressor and has a folding stock and bipod.*

Above: A sniper from 51st Squadron RAF Regiment aims an Accuracy International L96 sniper rifle from the top of a Land Rover in southern Iraq, 2003.

insurgents were firing from. The observer and the sniper scanned the area, using all their training and experience to try to discern where an enemy sniper might hide and trying to suppress the urge to rush caused by the urgency of the appeals of the men who were trapped and wounded. At last they spotted the position of an AK47. The only problem was that the range was over 800m (875 yards). The sniper adjusted his sights for range and left the windage adjustment as there was barely a breeze. Then he went through the calming breathing routine and slowly squeezed the trigger. The round sped to its unseen target and the AK47 fell silent. The trapped soldiers took advantage of the break in the firing and fired back before Warriors arrived to rescue them.

Operation "Phantom Fury"

The city of Fallujah became a bête noir for occupying forces in Iraq after an incident involving 82nd Airborne Division on April 2003 when a crowd protested against the occupation of a primary school by the U.S. troops. After shots were fired, the situation went downhill. By March 2004, after much fighting with insurgents, American forces had withdrawn from the city. On April 1, the 1st Marine Expeditionary Force was ordered to conduct a major operation against Fallujah, an order they apparently did not welcome as they did not want to get bogged down in a protracted city battle, preferring to conduct pinpoint raids against insurgents where appropriate. U.S. forces laid siege to the city, cutting off transport links, and many residents of the city left. As the Marines moved in, their scout/snipers formed an essential element of their armory and they began to take a heavy toll on the insurgents.

In November 2004, the U.S. forces returned to Fallujah, with additional backup from the British Black Watch regiment. In both battles, Fallujah proved to be a haven for snipers on both sides. Sergeant John Crane, a scout/sniper of the U.S.

Marines, quickly notched up a kill score of eleven insurgents. In Fallujah it was either kill or be killed and snipers on both sides struggled to gain the best vantage points high up in buildings or on flat roofs in order to pin down their adversaries. Crane led a squad of Marine snipers who were located in the north of the city. Watching by day and by night, using heat-sensitive binoculars, they made it perilous for anyone to venture out of doors.

On one occasion, the Marines spotted an insurgent sniper armed with a Dragunov SVD sniper rifle. Although the insurgent was in full view and looking for targets, he was also unaware that he was in the sights of a U.S. Marine sniper. It was to be his lucky day, however, for a slight misalignment in the Marine's sight settings meant that the bullet missed.

For the Marines, it was a bit uncomfortable as well. They were limited in their movements by standing orders and snipers instinctively do not like returning to the same place too often as the enemy will know where to find them and know to keep out of the way. The U.S. Marines scout/snipers did their best to make less obvious shooting positions, by making holes through buildings and concealing themselves in the backs of rooms. Iraqi gunmen on their way to "work," therefore, had a tough job trying to survive. Sometimes they would hide behind civilians and sometimes make super-fast dashes or rolls across open ground so that a sniper would not have time to fire.

One of the Marine snipers in the Fallujah battle was Corporal Paul W. Leicht. Located on a rooftop

Below: A *U.S. Marine Corps sniper uses the telescopic sight on his M40A1 sniper rifle to observe a cement factory near Bahkit, Iraq on July 3, 2008, for possible insurgent activity.*

THE MODERN SPECIALIST

across the Euphrates River, Leicht watched carefully through the scope of his M40A3 sniper rifle for targets of opportunity. As part of Company B, 1st Battalion, 23rd Marine Regiment, Leicht was briefed to take out insurgents as U.S. forces had their second stab at Fallujah.

A group of Iraqi insurgents started firing mortar rounds at the Marines and Leicht took them up in his sight. This was routine so far. This was the enemy and they were definitely in an offensive mode. They were, however, over 914m (1000 yards) from Leicht's position. Nevertheless, Leicht carefully squeezed the trigger and one insurgent went down. Then he fired again and dropped another.

The Marines were demonstrating once again that the sniper is one of the essential tools of the modern

Below: *A U.S. Marine Corps sniper of 1st Battalion, 8th Marine Regiment aims a M16A2 rifle with M203 grenade launcher through a hole during a Security and Stabilization Operation (SAS) as part of Operation "Al Fajr" in Fallujah, Iraq. He is using his helmet to support the weapon.*

Opposite: *A sniper of the Mahdi army of the radical Iraqi Shiite leader Moqtada al-Sadr in Najaf old town on August 19, 2004. Apart from his Dragunov SVD sniper rifle, the sniper has minimal equipment, merely a pouch presumably used to store ammunition. His head scarf would make him very conspicuous.*

battlefield. Sergeant Herbert B. Hancock, the chief scout/sniper, was confident about the ability of snipers to deal with insurgents. Hancock took a team and found a position from where they could reach the insurgents. Before that, they needed some fireworks to keep the insurgents entertained while they moved into position. So they called in suppressive fire. As this demonstrates, Marine scout/snipers were not just useful for sniping. Their skill set also included forward observation and the ability to decide on the best tactical options. With their ever-watchful gaze, snipers could begin to piece together what was going on in the battlefield in a way that was not possible for regular soldiers who were constantly on the move. Hancock's sniper team noted, for example, that certain vehicles appeared at about the same time that mortars were fired at the Marine positions. Someone giving a passing glance at these civilian vehicles would not have noticed anything strange about them. Hancock and his team, however, worked out that they were spotters for the mortars and, as such, they were a legitimate target. After this incident, Hancock and his team took out a mortar position not just with sniper rifles but with friendly mortars, playing the dual role of sniper and observer.

The Marines in Fallujah were high-scoring against a determined enemy. The level of the battle can be gauged by the performance of Sergeant John Ethan Place who had thirty-two confirmed kills in a period of thirteen days. He was awarded the Silver Star.

TIMOTHY L. KELLNER

Timothy L. Kellner is a U.S. Army sniper who has been credited with 139 confirmed kills. He is also thought to have achieved a much larger number of unconfirmed kills, some sources crediting with him more than 300.

Like so many naturally gifted snipers, Kellner was a keen hunter as a young man, before joining the U.S. Army in 1996. His hunting background gave him a special advantage in fieldcraft and he was an expert in covert movement and concealment.

Kellner favored the M24 Sniper Weapon System, which was the military version of the Remington 700 rifle. This had an effective range of about 800 meters (875 yards).

Although Iraq's open deserts may seem like an ideal arena for long-range shooting, most of the sniping in Iraq tends to be at relatively short ranges and in urban areas. This environment

Below: *Using the same weapon as used by Timothy L. Kellner, the M24 sniper rifle, A U.S. Army sniper of the 25th Infantry Division scans the rooftops in Baghdad Province, Iraq, during a joint cordon and search mission with 6th Iraqi National Police.*

Right: *A U.S. Marine sniper with the 6th Marine Regiment armed with a Barrett M82A1 anti-materiel rifle provides security somewhere in Iraq, 2010.*

poses different challenges for the sniper, though the basic principles still apply. Stealth, concealment and patience are always required, as well as excellent marksmanship.

Cities have relatively few long fields of fire, and there is plenty of cover for hostiles to disappear behind. There is also the civilian population to consider, both as potential collateral damage and as what amounts to camouflage for the enemy. Iraqi gunmen rarely dress very differently to the civilian population, posing a problem in terms of spotting and confirming a legitimate target.

Urban sniping

The same skills used to detect a camouflaged machine-gun post or likely route for enemy patrols are used by Kellner and his colleagues in the urban environment. Observation of the habits of non-combatant populace allows snipers to pick out anyone who seems to be out of place. By watching good ambush points or routes to and from them, a skilled marksman can identify insurgents as they move into position or retire after an attack.

> *"Every shot has to be measured against the Rules of Engagement [ROE], positive identification and proportionality."*
>
> United States Army Staff Sergeant
> Jim Gilliland

The sniper who thinks he has spotted a legitimate target must decide quickly whether or not to shoot. Opportunities are often fleeting and there is always the possibility that an over-penetrating round or a ricochet – or perhaps a missed shot – might hit a non-combatant.

There is also the problem of confirmation; it is not always possible to check a body or even to find it. Thus many of Kellner's kills are listed as probable but unconfirmed. However, it is the impact an effective sniper has on the enemy that matters. In terms of restricting enemy movements and diminishing morale, Kellner's contribution to the war in Iraq is far greater than a kill-count, no matter how high, can possibly indicate.

Unfortunately, even Kellner's exceptional abilities did not make him proof to the random effects of IEDs and in 2003 he was critically wounded by an explosion. He returned home to a hero's welcome and, after recovering, continued to work with the sniper community.

Urban sniping

In December 2003 in Samarra, Sergeant Randall Davis of B Company, 5th Battalion, 20th Infantry Regiment peered through the sight of his M14 rifle at sunset and saw an Iraqi insurgent sniper silhouetted against the light. The insurgent was in the process of maneuvering himself into a position whereby he could take aim at Davis's colleagues in a courtyard below. He would certainly have been successful had he not been in the sights of an M14 with a trained U.S. Army sniper behind it. By taking out the Iraqi insurgent, Davis certainly saved the lives of some of his fellow soldiers and he was also a testimony to the value of sniper training, such as at Fort Benning, United States, where they were specializing in urban sniper training. Sergeant Davis had been credited with eight kills in about two weeks.

Urban sniping presented all sorts of challenges, not least the fact that insurgents were prepared to use civilians for protection when they were out in the streets. The members of Fox company, Battalion Landing Team, 2nd Battalion, 2nd Marines, 24th Expeditionary Force were faced with just such a challenge on one occasion when they received an order to recover the body of one of their fellow soldiers who had been killed in an ambush. Unfortunately, the Iraqi insurgents wanted to stop them, so the sniper team got themselves into position to provide essential backup. Then they spotted an insurgent holding an AK47 in one hand

Below: U.S. Army Specialist Chantah Bun (foreground) looks through the AN/PVS-10 Day and Night Vision sniper scope of his tripod-mounted M40A1 sniper rifle. He is supported by another sniper armed with an M21 sniper rifle. Both are Bravo Company Snipers, 1st Battalion, 24th Infantry Regiment, 1st Brigade, 25th Infantry Division, Stryker Brigade Combat Team. They are guarding an Iraqi police station in Mosul, Iraq.

THE MODERN SPECIALIST

and with his other hand on the shoulder of a child. The Marine scout/sniper deliberately aimed away from the insurgent and child, sending a round smashing into the building a few feet away. This created enough of a distraction for the child to take the opportunity to run away. The insurgent made the mistake of coming out to inspect the damage from the shot as the second Marine scout/sniper had him in his sights.

On another occasion, in Baghdad, two U.S. Army snipers were tasked with the mission of taking out an insurgent machine-gun position that had been causing persistent problems for troops in a compound. As ever, the challenge for the sniper is to get into the optimum position with clear lines of sight so that they can see without being seen. On this occasion, the two army snipers worked their way to the top of a building and set up their equipment on a flat roof. It was night time so they used their night-vision equipment to scan the scene. Unfortunately for them, on this night there was a celebration going on in the streets, with people firing guns in the air. It was

Above: *This 2005 photograph shows U.S. Army soldiers escorting a sniper team to a hidden location near the Euphrates River, Iskandariyah, Iraq, in an operation to stop the placing of improvised explosive devices along a nearby road.*

therefore difficult to pick out the noise of the enemy machine-gun position in the confusion. Patience is one of the essential pieces of equipment that the sniper carries with him and as the two army snipers waited and prepared their weapons, the commotion gradually died down leaving only the stillness of the night. Then one sound began to penetrate the relative silence – the juddering fire of a 12.7mm (0.5in) machine gun.

The army snipers pinpointed the position of the gun and discerned that it was manned by four men. They were 731m (800 yards) away so it would require fast and accurate shooting to get all of them. They made the final preparations with their M24 rifles and fired almost simultaneously, bringing down two insurgents. The other two tried to get away but it was

"JUBA"

In 2005 in Baghdad a singular phenomenon arose among the usual exchange of sniping and sharpshooting. The Army 1-64 Battalion lost two men to a particular sniper in February and six more were wounded.

The shots seemed to follow a pattern. Other regiments may also have suffered from the same sniper. In June 2005 four U.S. Marine scout/snipers were shot in the head. Known as "Juba," this sniper's trademark was to target coalition forces and to have an uncanny ability to get around body armor. Another "Juba" trademark was that he did not fire a second shot and therefore it was extremely difficult to pinpoint where he was firing from.

Whether "Juba" was in fact a single individual or whether he represented a particularly effective team of Iraqi insurgent snipers is unknown. What is clear is that the name had a psychologically negative effect on American troops in theater who whenever they went out on patrol felt the eyes of "Juba" upon them.

The Internet provided a useful means of extending the "Juba" myth, with videos being circulated of American soldiers being shot and victorious insurgents returning to base. The fact that no positive identification of the super-sniper was provided rather suggests that "Juba" may have been a particularly effective sniper in the area at the time, or that he worked as part of an effective team. Whatever the truth behind the legend, eventually American forces shrugged off the "Juba" scare and got on with their duties, knowing that the best counter-measure was good battle drills and effective counter-sniper operations.

Below: An Iraqi militiaman aims his AK47 sniper rifle during clashes with coalition forces in Basra on August 22, 2004.

too late. The two rifles fired again in unison and the other two insurgents also fell. The snipers then withdrew from their position before any insurgents had a chance to pinpoint them.

Patience

In April 2007, Sergeant 1st Class Brandon McGuire of Alpha Troop, 1st Battalion (Airborne), 509th Infantry Regiment and his spotter companion were deployed to a Forward Observation Base at Iskandaryia in Iraq to scan the area for insurgent activity. The area had been notorious for the prevalence of Improvised Explosive Devices (IEDs) and also for a significant amount of mortar activity. Although the IEDs had by now largely been cleared, the U.S. forces certainly did not want anyone putting new ones in. Several U.S. soldiers had been either killed or wounded by these devices or by mortars.

McGuire and his companion had taken up position in an abandoned shed and waited patiently for anything unusual to happen. At length, a man appeared, walking nonchalantly through the canals in the area. After a while, the man started digging into the side of one of the canals and then pulled out a mortar tube. McGuire quickly contacted his HQ for target permission, which he soon received. Although this was a verifiable enemy target, the range was extreme at 1310m (1433 yards). On top of this there was a crosswind of about eight or ten knots as well as an imminent sand storm, which could effectively ruin their chances. Another problem was that the target was on the move over uneven ground, meaning that the calculations were changing at every moment.

The name of the game for snipers is patience and McGuire and his companion restrained the impulse to get off a lucky shot for about two hours. McGuire's plan was to get a first shot off for measurement purposes, allowing his spotter to report the fall of shot, and then follow up with the killer shot. McGuire squeezed the trigger and fired. The target disappeared. After this, the problem with IEDs in the area died down, which meant no more American soldiers or civilians would be maimed or killed.

AFGHANISTAN TODAY

After the September 11, 2001 attacks in New York, the North Atlantic Treaty Organization (NATO) made history by invoking for the first time Article 5 of its founding charter, which provided for mutual assistance in the face of attack. After the Bonn Conference of 2001, the International Security Assistance Force (ISAF) was set up in coordination with the United Nations Assistance Mission in Afghanistan and the Afghan Transitional Authority. After a period of rotational forces on the ground, on August 11, 2003 NATO assumed command of ISAF, which provided stronger coordination and leadership for the mission in the face of significant odds. Although ISAF's initial mission was to provide protection for Kabul, by October 2003 this had been extended to the whole of Afghanistan.

ISAF's mission was to reduce the capability of the insurgency in the country as well as training the Afghan Army and helping with reconstruction. In April 2010, there were 46 contributing nations in ISAF with a total strength of approximately 102,500 men. The country was divided into a number of regional commands in addition to HQ ISAF in Kabul. Each of the commands (Capital, North, South, West, East) had a lead nation responsible for operations in that area with the assistance of other nations. At the time of writing, Regional Command North was under German command, Regional Command East under U.S. command, Regional Command South under British command and Regional Command West under Italian command. The United States had by far the largest presence in the country (62,415), with the United Kingdom the second largest contributor (9500).

U.S. Snipers in Afghanistan

The war in Afghanistan is a very different combat environment from that of Iraq. Snipers in Iraq spend most of their time observing streets through the restricted viewpoint of a window or from a rooftop. Their shots are mostly at relatively short range against an enemy that can quickly disappear through a doorway or around a corner and get away.

In Afghanistan, there is no shortage of cover but most combat is in the open, in remote areas with little in the way of urbanization. Combat ranges are longer, often beyond the distance where the average gunman or even trained soldier can shoot accurately with a typical assault rifle. As generations of British and Soviet soldiers discovered before them, U.S. forces have learned that Afghanistan is prime country for the expert rifleman, a place where ordinary soldiers are often reduced to the level of ambush targets. It is then that the specialist skills of the sniper are needed. Snipers are effective in guarding installations or ambushing enemy forces, but equally they have proven their worth as part of a field force.

Convoy ambush

The experiences of one U.S. Army sniper, who prefers to remain anonymous, show just how vital snipers are as part of regular operations. Snipers are often dropped off by convoys headed out to carry out

Below: *A U.S. Army sniper team from Jalalabad Provincial Reconstruction Team (PRT) scans the horizon from a concealed position in an abandoned building after reports of enemy activity in the hilltops near Dur Baba, Afghanistan, 2006. The sniper (left) is armed with an M40A3 sniper rifle, while their escort (right) is armed with an M4 carbine.*

THE MODERN SPECIALIST

a specific mission, providing overwatch until they are picked up on the way back to base. Other times they ride with the convoy and respond to any incident with their unique skills.

The anonymous sniper was part of a convoy of U.S. and Afghan army vehicles sent out with the deliberate intent of drawing out Taliban fighters into an engagement. In due course, the convoy was ambushed from high ground on both sides of the road. As rocket-propelled grenades and small-arms fire hit the convoy, vehicles halted and troops dismounted to return fire.

As was fairly common, the ambush was undertaken from fairly long range – 500 meters (550 yards) or more – with the Taliban fighters shooting at the vehicles from high up in the rocks and the defenders lacking clear targets. Although their rifles were accurate at this range, most of the troops in the convoy could not hit a man-sized target at that distance, especially under the stress of combat.

Above: A U.S. Navy SEAL takes up a defensive position with a FN SCAR (SOF Combat Assault Rifle) in Zabul province, Afghanistan, April 2010. The FN SCAR is a modular series rather than a single weapon. The core of the rifles remains a gas-operated, rotating-bolt system, while the stock is adjustable for comb height and length of pull. The gun can take various optical sights or rely on folding, adjustable iron sights.

Neither could their enemies, but the convoy as a whole was under heavy automatic fire, creating a danger that was no less severe for being fairly indiscriminate.

Sniper response

The machine guns aboard U.S. Army Humvees had the range to engage the enemy, but it was the handful of snipers in the convoy who made the most effective response. Taking cover behind a bush, the anonymous sniper estimated the size of the enemy force based on a quick impression of muzzle flashes, and figured out

175

a rough idea of the range and elevation. Shooting uphill at a barely seen enemy, the sniper took a best guess based on muzzle flash and fired. The firing from that position stopped. Another muzzle flash drew his attention so he repeated the process, and kept doing it until the fighting died down. He could not be sure if his shots had struck the target or not, but some of the enemy guns ceased firing. That was what mattered.

Gradually the fighting died down and the enemy began to withdraw into the hills, away from the road. Spotting a promising retirement route, the sniper took a precise range with his laser rangefinder and waited. In due course a gunman appeared, walking right into a shot the sniper had already set up. He was hit in the head at over 700 meters (760 yards).

The action ended with relatively little damage to the convoy despite the immense volume of fire going both ways. After checking the enemy bodies as best they could – most were out of reach, high in the rocks – the convoy called in air support on the withdrawing Taliban force and began to pull back, having achieved its mission aim.

Enemy casualties were probably light in the engagement, though an air strike as the Taliban forces withdrew probably inflicted more. The U.S./Afghan force only suffered damage to vehicles. The sniper had good reason to believe that he had inflicted at the very least some wounds among the enemy in addition to his definite kill.

Long-range specialists

Incidents like this one, and the support given to operations "Anaconda" and "Harpoon" as related elsewhere, indicate the value of including snipers within a combat force, especially in an environment like that of Afghanistan. At times the sniper may be able to change the course of an engagement or take the pressure off his comrades by eliminating an artillery observer, machine-gunner or leader. On other occasions he functions much like any other soldier, firing at the enemy wherever they are seen. In a long-range engagement, the snipers may be the only elements of a force that have any real chance of hitting the enemy without vast expenditure of ammunition. The snipers' skills and possession of highly accurate rifles with long-range sights are far better suited to this kind of combat than the typical infantry squad armed with assault rifles. The snipers may only inflict a handful of casualties but in an inconclusive long-range firefight that might be enough to turn the engagement.

British snipers in Afghanistan

In September 2007 the British Special Boat Squadron (SBS) were involved in a raid to rescue two Italian intelligence officers and an interpreter who had been

Left: *Two snipers from the U.S. 82nd Airborne Division provide overwatch security from a rooftop for local Afghan forces during a civil meeting in Dey Yak, Afghanistan, 2007. The sniper on the right is armed with a new sniper version of the M14 rifle, the Mk.14 Mod 0 EBR.*

captured by the Taliban and taken to Farah province. The SBS worked alongside an Italian special operations unit, the plan being that the SBS would provide aerial support and cut-off operations while the Italians stormed the building.

As the Italians went in, the Taliban attempted to escape with their captives in nearby vehicles. The SBS sniper team was positioned in Westland Lynx helicopters overhead and shot out the engines of the vehicles. They then provided fire support as a Chinook helicopter landed another SBS team to cut off the Taliban and rescue the hostages. Unfortunately, one of the Italian intelligence officers was mortally wounded in the raid.

Bravery under fire
British and American snipers were up against a common enemy in Afghanistan. Sometimes they took the battle to the enemy and sometimes the battle came to them. In unexpected situations, high levels of training would often pay off. Lance-Corporal Oliver "Teddy" Ruecker of 1st Battalion Royal Anglian Regiment was trained as a sniper and proved to be one of the best in the region. When he and his sniper companion Dean Bailey were ambushed by Taliban fighters in their Viking patrol vehicle in September 2008, another kind of training took over. A rocket-propelled grenade hit the Viking amidships and Ruecker got out of the burning vehicle fast. As he ran for cover, he came across a Taliban fighter shooting an AK47 into the air by way of celebration. With the skill of a Wild West gunfighter, he drew his Browning L9A1 pistol and swiftly shot the insurgent.

At this point he realized that his mate Dean was not with him and must still be in the burning vehicle. Under heavy machine-gun and small-arms fire, Ruecker ran back to the Viking and dragged out his unconscious friend. Still under fire, he managed to pull him over to the relative safety of another Viking and they got out of the area. As a result of this action, Ruecker was awarded the Military Cross.

As part of 11 Light Brigade, the Rifles were deployed in Afghanistan from 2009 to 2010. The Rifles had a distinguished history in the field of marksmanship, tracing their roots back to the sharpshooters of the Peninsular War, immortalized by Captain John Kincaid in *Adventures in the Rifle Brigade* and by Bernard Cornwell in the *Sharpe* series of books and subsequent TV series. Number 3 Company of the Rifles were located in Sangin, equipped with the L115A1 rifle. Their presence in the area coincided with the presence of a Taliban super-sniper who targeted the British snipers and scored several fatal hits. The stand-off had an uncanny resemblance to the battle between Vassili Zaitsev and the German super-sniper in Stalingrad during World War II. Things got so serious that the British drafted in the SAS and the Special Reconnaissance Regiment to track him down but this sniper knew how to get out of the way when necessary.

To make matters more difficult, the Taliban snipers often used an intricate network of caves and tunnels, which made it easy for their snipers to evaporate when the enemy came too close. In order to counter the Taliban insurgents and snipers, the Rifles maintained a series of forward observation posts, including Forward Observation Post Jackson where the fire support team were emplaced with L115A sniper rifles, machine guns, Javelin missiles and advanced observation equipment.

Sniper hunting
In Helmand Province in 2010 snipers of the reconnaissance platoon of 1st Battalion Grenadier Guards went out to track down some Taliban snipers who had already killed the company sergeant-major. This loss provided an extra edge to their determination. They were equipped with the Accuracy International L115A1 rifle, firing 8.59mm (0.338in) Lapua, a rifle once restricted to Special Forces but now increasingly available to regular sniper units.

As they were confronting snipers, the Guardsmen knew that they were targets themselves and that they

L115A3 RIFLE

This rifle formed part of the British Army Sniper System Improvement Program (SSIP). The heavier caliber and 8.59mm (0.338in) Lapua round provided extra range and stability enhanced by day/night all-weather optical sights.

The rifle features a folding stock, which makes it easier to transport the weapon. The back of the stock is fitted with a cheek piece. The rifle is fitted with a folding bipod, which can be deployed to provide essential stability, and has an effective range of 1100m (1203 yards). At the end of the barrel, it is fitted with a suppressor that reduces both flash and noise signature. The rifle has a five-round magazine.

Country of Origin	United Kingdom
Caliber	8.59mm (0.338in)
Overall length	1300mm (51in)
Barrel length	686mm (27in)
Weight	6.8kg (15lbs)

Below: *British Royal Marines train with the Accuracy International L115A3 rifle, one of them using an improvised tripod. Carrying cases for the rifles lie alongside.*

LONG-RANGE SNIPER RECORD

Snipers influence the course of a conflict the most when they eliminate high-value targets, or protect their own side's key personnel. Two British snipers recently demonstrated both sides of this coin in Afghanistan, eliminating and rescuing senior personnel respectively.

Corporal Christopher Reynolds' contribution to the war in Afghanistan was to kill a Taliban warlord known as Mula. Senior commanders and insurgent leaders generally try to stay some distance away from the fighting, and even when they are in the field, opportunities to eliminate them are likely to be few and fleeting.

Reynolds' unit was involved in heavy fighting, but this did not prevent him taking up position on a roof and remaining there for three days awaiting a suitable opportunity. Finally, he noticed a group of Taliban personnel in the distance, which appeared to include a prominent leader.

This individual gave away his status in ways any sniper would recognize; pointing, giving orders that were seen to be obeyed, and using a radio. Realizing that this was someone important, Corporal Reynolds decided to shoot him and began calculating range and wind speed.

Reynolds' first shot, at a range of 1853 meters (2026 yards), went a little wide. The warlord did not apparently realize he was under fire, so Reynolds recalculated and fired again. His weapon was not pointed at the target but at a nearby door frame to compensate for trajectory variations cased by the wind. The Taliban leader was hit in the chest and killed; his comrades scattered and fled.

"The second insurgent grabbed the weapon and turned as my second shot hit him in the side. He went down, too. They were both dead."

Corporal of Horse Craig Harrison

During the same engagement, another member of Reynolds' force demonstrated the risks facing snipers when he used a Javelin missile launcher – normally an anti-tank system – to eliminate an enemy marksman. Only a high-value target like a sniper would justify the expenditure of such a weapon.

Record-breaking hit
Perfect environmental conditions, including thin air and no wind, allowed Corporal of Horse Craig Harrison to rescue his troop commander in November 2009. With the commander's vehicle stuck in difficult terrain and under small-arms fire, Harrison decided to intervene. This required a prodigious shot that greatly exceeded the 1500 meters (1640 yards) effective range of his L115A3 long range rifle.

Although the distance to the target was far beyond the rifle's official capability, Harrison

Above: A sniper team from the British Royal Marines search for targets in Lakari Bazaar, Afghanistan, July 2009. The sniper is armed with an L96 sniper rifle, which he has covered with material to avoid the rifle barrel and stock reflecting light and giving away their position.

decided to try, taking several ranging shots before engaging. He was thus able to shoot both machine-gunners and their weapon in quick succession, hitting three times with three shots and destroying the machine gun as well as killing the crew. These three incredible shots were made at a range of 2475 meters (2700 yards), the longest ever confirmed kill by a sniper to date.

Harrison's tour in Afghanistan was eventful in other ways, too. When his vehicle was ambushed and riddled with automatic fire, one round penetrated his helmet but was deflected out of the top rather than into the sniper's brain. He later broke both arms as a result of a roadside bomb but recovered and returned to duty.

would need to employ all their training in covert movement if they were to remain alive. They were out seeking their targets before first light and were in position by 5:00 a.m. Apart from their regular equipment, the Guardsmen had a target indicator for the Javelin missile system as a backup. They waited patiently, as snipers do, until at about 8 o'clock when they began to notice some movement. There was one insurgent sniper on a roof, which one of the Guardsmen managed to eliminate. The Javelin system provided a target indication for the second sniper, who was also then dispatched.

Helmand firefight

Snipers provided essential cover for 1st Battalion Coldstream Guards as they took part in Operation "Lion's Leap" when they were inserted by Chinook helicopter deep into enemy territory to establish dominance in the area and to provide the basis for building relationships with the local people and reconstruction. Near Babaji, No. 1 Company of the Coldstream came under fire and it is in scenarios such as these that the sniper team can provide essential fire support.

The snipers of Fire Support Company, 1st Battalion the Royal Welsh found themselves in a firefight with enemy insurgents near Shahzad in the southwest of Helmand province. The Welsh snipers had been tasked with providing protection for an Army Bomb Disposal team near a compound, but as they approached their location they came under fire from insurgents in the area.

L129A1 SHARPSHOOTER RIFLE

Although not designed specifically for snipers, the new L129A1 sharpshooter rifle issued to some British Army units in 2010, including members of the Parachute Regiment, fulfilled requirements for soldiers trained to sharpshooter level who needed a rifle with greater range and accuracy than the standard-issue automatic SA-80. The new rifle replaced the L96 sniper rifle, which had also been partly replaced by the new L115 long-range sniper rifle, and it provides accuracy up to 800m (875 yards).

The L129A1 has a monolithic rail platform that allows the barrel to be changed without any modifications to the rest of the weapon. It has a retractable stock and a Picatinny rail for attaching night-vision sights. It also has an adjustable bipod for stability in the prone position. It can be held by a folding fore-grip. In automatic mode it is capable of firing twenty rounds in about twenty seconds.

Country of Origin	United Kingdom
Caliber	7.62mm (0.3in)
Overall length	not known
Barrel length	305mm (12in), 406mm (16in) and 508mm (20in)
Weight	5kg (11lb)

Despite the rounds coming in, the snipers managed to fight their way through to the compound using their standard infantry battle drills. Once inside the compound, the snipers worked their way up to the roof. From here, they could start to observe where the enemy were located but, as they did so, incoming rounds thudded into the exterior of the compound wall. To make matters more complicated, the insurgent gunmen were using local people as human shields. Unfortunately for the insurgents, they were not up against regular soldiers with automatic weapons but highly trained snipers armed with the precision L115A1 rifle. One of the Royal Welsh snipers scanned the buildings in which the insurgents had taken cover, searching for firing holes. He saw an insurgent aim and fire a burst from his automatic

Above: *A U.S. Marine sniper from the 3rd Marine Regiment seeks targets through a hole with an M82 Barrett .50 caliber rifle near Marjah, Afghanistan, 2010. The high-powered Barrett has an effective range of 1800 meters (1969 yards).*

weapon and immediately engaged him with sniper fire. From now on, the battle could only go one way, and the insurgents were soon cleared.

CONCLUSION

The story of sniping covers every form of warfare where an accurate rifle has been used. It extends beyond that to the art of hunting, where it has its roots, for many of the best snipers have been hunters. They have had the talent of marksmen alongside the natural instinct for fieldcraft, which is an essential

THE MODERN SPECIALIST

part of the sniper's art. A form of warfare that has a redolence of Daniel Boone with a Kentucky rifle might have become irrelevant in the realms of modern warfare with precision laser-guided weapons delivered by fighter bombers, heavy-caliber machine guns and heat-seeking missiles.

The opposite is in fact the case. In both the small wars of the late twentieth century and the larger wars in the Middle East, including both Iraq and Afghanistan, the sniper has become an essential precision tool of the modern battlefield, providing not only support fire for other missions but also

Left: *A Canadian sniper team scan the landscape during an operation to arrest suspected Taliban in the Panjwayi district, southern Kandahar province, April 2006. These men are armed with the recently deployed M110 semi-automatic sniper system, which is gradually replacing the M24 rifle for all U.S. forces.*

combat situation without either its own team of snipers deployed or Special Forces or elite regiment snipers on hand.

New weapons, new role

As has been seen, sniper training has increased exponentially and sniper equipment, including both rifles and sights, has grown alongside. A wide variety of sniper rifles are now available to suit the differing needs and tastes of various units, from the U.S. Barrett M82 .50 caliber and L115 .338 Lapua heavy rifles through the M14 and Winchester rifles to the U.S. Special Forces Mk12 (SPR) rifle.

In theaters such as Afghanistan, where ISAF forces have a priority in reconstruction and winning the hearts and minds of the local population, the sniper has provided a useful precision tool, acting as an effective deterrent against insurgents, with far less risk of collateral damage than an air mission.

Whereas the sniper was once regarded as a bit of an oddity, at the time of writing it is rare for a month to go by without one or more snipers being hailed in the press for their gallant work. There is now a realization that these soldiers are doing a very difficult job that requires a high degree of training and also an awareness that their opponents are regularly killing American, British and other national soldiers. Snipers not only provide target interdiction but also essential battlefield intelligence and target identification.

focused interdiction of insurgents, often in an urban setting.

Whereas even in the Korean and early part of the Vietnam wars commanders had to search for suitable marksmen to fulfill sniping roles, by the twenty-first century no regiment would think of entering a

The modern sniper is not an assassin but a specialist fighting in the very difficult circumstances of modern, often urban, warfare. Their overwatch may have meant that countless soldiers have been able to return home safely after completing their mission.

APPENDICES

TOP SNIPERS THROUGH THE AGES

Country	Sniper	Conflict	Confirmed Kills
U.S.	Timothy Murphy	American Revolutionary War	not known
UK	Patrick Ferguson	American Revolutionary War	not known
UK	Thomas Plunkett	Peninsular War	not known
U.S.	Sgt Ben Powell	American Civil War	not known
Canada	Francis Pegahmagabow	World War I	378
Australia	Billy Sing	World War I	150
U.S.	Henry Norwest	World War I	115
Finland	Simo Häyhä	Winter War (Finland v. Soviet Union)	705
Soviet Union	Lt. Vassil Zaitsev	World War II	225
Germany	Pvte Matthias Hetzenauer	World War II	345
Germany	Josef "Sepp" Allerberger	World War II	257
Soviet Union	Lyudmila Pavlichenko	World War II	309
UK	Alfred Hulme VC	World War II	33
China	Zhang Taofang	Korean War	214
U.S.	Adelbert F. Waldron	Vietnam War	109
U.S.	Carlos Hathcock	Vietnam War	93
U.S.	Chuck Mawhinney	Vietnam War	103
U.S.	Frank Grieci	Operation "Desert Storm"	15
U.S.	Scott Dennison	Operation "Desert Storm"	14
U.S.	Timothy L. Kellner	Operation "Iraqi Freedom"	139

RECORD SHOTS

Country	Sniper	Conflict	Rifle	Distance
UK	Craig Harrison	Afghanistan/ISAF	Accuracy International L115A3	2475m/2707yds
Canada	Rob Furlong	Afghanistan	TAC™-50 McMillan Tactical Rifle	2430m/2657yds
Canada	Aaron Perry	Afghanistan	TAC™-50 McMillan Tactical Rifle	2310m/2526yds
UK	Christopher Reynolds	Afghanistan	Accuracy International L115A3	1853m/2026yds
U.S.	Brandon McGuire	Iraq	Barrett .50 M82	1310m/1433yds

APPENDICES

Left: *A U.S. Army sniper team from the 4th Infantry Regiment provide sniper overwatch during a foot patrol near Mizan, Afghanistan, February 2009. The sniper is armed with a high-powered M82A1 Barrett .50 caliber semi-automatic rifle.*

BEST SNIPER RIFLES

Rifle	Country	Caliber	Effective Range
Kentucky Long rifle	American colonies	0.60in/15.2mm	100–250yds
Whitworth rifle	United Kingdom	0.451in/11.5mm	800–1000yds/730–910m
Ferguson rifle	United Kingdom	17.27mm/0.68in	Variable
Baker rifle	United Kingdom	11.43mm/0.45in	Variable 100–300yds/ 91–270m
Mauser Gewehr 98	Germany	7.92mm/0.31in	800m/875yds
Gewehr 41	Germany	7.92mm/0.31in	400m/437yds
Lee-Enfield No.4 Mk 1	United Kingdom	0.303in (7.7mm)	550m/550yds
M1 Garand	United States	0.30in/7.62mm	440yds/402m
Mosin-Nagant 1891/30	Soviet Union	7.62mm/0.30in	750m/820yds
Karabiner 98K	Germany	7.92mm/0.31in	800m/875yds
Type 99	Japan	6.5mm/0.25in	–
Springfield 1903A4	United States	0.30in/7.62mm	–
L42A1	United Kingdom	7.62mm/0.30in	750m/820yds
M40A1	United States	7.62mm/0.30in	800m/875yds
M14	United States	7.62mm/0.30in	800m/875yds
M21	United States	7.62mm/0.30in	690m/750yds
Dragunov SVD	Soviet Union	7.62mm/0.30in	1300m/1422yds
L96 rifle	United Kingdom	7.62mm/0.30in	1094m/1000yds
M82A1 Barrett .50	United States	12.7mm/0.5in	1830m/2000yds
Heckler & Koch G3 SG-1	Germany	7.62mm	400m/437yds
Heckler & Koch PSG-1	Germany	7.62mm	800m/820yds
Mk12 Special Purpose rifle	United States	5.56mm/0.223in	550m/600yds
Accuracy International L115A3 rifle	United Kingdom	8.59mm/0.338in	1400m/1531yds
TAC-50 McMillan Tactical rifle	United States	.50 BMG/12.7x99mm	2000m/2190yds

BIBLIOGRAPHY

Books:

Brookesmith, Peter. *Sniper.* Spellmount Publishers Ltd, 2000.

Cabell, Craig and Richard Brown. *Snipers.* John Blake Publishing Ltd, 2005.

Gilbert, Adrian D. *Sniper: The Skills, the Weapons and the Experiences.* St. Martin's Press, 1996.

Gilbert, Adrian D. *Stalk and Kill: The Sniper Experience.* Sidgwick and Jackson, 1997.

Haskew, Michael E. *The Sniper at War: From the American Revolutionary War to the Present Day.* St. Martin's Press, 2004.

Mills, Sergeant Dan. *Sniper One.* Penguin, 2008.

Pegler, Martin M. *Out of Nowhere: A History of the Military Sniper.* Osprey Publishing, 2006.

Sasser, Charles W. and Craig Roberts. *One Shot, One Kill.* Pocket Books, 1994.

Shore, Captain C. *With British Snipers to the Reich.* Greenhill, 1997.

Spicer, Mark. *Illustrated Manual of Sniper Skills.* Zenith Press, 2006.

Websites:

From an account of Canadian snipers in Afghanistan:

http://www.macleans.ca/canada/national/article.jsp?content=20060515_126689_126689

INDEX

Page numbers in *italics* refer to illustrations.

21 Army Group Sniper School 61–3
95th Rifles 12–14

A

A Bridge Too Far (Ryan) 72
"Abdul the Terrible" 36–7
Accuracy International
  AWM-F 152
  L96A1 156, 162, *164, 181,* 187
  L115A1 162, *163,* 178, 185
  L115A3 *179,* 180–1, 186, 187
  PM 160
  SR-98 158
Aden Emergency (1963–67) 115–17
Adventures in the Rifle Brigade (Kincaid) 178
Afghanistan 7, 18–21, 137, 146–50, 173–8, 180–3, 184, 185, 186, *187*
AK47, Kalashnikov *142,* 156, 157, 160, 170, *172,* 178
Al-Qaeda 146

Al Wafrah, Kuwait 134–5
Alexander, General 65
Allerberger, Josef "Sepp" 50, 54, 56–9, 186
American Civil War (1861–65) 15–16, *17,* 18, 32, 186
American War of Independence (1775–83) *8,* 9–12, 15, 186
Anaconda, Operation 146, 148–9, 177
Anglo-Afghan Wars
  First (1839–42) 18, 20–1
  Second (1879–80) 21
Ansar al-Islam 160
Antwerp 73
Argentina 124–5, *126,* 127–30
Arnold, General Benedict 11
Artists' Rifles 34
AWM-F, Accuracy International 152

B

Baghdad, Iraq 160, 162
Bailey, Dean 178
Baker, Ezekiel 12

Baker rifle 7, 12, *13,* 187
Barbarossa, Operation 40, 44–6
Barrett
  M82A1 7, 105, *136,* 146, *148,* 160, *169, 183,* 185, 186, 187
  M107 105, 152
Basra, Iraq 155–7, 159, *161*
Bastille, Operation *153*
Beirut, Lebanon 120–1
Berdan, Hiram 15–16
Berdan rifle 16
Berdan's Sharpshooters 15–16
"Bob the Nailer" 21
Boer Wars 32
  First (1880–81) 21–2
  Second (1899–1902) 22, *23*
Boone, Daniel 9, 184
Borneo 115
Bosnia 140–6
Boys anti-tank rifle 83, 85
Braddon, Russell 83, 85
Bren gun 80, 85

INDEX

Briggs, Lance-Sergeant Chris *161*
Brophy, Ordnance Captain William S. 86
Browning L9A1 178
Brydon, Dr. William 20
Buenos Aires 14
Bun, Specialist Chantah *170*
Burgoyne, General 11
Burnes, Sir Alexander 18

C

caçadores 13
Cameron, Sergeant Mick 159
camouflage
    American Civil War 15–16, 32
    American War of Independence *8*
    Boer Wars 22, 32
    French Revolutionary War 12–13
    Korean War *87*
    modern *6*, *92*, 106–7
    Palestinian *119*
    Winter War 42
    World War I 32–3, 34
    World War II *38*, 44, *53*, *55*, 61, 62, *63*, *75*, *77*
Canham, Colonel 69
Cass Jr., Marine Private Daniel Webster 76, 78
Central Women's Sniper Training School, Moscow 52
Chechnya 137–9
CheyTac Intervention 152
Chuikov, Marshal 46
Clarke, Sir Francis 11
Colbert, Auguste-Marie-François 14
Colley, Sir George 22
Collingwood, Midshipman Francis Edward 15
Colt revolving rifle 16
Copse 125 (Junger) 26–7, 29
Cornwell, Bernard 13, 178
Corunna 14
Cowpens, Battle of (1781) 11
Crane, Anthony 72
Crane, Sergeant John 164–5
Craufurd, Robert "Black Bob" 13
Crete 60–1

D

D-Day landings 61, 66–72
Dardanelles 35
Davis, Sergeant Randall 170
Delta Force 136, 151
Denison smock 62, 75
Dennison, Scott 186
Desert Shield, Operation *134*
Desert Storm, Operation 134–6, 186
The Devil's Anvil (Hallas) 84
Devil's Den 16
Diadem, Operation 65

Dimick rifle 16
dogs, anti-sniper 84
Doyle, Sir Arthur Conan 21
Dragunov
    SVD 137, *138*, *139*, *157*, 165, *167*, 187
    SVDS 137
DShK machine gun 154
Dunkirk 61

E

Enduring Freedom, Operation 146–50
Enfield rifle 16, 21

F

Falklands War (1982) 124–5, *126*, 127–30, 135, 141
Fallschirmjäger 64–5
Fallujah, Iraq 164–7
Farrell, Major 155–6
Ferguson, Major Patrick 12, 186
Ferguson rifle 12, *14*, 187
Ferguson's Rifle Corps 12
FG42 *64*, 65
Fiedler, August 31
fieldcraft 106–7
Fiji 80
Finland, Winter War (1939–40) 40, *41*, 42–3, 46, 186
First Army Sniping, Observation and Scouting School 30, 32, 34
Fish, Marine Corporal Ernest R. 88–9
FN MAG GPMG 130
FN SCAR (Special Forces Combat Assault Rifle) *175*
Frank, Benis M. 121
Fraser, General Simon 11
French Revolutionary War (1792–1802) 12–14
Freyberg, Major-General Bernard 60
Fulcher, Sergeant John 68–9
Furlong, Master Corporal Rob 148, 149, 186

G

Gaza Strip 119
Gettysburg, Battle of (1863) 16
Gewehr 33/40 65
Gewehr 41/43 7, 57, *59*, 187
Gewehr 43/K43 65
Gewehr 98, Mauser 26, *27*, *31*
ghillie suits *6*, 32, 34, 61, 107
Gilbert, Adrian 74, 76, 82–3, 129
Gilliland, Staff Sergeant Jim 169
Goerz telescopic sights 26, 30
GP-25 grenade launcher 137
The "Great Game" 18, 20
The Great Game: On Secret Service in High Asia (Hopkirk) 20
Grenada 130–1
Grieci, Frank 186

GROM special forces (Poland) 152, 155
Grozny, Chechnya 137
Guadalcanal 78
Guderian, General Heinz 44

H

Halder, General Franz Ritter von 44
Hallas, H. 84
Hamilton, Chester F. "Chet" 86–8
Hancock, Sergeant Herbert B. 166–7
Hardee, William 16
Harpoon, Operation 177
Harris
    M-86 *150*
    M-89 *151*
Harrison, Corporal of Horse Craig 180–1, 186
Harrison, Mick 116–17
Harvey, Corporal 157
Hathcock, Marine Sergeant Carlos 100–5, 112, 186
Hawkins Position 33
Häyhä, Simo 40, 42–3, 46, 47, 186
Heckler & Koch
    G3 SG-1 131, 187
    PSG-1 146, *147*, 152, 187
Helmand, Afghanistan 182–3
Hensoldt telescopic sights 26
Herzegovina 146
Hesketh-Prichard, Major H. 25, 29, 30, 32, 34, 51, 163
Hetzenauer, Matthias 50, 57, 186
Hopkirk, Peter 20
Horne, General Lord 25
Howell, Lance-Corporal J.W. *105*
Hulme, Alfred Clive 60–1, 186

I

Idriess, Ion 36
Improvised Explosive Devices (IEDs) 169, 173
India 18, 21
Indian Mutiny (1857) 21
International Security Assistance Force (ISAF) 173, 185
Iraq 7, *132*, 134–6, 150–2, *153*, 154–60, *161*, 162, 164–73, 184, 186
Iraqi Freedom, Operation *132*, 150–2, *153*, 154–60, *161*, 162, 164, 186
Israel 117–22, *123*, 125
Italy 63, 65–6

J

Javelin anti-tank missile 158, 178, 180, 182
Jezail 18, *19*, 20–1
Johnston, Sir John 10
Jones, William E. 73–4
"Juba" 172
Junger, Ernst 26–7, 29

INDEX

K

Kabul, Afghanistan 18, 173
KAC SR-25 152, 158
Kalashnikov AK47 *142*, 156, 157, 160, 170, *172*, 178
Karabiner 98K, Mauser *45*, 54, *56*, 57, 187
Kellner, Timothy L. 168–9, 186
Kentucky rifle 11–12, 184, 187
Khyber Pass 20–1
Kim (Kipling) 18
Kincaid, Captain John 13, 178
Kingsbury, Private Bruce 80–1
Kipling, Rudyard 18
Kokoda, New Guinea 80–1
Kollaa, Battle of (1940) 42
König, Major 46, 51
Korean War 85–91, 93, 148, 185, 186
Kulikov, Nikolai 49–50
Kursk, Battle of (1943) 53
Kuwait 134–5

L

L1A1 self-loading rifle *124*, *125*, *126*
L7 General Purpose Machine Gun 162
L9A1, Browning 178
L42A1, Lee-Enfield *116*, *117*, 187
L96A1, Accuracy International 156, 162, *164*, *181*, 187
L115A1, Accuracy International 162, *163*, 178, 185
L115A3, Accuracy International *179*, 180–1, 186, 187
L129A1 sharpshooter rifle *182*
la Drang, Battle of (1965) 97, 99
Laing, Lance-Corporal Pedro 156–7
Lalkova, Maria *58*
Land, Captain Jim 98, 112
Leatherwood, Captain Jim 111
Lebanon 119, 120–1
Lee-Enfield
   L42A1 *116*, *117*, 187
   No.1 Mk III 79
   No.4 Mk I 7, 61, 62, *66*, *73*, 74, 187
   SMLE Mk I 27, *28*, 29
   SMLE Mk III *30*, 31, 60, *62*
Leicht, Corporal Paul W. 165–6
Lingen, Company Sergeant-Major K.C. 73
Lithgow SMLE No.1 Mk III 79, *80*
Londonderry, Lord 25
Lovat Scouts 34, 59, 61, 106
Lucas, Captain 14
Lucknow, India 21
Lynch, Private Jessica 152

M

M1 Garand 7, 67, 68, *81*, 86, *87*, *88*, *89*, 187
M2 machine-gun 105, 154, 160
M4 carbine *122*, *153*, *174*
M14 100, 101, *102*, *103*, 111, 113, *115*, 170, 185, 187
M14 Mod 0 EBR *176*
M14 SWS 122
M16 110–11, 112
M16A2 *166*
M21 108, 110, 111, 112, 160, *170*, 187
M24 *107*, *123*, *132*, *140*, 146, 168, 171
M28, Mosin-Nagant *41*, 42, *43*
M40A1 *92*, *94*, *96*, *97*, *105*, *112*, *113*, *134*, 146, *165*, *170*, 187
M40A3 6, 166, *174*
M82A1, Barrett 7, 105, *136*, 146, *148*, 160, *169*, *183*, 185, 186, 187
M86, Mauser 152
M-86, Harris *150*
M-89, Harris *151*
M107, Barrett 105, 152
M110 semi-automatic sniper system *159*, *184–5*
M203 grenade launcher *153*, 166
M240 light machine-gun 160
MacArthur, General Douglas 85
McBride, Herbert 34
McGuire, Sergeant 1st Class Brandon 173, 186
McKay, Sergeant 130
McMeekin, Master Corporal Tim 149
McMillan Tac-50 *144*, 147, 148, *149*, 186, 187
Mafeking, Siege of (1899–1900) 22
Magersfontein, Battle of (1899) 22
Maiwand, Battle of (1880) 21
Majuba Hill, Battle of (1881) 21–2
Malaya 115
Manningham, Colonel Coote 12
Market Garden, Operation 72, 107
Marshall, Sergeant Harold A. 74
Mauser
   Gewehr 98 26, *27*, *31*
   Karabiner 98K *45*, 54, *56*, 57, 187
   M86 152
   model 1895 22, *23*
Mawhinney, Chuck 112–15, 186
Mekong Delta 108
Menendez, General 130
Mergott, Jack 104
MG34 machine gun 65
MG42 machine gun 65
Milan anti-tank missiles 129
Military Cross 178
Mills, Sergeant Dan 162
Mk12 rifle *154*, 155, 185, 187
Mk19 grenade launcher 154, 160
Monte Cassino 65–6
Moore, Sir John 14
Morgan, Company Sergeant-Major R. 73
Morgan, General Daniel 9, 10–11, 12, 15
Morgan's Sharpshooters *8*, 10–11, 15

Mosin-Nagant
   1891/30 7, 46, *47*, 51, *53*, 54, *55*, 85, 91, 96, 187
   M28 *41*, 42, *43*
Mount Harriet, Falklands 125, 126–7
Mount Longdon, Falklands 125, 127, 130
MP44/43 assault rifle 65
Murphy, Timothy 9–10, 11, 14, 186
muskets 12, 18, 19

N

Nanking Scotland II, Operation *109*
Napoleonic War (1803–15) 14–15
Nelson, Admiral Horatio 14–15
New Guinea 79–81
Newland, Corporal 129
night vision scopes *101*, *107*, *126*, 128, 130, 139, *150*, *153*, *170*
Normandy landings 61, 66–72
Norwest, Henry 34–5, 186
Notes on the Training of Snipers 59

O

Odessa 51–2
Okinawa 76, 78
Operations
   Anaconda 146, 148–9, 177
   Barbarossa 40, 44–6
   Bastille *153*
   Desert Shield *134*
   Desert Storm 134–6, 186
   Diadem 65
   Enduring Freedom 146–50
   Harpoon 177
   Iraqi Freedom *132*, 150–2, *153*, 154–60, *161*, 162, 164, 186
   Market Garden 72, 107
   Nanking Scotland II *109*
   Overlord 63, 66–72
   Phantom Fury 164–7
   Swift *105*
   Telic 155–7, 159
Osama bin Laden 146
OSV-96 139
Overlord, Operation 63, 66–72

P

Paulus, Field Marshal 46
Pavlichenko, Lyudmila 51–3, 186
Pegamagabow, Corporal Francis 34, 186
Pegler, Martin 137
Peninsular War (1808–14) *12*, 13–14, 178, 186
Pennsylvania rifle *8*, 11
Perry, Master Corporal Aaron 148, 149, 186
PGM 338 152
Phantom Fury, Operation 164–7
Place, Sergeant John Ethan 167

Plunkett, Thomas 13–14, 186
PM, Accuracy International 160
Pointe du Hoc 71–2
Pollard, Lieutenant John 15
Pollock, General George 20
Polus, Vincent 157, 159
Port Moresby, New Guinea 80
Port Stanley, Falklands 125, 130
Powell, Sergeant Ben 186
Princess Patricia's Canadian Light Infantry 147–50
PTRD anti-tank rifle 86

R

Ragsdale, Master Corporal Graham 148
reconnaissance 95, 166–7
Redoubtable (French man-of-war) 14–15
Remington
 Model 40x 112
 Model 700 *98*, 112, 168
Reynolds, Corporal Christopher 180, 186
Rice, Joh *115*
Rifle and Light Infantry Tactics (Hardee) 18
rocket-propelled grenades 119, 122, 134, 157, 175, 178
Rose, General Sir Michael 141–3
Rose, Private Nick 127, 130
Ross hunting rifle *25*
Royal Winnipeg Rifles 74–5
Rudder, Lieutenant-Colonel James E. 71
Ruecker, Lance-Corporal Oliver "Teddy" 178
Russell, Captain Robert A. 98, 112
Ryan, Cornelius 72

S

SA-80 162, 182
Saddam Hussein 135, 136, 151, 159
Saipan 82–3
SAKO TRG-22 152
Samoa 80
San Carlos, Falklands 125
Sanders, Corporal F.S. *105*
Sangin, Afghanistan 178, 182
Sarajevo 141–6
Saratoga, Battles of (1777) *10*, *11*
SASR (Australia) 147, 152, 158
Saudi Arabia 135
Scheldt, Battle of the (1944) 72–3
Schneider, Lieutenant-Colonel Max F. 71
Schoharie Creek 10
Scoon, Sir Paul 130
"Scud" missiles 136, 154
Second Chechen War (1999–2000) 137–8
Sedgwick, General John 16, *17*, 18
September 11, 2001 146
Serbia 141, 145–6
Sharpe novels (Cornwell) 13, 178

Sharps rifle 16
Shimshon Battalion 119
Shmel rocket flamethrower 137
Shore, Captain C. 59, 61, 66
Sing, William Edward 36–7, 186
Six-Day War (1967) 117–18
The Small Arms School, Sniping Wing 40
Sniper (Gilbert) 74, 76
Sniper One: The Blistering True Story of a British Battle Group Under Siege (Mills) 162
Sniping in France (Hesketh-Prichard) 25, 32
South Georgia 124
South Ossetia *138*
Special Air Service (SAS)
 Aden 116, 117
 Afghanistan 147
 Falklands War 124, 141
 Iraq 136, 152, 154, 155, 160, 162
 Malaya 115
Special Boat Service (SBS) 124, 155, 156, 177–8
Spencer magazine rifle 16
Spion Kop, Battle of (1900) 22
Spotsylvania Court House, Battle of (1864) 16, *17*, 18
Springfield Model 1903 *67*, *68*, 74, *82*, 83, 86, *87*, 187
SR-25, KAC 152, 158
SR-98, Accuracy International 158
Stalingrad 7, 45–51, 178
Stalk and Kill – The Sniper Experience (Gilbert) 82–3, 129
stalking tactics 62–3, 99
Storm of Steel (Junger) 26
Suomi KP/-31 43
Sutherland, Private Eugene 91
SV-98 140
SVD, Dragunov 137, *138*, *139*, *157*, 165, *167*, 187
SVT40, Tokarev *38*, 52, *58*, 59
Swift, Operation *105*

T

tactics
 Afghanistan 147, 149, 175–6, 178, 183
 American Civil War 16, 18
 American War of Independence 10, 11
 Anglo-Afghan Wars 18, 20–1
 Boer Wars 21–2
 Chechen 137
 counter sniper action 47–51, 73–4, 81, 83, 103, 121, 122, 144–5, 178, 182
 dogs, anti-sniper 84
 Falklands War 127, 128–9
 fieldcraft 106–7
 Grenada 130–1

Indian Mutiny 21
Iraq War 154–5, 157, 159, 162, 164, 168–9, 171
Korean War 91
Lebanon 121
Napoleonic War 14–15
Peninsular War 13–14
reconnaissance 95, 166–7
Serbian 141, 145–6
Six-Day War 118
stalking 62–3, 99
teamwork 50–1, *56*, 76, *174*
Vietnam War 96–7, 99–100, 101–2, 104
Winter War 42–3
World War I 26–7, *28*, 32–4, 36–7
World War II 48–51, 56, 58, 60–1, 68–9, 72
Taliban 146, 175, 177, 178, 180
Task Force 20 151–2
telescopic sights
 earliest 31
 Korean War *87*
 modern *107*, *131*, *138*, 139, 140, *150*, *159*, *163*, *170*
 Vietnam War *101*, *102*, *103*, 111, 112
 World War I 26, 27, 30, 31
 World War II *38*, *45*, 46, *47*, *55*, 61, *66–7*, 79
 see also night vision scopes
Telic, Operation 155–7, 159
Tet Offensive (1968) 99–100, 113
Tilley, Lance-Corporal John *116*
Timor 79
Tito, Marshal 145
Tokarev SVT40 *38*, 52, *58*, 59
Trafalgar, Battle of (1805) 14–15
training
 American War of Independence 8
 Korean War 85–6, 89
 modern *6*, *92*, 131, 163
 Russian 137
 Vietnam War *97*, 98–9, 104–5, 108, 111–12, 114
 World War I 26, 30, 32, 34, *35*, 37
 World War II 40, 44, 51, 52, 54, 59, 61–3, 68, 76, 79
Travis, Richard 37
Type 38 rifle 79
Type 97 rifle 79
Type 99 rifle *78*, 79, 187

U

UN Protection Force (UNPROFOR) 141, 144
U.S. Marine Corps Scout/Sniper School 98–9
U.S. Navy SEALs 130–1, 152, 155, *175*
U.S. Marines in Lebanon 1982–84 (Frank) 121

INDEX

V
V-94 139
Victoria Cross 60, 81
Victory, HMS 14–15
Vietnam War 93–105, 108–15, 185, 186
Vintorez silenced rifle 137, 139–40
Voigtlander telescopic sights 26, 30
Voroshilov Sharpshooter Badge 44, 51

W
Waldron, Adelbert F. 105, 108–10, 112, 186
Waring, Sergeant Eddie 156
Washington, General George 12
Waterloo, Battle of (1815) 13
weapons
  Accuracy International AWM-F 152
  Accuracy International L96A1 156, 162, *164*, *181*, 187
  Accuracy International L115A1 162, *163*, 178, 185
  Accuracy International L115A3 *179*, 180–1, 186, 187
  Accuracy International PM 160
  Accuracy International SR-98 158
  Baker rifle 7, 12, *13*, 187
  Barrett M82A1 7, 105, *136*, 146, *148*, 160, *169*, *183*, 185, 186, 187
  Barrett M107 105, 152
  Berdan rifle 16
  Boys anti-tank rifle 83, 85
  Bren gun 80, 85
  Browning L9A1 178
  CheyTac Intervention 152
  Colt revolving rifle 16
  Dimick rifle 16
  Dragunov SVD 137, *138*, *139*, 157, 165, *167*, 187
  Dragunov SVDS 137
  DShK machine gun 154
  Enfield rifle 16, 21
  Ferguson rifle 12, *14*, 187
  FG42 *64*, 65
  FN MAG GPMG 130
  FN SCAR (Special Forces Combat Assault Rifle) *175*
  Gewehr 33/40 65
  Gewehr 41/43 7, 57, *59*, 187
  Gewehr 43/K43 65
  Harris M-86 *150*
  Harris M-89 *151*
  Heckler & Koch G3 SG-1 131, 187
  Heckler & Koch PSG-1 146, *147*, 152, 187
  Improvised Explosive Devices (IEDs) 169, 173
  Javelin anti-tank missile 158, 178, 180, 182
  Jezail 18, *19*, 20–1
  KAC SR-25 152, 158

  Kalashnikov AK47 *142*, 156, 157, 160, 170, *172*, 178
  Kentucky rifle 11–12, 184, 187
  L1A1 self-loading rifle *124*, *125*, *126*
  L7 General Purpose Machine Gun 162
  L42A1 *116*, *117*, 187
  L129A1 sharpshooter rifle *182*
  Lee-Enfield No.1 Mk III 79
  Lee-Enfield No.4 Mk I 7, 61, 62, *66*, *73*, 74, 187
  Lee-Enfield SMLE Mk I 27, *28*, 29
  Lee-Enfield SMLE Mk III *30*, 31, 60, *62*
  Lithgow SMLE No.1 Mk III 79, *80*
  M1 Garand 7, 67, 68, *81*, 86, *87*, 88, 89, 187
  M2 machine-gun 105, 154, 160
  M4 carbine *122*, *153*, *174*
  M14 100, 101, *102*, *103*, 111, 113, *115*, 170, 185, 187
  M14 Mod 0 EBR *176*
  M14 SWS 122
  M16 110–11, 112
  M16A2 *166*
  M21 108, 110, 111, 112, 160, *170*, 187
  M24 *107*, *123*, *132*, *140*, 146, 168, 171
  M40A1 *92*, *94*, *96*, *97*, 105, *112*, 113, *134*, 146, *165*, *170*, 187
  M40A3 *6*, *166*, *174*
  M110 semi-automatic sniper system *159*, 184–5
  M203 grenade launcher *153*, *166*
  M240 light machine-gun 160
  McMillan Tac-50 *144*, 147, 148, *149*, 186, 187
  Mauser Gewehr 98 26, *27*, *31*
  Mauser Karabiner 98K *45*, 54, *56*, 57, 187
  Mauser M86 152
  Mauser model 1895 22, *23*
  MG34 machine gun 65
  MG42 machine gun 65
  Milan anti-tank missiles 129
  Mk12 rifle *154*, 155, 185, 187
  Mk19 grenade launcher 154, 160
  Mosin-Nagant 1891/30 7, 46, *47*, 51, *53*, 54, 85, 91, 96, 187
  Mosin-Nagant M28 *41*, 42, *43*
  MP44/43 assault rifle 65
  muskets 12, 18, 19
  OSV-96 139
  Pennsylvania rifle *8*, 11
  PGM 338 152
  PTRD anti-tank rifle 86
  Remington Model 40x 112
  Remington Model 700 *98*, 112, 168
  rocket-propelled grenades 119, 122, 134, 157, 175, 178
  Ross hunting rifle *25*
  SA-80 162, 182

  SAKO TRG-22 152
  "Scud" missiles 136, 154
  Sharps rifle 16
  Shmel rocket flamethrower 137
  Spencer magazine rifle 16
  Springfield Model 1903 *67*, 68, 74, *82*, 83, 86, *87*, 187
  Suomi KP/31 43
  SV-98 140
  Tokarev SVT40 *38*, 52, *58*, 59
  Type 38 rifle 79
  Type 97 rifle 79
  Type 99 rifle *78*, 79, 187
  V-94 139
  Vintorez silenced rifle 137, 139–40
  Whitworth rifle 7, 16, 18, 187
  Winchester Model 70 86, 100, *101*, 112
Welch, Mark 134
WerBell, Colonel Mitchell 109
Westerfield, Hargis 81, 83
Whitworth rifle 7, 16, 18, 187
Winchester Model 70 86, 100, *101*, 112
Winter War, Finland (1939–40) 40, *41*, 42–3, 46, 186
World War I 7, 25–7, 147, 186
  Gallipoli *30*, 32, *33*, 34, 35–7
  Western Front *24*, *28*, 29–30, *31*, 34–5, 37
World War II 62, 75, 148, 186
  Eastern Front 7, *38*, 40, 44–54, *55*, 56–9, 178
  Italy 63, 65–6
  Pacific theatre 74, 76, *77*, 78–85
  Western Europe 40, 59–61, 66–74, 107

Y
Yaremchoock, Guards Sergeant A.M. *47*
Yom Kippur War (1973) 118–19
Yugoslavia 141, 145

Z
Zaitsev, Vassil 46–51, 107, 178, 186
Zeiss telescopic sights 26, 30, *45*, 140
Zhang Taofang 85, 86, 90–1, 186